ASPEN PUBLISHERS

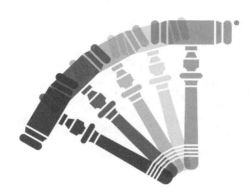

Casenote™ Legal Briefs

ENVIRONMENTAL LAW

Keyed to Courses Using

Percival, Schroeder, Miller, and Leape's
Environmental Regulation

Sixth Edition

Wolters Kluwer
Law & Business

AUSTIN   BOSTON   CHICAGO   NEW YORK   THE NETHERLANDS

This publication is designed to provide accurate and authoritative information in regard to the subject matter covered. It is sold with the understanding that the publisher is not engaged in rendering legal, accounting, or other professional services. If legal advice or other expert assistance is required, the services of a competent professional person should be sought.

> — From a Declaration of Principles adopted jointly by a Committee of the American Bar Association and a Committee of Publishers and Associates

To contact Customer Care, e-mail customer.care@aspenpublishers.com, call 1-800-234-1660, fax 1-800-901-9075, or mail correspondence to:

Aspen Publishers
Attn: Order Department
P.O. Box 990
Frederick, MD 21705

Printed in the United States of America.

1 2 3 4 5 6 7 8 9 0

ISBN 978-0-7355-8591-1

About Wolters Kluwer Law & Business

Wolters Kluwer Law & Business is a leading provider of research information and workflow solutions in key specialty areas. The strengths of the individual brands of Aspen Publishers, CCH, Kluwer Law International and Loislaw are aligned within Wolters Kluwer Law & Business to provide comprehensive, in-depth solutions and expert-authored content for the legal, professional and education markets.

CCH was founded in 1913 and has served more than four generations of business professionals and their clients. The CCH products in the Wolters Kluwer Law & Business group are highly regarded electronic and print resources for legal, securities, antitrust and trade regulation, government contracting, banking, pension, payroll, employment and labor, and health-care reimbursement and compliance professionals.

Aspen Publishers is a leading information provider for attorneys, business professionals and law students. Written by preeminent authorities, Aspen products offer analytical and practical information in a range of specialty practice areas from securities law and intellectual property to mergers and acquisitions and pension/benefits. Aspen's trusted legal education resources provide professors and students with high-quality, up-to-date and effective resources for successful instruction and study in all areas of the law.

Kluwer Law International supplies the global business community with comprehensive English-language international legal information. Legal practitioners, corporate counsel and business executives around the world rely on the Kluwer Law International journals, loose-leafs, books and electronic products for authoritative information in many areas of international legal practice.

Loislaw is a premier provider of digitized legal content to small law firm practitioners of various specializations. Loislaw provides attorneys with the ability to quickly and efficiently find the necessary legal information they need, when and where they need it, by facilitating access to primary law as well as state-specific law, records, forms and treatises.

Wolters Kluwer Law & Business, a unit of Wolters Kluwer, is headquartered in New York and Riverwoods, Illinois. Wolters Kluwer is a leading multinational publisher and information services company.

Format for the Casenote Legal Brief

Nature of Case: This section identifies the form of action (e.g., breach of contract, negligence, battery), the type of proceeding (e.g., demurrer, appeal from trial court's jury instructions), or the relief sought (e.g., damages, injunction, criminal sanctions).

Party ID: Quick identification of the relationship between the parties.

Fact Summary: This is included to refresh your memory and can be used as a quick reminder of the facts.

Rule of Law: Summarizes the general principle of law that the case illustrates. It may be used for instant recall of the court's holding and for classroom discussion or home review.

Facts: This section contains all relevant facts of the case, including the contentions of the parties and the lower court holdings. It is written in a logical order to give the student a clear understanding of the case. The plaintiff and defendant are identified by their proper names throughout and are always labeled with a (P) or (D).

Concurrence/Dissent: All concurrences and dissents are briefed whenever they are included by the casebook editor.

Analysis: This last paragraph gives you a broad understanding of where the case "fits in" with other cases in the section of the book and with the entire course. It is a hornbook-style discussion indicating whether the case is a majority or minority opinion and comparing the principal case with other cases in the casebook. It may also provide analysis from restatements, uniform codes, and law review articles. The analysis will prove to be invaluable to classroom discussion.

Issue: The issue is a concise question that brings out the essence of the opinion as it relates to the section of the casebook in which the case appears. Both substantive and procedural issues are included if relevant to the decision.

Holding and Decision: This section offers a clear and in-depth discussion of the rule of the case and the court's rationale. It is written in easy-to-understand language and answers the issue presented by applying the law to the facts of the case. When relevant, it includes a thorough discussion of the exceptions to the case as listed by the court, any major cites to the other cases on point, and the names of the judges who wrote the decisions.

Quicknotes: Conveniently defines legal terms found in the case and summarizes the nature of any statutes, codes, or rules referred to in the text.

Palsgraf v. Long Island R.R. Co.

Injured bystander (P) v. Railroad company (D)

N.Y. Ct. App., 248 N.Y. 339, 162 N.E. 99 (1928).

NATURE OF CASE: Appeal from judgment affirming verdict for plaintiff seeking damages for personal injury.

FACT SUMMARY: Helen Palsgraf (P) was injured on R.R.'s (D) train platform when R.R.'s (D) guard helped a passenger aboard a moving train, causing his package to fall on the tracks. The package contained fireworks which exploded, creating a shock that tipped a scale onto Palsgraf (P).

🏛 RULE OF LAW
The risk reasonably to be perceived defines the duty to be obeyed.

FACTS: Helen Palsgraf (P) purchased a ticket to Rockaway Beach from R.R. (D) and was waiting on the train platform. As she waited, two men ran to catch a train that was pulling out from the platform. The first man jumped aboard, but the second man, who appeared as if he might fall, was helped aboard by the guard on the train who had kept the door open so they could jump aboard. A guard on the platform also helped by pushing him onto the train. The man was carrying a package wrapped in newspaper. In the process, the man dropped his package, which fell on the tracks. The package contained fireworks and exploded. The shock of the explosion was apparently of great enough strength to tip over some scales at the other end of the platform, which fell on Palsgraf (P) and injured her. A jury awarded her damages, and R.R. (D) appealed.

ISSUE: Does the risk reasonably to be perceived define the duty to be obeyed?

HOLDING AND DECISION: (Cardozo, C.J.) Yes. The risk reasonably to be perceived defines the duty to be obeyed. If there is no foreseeable hazard to the injured party as the result of a seemingly innocent act, the act does not become a tort because it happened to be a wrong as to another. If the wrong was not willful, the plaintiff must show that the act as to her had such great and apparent possibilities of danger as to entitle her to protection. Negligence in the abstract is not enough upon which to base liability. Negligence is a relative concept, evolving out of the common law doctrine of trespass on the case. To establish liability, the defendant must owe a legal duty of reasonable care to the injured party. A cause of action in tort will lie where harm, though unintended, could have been averted or avoided by observance of such a duty. The scope of the duty is limited by the range of danger that a reasonable person could foresee. In this case, there was nothing to suggest from the appearance of the parcel or otherwise that the parcel contained fireworks. The guard could not reasonably have had any warning of a threat to Palsgraf (P), and R.R. (D) therefore cannot be held liable. Judgment is reversed in favor of R.R. (D).

DISSENT: (Andrews, J.) The concept that there is no negligence unless R.R. (D) owes a legal duty to take care as to Palsgraf (P) herself is too narrow. Everyone owes to the world at large the duty of refraining from those acts that may unreasonably threaten the safety of others. If the guard's action was negligent as to those nearby, it was also negligent as to those outside what might be termed the "danger zone." For Palsgraf (P) to recover, R.R.'s (D) negligence must have been the proximate cause of her injury, a question of fact for the jury.

▶ ANALYSIS
The majority defined the limit of the defendant's liability in terms of the danger that a reasonable person in defendant's situation would have perceived. The dissent argued that the limitation should not be placed on liability, but rather on damages. Judge Andrews suggested that only injuries that would not have happened but for R.R.'s (D) negligence should be compensable. Both the majority and dissent recognized the policy-driven need to limit liability for negligent acts, seeking, in the words of Judge Andrews, to define a framework "that will be practical and in keeping with the general understanding of mankind." The Restatement (Second) of Torts has accepted Judge Cardozo's view.

Quicknotes

FORESEEABILITY A reasonable expectation that change is the probable result of certain acts or omissions.

NEGLIGENCE Conduct falling below the standard of care that a reasonable person would demonstrate under similar conditions.

PROXIMATE CAUSE The natural sequence of events without which an injury would not have been sustained.

Aspen Publishers is proud to offer *Casenote Legal Briefs*—continuing thirty years of publishing America's best-selling legal briefs.

Casenote Legal Briefs are designed to help you save time when briefing assigned cases. Organized under convenient headings, they show you how to abstract the basic facts and holdings from the text of the actual opinions handed down by the courts. Used as part of a rigorous study regimen, they can help you spend more time analyzing and critiquing points of law than on copying bits and pieces of judicial opinions into your notebook or outline.

Casenote Legal Briefs should never be used as a substitute for assigned casebook readings. They work best when read as a follow-up to reviewing the underlying opinions themselves. Students who try to avoid reading and digesting the judicial opinions in their casebooks or online sources will end up shortchanging themselves in the long run. The ability to absorb, critique, and restate the dynamic and complex elements of case law decisions is crucial to your success in law school and beyond. It cannot be developed vicariously.

Casenote Legal Briefs represents but one of the many offerings in Aspen's Study Aid Timeline, which includes:

- *Casenote Legal Briefs*
- *Emanuel Law Outlines*
- *Examples & Explanations* Series
- *Introduction to Law* Series
- Emanuel *Law in a Flash* Flashcards
- Emanuel *CrunchTime* Series

Each of these series is designed to provide you with easy-to-understand explanations of complex points of law. Each volume offers guidance on the principles of legal analysis and, consulted regularly, will hone your ability to spot relevant issues. We have titles that will help you prepare for class, prepare for your exams, and enhance your general comprehension of the law along the way.

To find out more about Aspen Study Aid publications, visit us online at *http://lawschool.aspenpublishers.com* or email us at *legaledu@wolterskluwer.com*. We'll be happy to assist you.

Get this Casenote Legal Brief as an AspenLaw Studydesk eBook today!

By returning this form to Aspen Publishers, you will receive a complimentary eBook download of this Casenote Legal Brief in the AspenLaw Studydesk digital format.* Learn more about AspenLaw Studydesk today at *www.AspenLaw.com*.

Name	Phone ( )	
Address		**Apt. No.**
City	**State**	**ZIP Code**
Law School	**Year** (check one) ☐ 1st ☐ 2nd ☐ 3rd	

Cut out the UPC found on the lower left corner of the back cover of this book. Staple the UPC inside this box. Only the original UPC from the book cover will be accepted. (No photocopies or store stickers are allowed.)

Attach UPC inside this box.

Email (Print legibly or you may not get access!)

Title of this book (course subject)

ISBN of this book (10- or 13-digit number on the UPC)

Used with which casebook (provide author's name)

Mail the completed form to:

Aspen Publishers, Inc.
Legal Education Division
130 Turner Street, Bldg 3, 4th Floor
Waltham, MA 02453-8901

* Upon receipt of this completed form, you will be emailed a code for the digital download of this book in AspenLaw Studydesk format. The AspenLaw Studydesk application is available as a 60-day free trial at *www.AspenLaw.com*.

For a full list of print titles by Aspen Publishers, visit *lawschool.aspenpublishers.com*.
For a full list of digital eBook titles by Aspen Publishers, visit *www.AspenLaw.com*.

Make a photocopy of this form and your UPC for your records.

For detailed information on the use of the information you provide on this form, please see the PRIVACY POLICY at www.aspenpublishers.com.

A. Decide on a Format and Stick to It

Structure is essential to a good brief. It enables you to arrange systematically the related parts that are scattered throughout most cases, thus making manageable and understandable what might otherwise seem to be an endless and unfathomable sea of information. There are, of course, an unlimited number of formats that can be utilized. However, it is best to find one that suits your needs and stick to it. Consistency breeds both efficiency and the security that when called upon you will know where to look in your brief for the information you are asked to give.

Any format, as long as it presents the essential elements of a case in an organized fashion, can be used. Experience, however, has led *Casenotes* to develop and utilize the following format because of its logical flow and universal applicability.

NATURE OF CASE: This is a brief statement of the legal character and procedural status of the case (e.g., "Appeal of a burglary conviction").

There are many different alternatives open to a litigant dissatisfied with a court ruling. The key to determining which one has been used is to discover *who is asking this court for what.*

This first entry in the brief should be kept as *short as possible.* Use the court's terminology if you understand it. But since jurisdictions vary as to the titles of pleadings, the best entry is the one that addresses who wants what in this proceeding, not the one that sounds most like the court's language.

RULE OF LAW: A statement of the general principle of law that the case illustrates (e.g., "An acceptance that varies any term of the offer is considered a rejection and counteroffer").

Determining the rule of law of a case is a procedure similar to determining the issue of the case. Avoid being fooled by red herrings; there may be a few rules of law mentioned in the case excerpt, but usually only one is *the* rule with which the casebook editor is concerned. The techniques used to locate the issue, described below, may also be utilized to find the rule of law. Generally, your best guide is simply the chapter heading. It is a clue to the point the casebook editor seeks to make and should be kept in mind when reading every case in the respective section.

FACTS: A synopsis of only the essential facts of the case, i.e., those bearing upon or leading up to the issue.

The facts entry should be a short statement of the events and transactions that led one party to initiate legal proceedings against another in the first place. While some cases conveniently state the salient facts at the beginning of the decision, in other instances they will have to be culled from hiding places throughout the text, even from concurring and dissenting opinions. Some of the "facts" will often be in dispute and should be so noted. Conflicting evidence may be briefly pointed up. "Hard" facts must be included. Both must be *relevant* in order to be listed in the facts entry. It is impossible to tell what is relevant until the entire case is read, as the ultimate determination of the rights and liabilities of the parties may turn on something buried deep in the opinion.

Generally, the facts entry should not be longer than three to five *short* sentences.

It is often helpful to identify the role played by a party in a given context. For example, in a construction contract case the identification of a party as the "contractor" or "builder" alleviates the need to tell that that party was the one who was supposed to have built the house.

It is always helpful, and a good general practice, to identify the "plaintiff" and the "defendant." This may seem elementary and uncomplicated, but, especially in view of the creative editing practiced by some casebook editors, it is sometimes a difficult or even impossible task. Bear in mind that the *party presently* seeking something from this court may not be the plaintiff, and that sometimes only the cross-claim of a defendant is treated in the excerpt. Confusing or misaligning the parties can ruin your analysis and understanding of the case.

ISSUE: A statement of the general legal question answered by or illustrated in the case. For clarity, the issue is best put in the form of a question capable of a "yes" or "no" answer. In reality, the issue is simply the Rule of Law put in the form of a question (e.g., "May an offer be accepted by performance?").

The major problem presented in discerning what is *the* issue in the case is that an opinion usually purports to raise and answer several questions. However, except for rare cases, only one such question is really the issue in the case. Collateral issues not necessary to the resolution of the matter in controversy are handled by the court by language known as *"obiter dictum"* or merely *"dictum."* While dicta may be included later in the brief, they have no place under the issue heading.

To find the issue, ask *who wants what* and then go on to ask *why did that party succeed or fail in getting it.* Once this is determined, the "why" should be turned into a question.

The complexity of the issues in the cases will vary, but in all cases a single-sentence question should sum up the issue. *In a few cases,* there will be two, or even more rarely, three issues of equal importance to the resolution of the case. Each should be expressed in a single-sentence ·question.

Since many issues are resolved by a court in coming to a final disposition of a case, the casebook editor will reproduce the portion of the opinion containing the issue or issues most relevant to the area of law under scrutiny. A noted law professor gave this advice: "Close the book; look at the title on the cover." Chances are, if it is Property, you need not concern yourself with whether, for example, the federal government's treatment of the plaintiff's land really raises a federal question sufficient to support jurisdiction on this ground in federal court.

The same rule applies to chapter headings designating sub-areas within the subjects. They tip you off as to what the text is designed to teach. The cases are arranged in a casebook to show a progression or development of the law, so that the preceding cases may also help.

It is also most important to remember to *read the notes and questions* at the end of a case to determine what the editors wanted you to have gleaned from it.

HOLDING AND DECISION: This section should succinctly explain the rationale of the court in arriving at its decision. In capsulizing the "reasoning" of the court, it should always include an application of the general rule or rules of law to the specific facts of the case. Hidden justifications come to light in this entry; the reasons for the state of the law, the public policies, the biases and prejudices, those considerations that influence the justices' thinking and, ultimately, the outcome of the case. At the end, there should be a short indication of the disposition or procedural resolution of the case (e.g., "Decision of the trial court for Mr. Smith (P) reversed").

The foregoing format is designed to help you "digest" the reams of case material with which you will be faced in your law school career. Once mastered by practice, it will place at your fingertips the information the authors of your casebooks have sought to impart to you in case-by-case illustration and analysis.

B. Be as Economical as Possible in Briefing Cases

Once armed with a format that encourages succinctness, it is as important to be economical with regard to the time spent on the actual reading of the case as it is to be economical in the writing of the brief itself. This does not mean "skimming" a case. Rather, it means reading the case with an "eye" trained to recognize into which "section" of your brief a particular passage or line fits and having a system for quickly and precisely marking the case so that the passages fitting any one particular part of the brief can be easily identified and brought together in a concise and accurate manner when the brief is actually written.

It is of no use to simply repeat everything in the opinion of the court; record only enough information to trigger your recollection of what the court said. Nevertheless, an accurate statement of the "law of the case," i.e., the legal principle applied to the facts, is absolutely essential to class preparation and to learning the law under the case method.

To that end, it is important to develop a "shorthand" that you can use to make margin notations. These notations will tell you at a glance in which section of the brief you will be placing that particular passage or portion of the opinion.

Some students prefer to underline all the salient portions of the opinion (with a pencil or colored underliner marker), making marginal notations as they go along. Others prefer the color-coded method of underlining, utilizing different colors of markers to underline the salient portions of the case, each separate color being used to represent a different section of the brief. For example, blue underlining could be used for passages relating to the rule of law, yellow for those relating to the issue, and green for those relating to the holding and decision, etc. While it has its advocates, the color-coded method can be confusing and time-consuming (all that time spent on changing colored markers). Furthermore, it can interfere with the continuity and concentration many students deem essential to the reading of a case for maximum comprehension. In the end, however, it is a matter of personal preference and style. Just remember, whatever method you use, underlining must be used sparingly or its value is lost.

If you take the marginal notation route, an efficient and easy method is to go along underlining the key portions of the case and placing in the margin alongside them the following "markers" to indicate where a particular passage or line "belongs" in the brief you will write:

N   (NATURE OF CASE)
RL   (RULE OF LAW)
I   (ISSUE)
HL   (HOLDING AND DECISION, relates to the RULE OF LAW behind the decision)
HR   (HOLDING AND DECISION, gives the RATIONALE or reasoning behind the decision)
HA   (HOLDING AND DECISION, APPLIES the general principle(s) of law to the facts of the case to arrive at the decision)

Remember that a particular passage may well contain information necessary to more than one part of your brief, in which case you simply note that in the margin. If you are using the color-coded underlining method instead of margin notation, simply make asterisks or checks in the margin next to the passage in question in the colors that indicate the additional sections of the brief where it might be utilized.

The economy of utilizing "shorthand" in marking cases for briefing can be maintained in the actual brief writing process itself by utilizing "law student shorthand" within the brief. There are many commonly used words and phrases for which abbreviations can be substituted in your briefs (and in your class notes also). You can develop abbreviations that are personal to you and which will save you a lot of time. A reference list of briefing abbreviations can be found on page xii of this book.

C. Use Both the Briefing Process and the Brief as a Learning Tool

Now that you have a format and the tools for briefing cases efficiently, the most important thing is to make the time spent in briefing profitable to you and to make the most advantageous use of the briefs you create. Of course, the briefs are invaluable for classroom reference when you are called upon to explain or analyze a particular case. However, they are also useful in reviewing for exams. A quick glance at the fact summary should bring the case to mind, and a rereading of the rule of law should enable you to go over the underlying legal concept in your mind, how it was applied in that particular case, and how it might apply in other factual settings.

As to the value to be derived from engaging in the briefing process itself, there is an immediate benefit that arises from being forced to sift through the essential facts and reasoning from the court's opinion and to succinctly express them in your own words in your brief. The process ensures that you understand the case and the point that it illustrates, and that means you will be ready to absorb further analysis and information brought forth in class. It also ensures you will have something to say when called upon in class. The briefing process helps develop a mental agility for getting to the *gist* of a case and for identifying, expounding on, and applying the legal concepts and issues found there. The briefing process is the mental process on which you must rely in taking law school examinations; it is also the mental process upon which a lawyer relies in serving his clients and in making his living.

Abbreviations for Briefs

Table of Cases

CHAPTER 2

Environmental Law: Overview

Quick Reference Rules of Law

Madison v. Ducktown Sulphur, Copper & Iron Co.

Landowner (P) v. Mining companies (D)

Tenn. Sup. Ct., 113 Tenn. 331, 83 S.W. 658 (1904).

NATURE OF CASE: Appeal from injunction in a nuisance action.

FACT SUMMARY: Claiming that their timber and crop interests had been badly injured by the smoke and noxious vapors from Ducktown Sulphur, Copper & Iron Co.'s (Ducktown) (D) copper reduction plants, Madison (P) and other landowners in the vicinity sought to enjoin Ducktown's (D) operation.

RULE OF LAW
The granting of an injunction is not a matter of absolute right but rests in the sound discretion of the court, after a full and careful consideration of every element pertaining to the injury.

FACTS: Madison (P) and other small landowners (P) filed suit, seeking to enjoin Ducktown (D) and the Tennessee Copper Co. (D) from operating their copper reduction plants. The smelters reduced copper ores through the use of open-air roast piles, which emitted large volumes of smoke then carried by air currents over land belonging to Madison (P) and the other landowners (P). They alleged that the smoke made it impossible for them to raise and harvest their customary crops and that their timber had been largely destroyed. The court of chancery appeals found that Ducktown (D) and Tennessee Copper (D) were conducting their businesses in a lawful way, without any desire to injure Madison (P) or the other landowners (P), that this was the only known means by which the copper could be reduced, and that Ducktown (D) and Tennessee Copper (D) had made every effort to get rid of the smoke and noxious vapors. Nevertheless, it issued an injunction. Ducktown (D) and Tennessee Copper (D) appealed.

ISSUE: Is the granting of an injunction a matter of absolute right?

HOLDING AND DECISION: (Neil, J.) No. The granting of an injunction is not a matter of absolute right but rests in the sound discretion of the court, after a full and careful consideration of every element pertaining to the injury. Madison (P) and the other landowners (P) are entitled, as a matter of absolute right, to recover damages. However, if an injunction is granted, it would wreck Ducktown's (D) and Tennessee Copper's (D) enterprises, make their property practically worthless, and deprive them of all their rights. In a case of conflicting rights, the law must make the best arrangement it can between contending parties, while preserving to each the largest measure of liberty possible. Madison (P) and the other landowners (P) are entitled to an award of damages, but the injunction is denied.

► ANALYSIS

Liability theories based on fault entail a balancing of equities, or hardships; pollution cases involving modern technologies sorely test the viability of nuisance law. *Madison* is a leading case in favor of balancing. Significantly, the court in the above case summed up the two sides of the scale this way: "In order to protect by injunction several small tracts of land, aggregating in value to less than $1,000, we are asked to destroy other property worth nearly $2 million, and wreck two great mining and manufacturing enterprises . . . depopulate a large town, and deprive thousands of working people of their homes and livelihood . . . ."

Quicknotes

INJUNCTION A remedy imposed by the court ordering a party to cease the conduct of a specific activity.

Missouri v. Illinois

State (P) v. State (D)

200 U.S. 496 (1906).

NATURE OF CASE: Common law nuisance action seeking to enjoin sewage discharge.

FACT SUMMARY: When Illinois (D) began to discharge Chicago's raw sewage into a canal emptying into the Mississippi River, Missouri (P) brought suit to restrain such discharge, alleging that the water would be made unfit for use by its cities.

🏛 RULE OF LAW
Where a sovereign power deliberately permits discharges similar to those of which it complains, it must prove that its own conduct did not produce the complained-of result.

FACTS: The state of Missouri (P) brought suit to restrain the state of Illinois (D) from discharging Chicago's sewage through an artificial channel into the Des Plaines River, which emptied into the Illinois River, eventually emptying into the Mississippi about forty-three miles above the city of St. Louis. The suit alleged that the result of the discharge would be to send 1,500 tons of poisonous filth daily into the Mississippi. Missouri (P) alleged that typhoid fever had increased considerably since the canal was built and that the typhoid bacillus was able to survive the journey, reaching the intake of St. Louis in the Mississippi. However, Missouri (P) also permitted its own cities to discharge sewage into the Mississippi.

ISSUE: Where a sovereign power deliberately permits discharges similar to those of which it complains, must it prove that its own conduct did not produce the complained-of result?

HOLDING AND DECISION: (Holmes, J.) Yes. Where a sovereign power deliberately permits discharges similar to those of which it complains, it must prove that its own conduct did not produce the complained-of result. While there has been an increase in deaths from typhoid fever since the opening of the drainage canal, there has not been the enhanced rate of typhoid on the banks of the Illinois River that would be expected if the drainage canal were the true cause. Moreover, St. Louis must take preventive measures against the dangers created by Missouri's (P) own upriver discharge or from sources other than Illinois (D). The presence of causes of infection from Missouri's (P) own actions indicate that Missouri (P) has not proved cause in fact.

▶ ANALYSIS

The federal common law of nuisance is no longer a significant pollution control strategy, especially with the advent of comprehensive regulatory schemes that tend to preempt common law remedies. In addition, the nuisance doctrine cuts in favor of discharges in that it requires proof of cause. In fact, it permits courts to balance benefits against costs, and compliance with applicable regulations is a presumptive defense.

■■■

Quicknotes

ENJOIN The ordering of a party to cease the conduct of a specific activity.

■■■

Georgia v. Tennessee Copper Co.

State (P) v. Mining companies (D)

206 U.S. 230 (1907).

NATURE OF CASE: Bill in equity seeking to enjoin a defendant from discharging noxious gas.

FACT SUMMARY: Because Georgia's (P) air was being polluted and its forests, crops, and orchards were being destroyed by noxious gas emanating from the Ducktown (D) and Tennessee Copper Co. (D), Georgia (P) sought to enjoin the Copper Companies (D) from discharging the noxious gas over its territory.

🏛 RULE OF LAW
It is fair and reasonable for a sovereign to demand that the air over its territory, its forests, and its crops and orchards not be polluted or destroyed by sulfurous acid gas coming from a neighboring state.

FACTS: Georgia (P) sought to enjoin the Ducktown (D) and Tennessee Copper (D) smelters from discharging noxious gas from their works in Tennessee over Georgia's (P) territory. Georgia (P) alleged that the discharge resulted in pollution of its air and the wholesale destruction of its forests, orchards, and crops, with other injuries occurring in five counties of the state (P).

ISSUE: Is it fair and reasonable for a sovereign to demand that the air over its territory, its forests, and its crops and orchards not be polluted or destroyed by sulfurous acid gas coming from a neighboring state?

HOLDING AND DECISION: (Holmes, J.) Yes. It is fair and reasonable for a sovereign to demand that the air over its territory, its forests, and its crops and orchards not be polluted or destroyed by sulfurous acid gas coming from a neighboring state. Given the evidence in this case, the pollution of the air and the magnitude of that pollution are not open to dispute. A preponderance of the evidence showed that the sulfurous fumes caused and threatened damage on a considerable scale to the forests and vegetable life, if not to health, within the State of Georgia (P). Thus, there is no alternative to issuing an injunction, after allowing a reasonable time to the Copper Companies (D) to complete the structures that they are now building and the efforts they are making to stop the fumes. Injunction to issue.

▶ ANALYSIS

The Court noted that states were somewhat more entitled to specific relief than a private party might be. A state should not be required to give up quasi-sovereign rights in exchange for damages. Apart from the difficulty of valuing such rights in money, a state may insist that its sovereign rights not be impaired. The Court also declared that it did not have quite the same freedom to balance the equities when the plaintiff was a sovereign state as it would have if deciding between two subjects of a single political power.

■━■

Quicknotes

BILL IN EQUITY First pleading in a lawsuit in which a plaintiff seeks equitable remedies.

INJUNCTION A remedy imposed by the court ordering a party to cease the conduct of a specific activity.

■━■

International Paper Co. v. Ouellette

Manufacturer (D) v. Lakeshore property owners (P)

479 U.S. 481 (1987).

NATURE OF CASE: Appeal of a denial of a motion to dismiss action for nuisance.

FACT SUMMARY: A district court applied Vermont law rather than the Clean Water Act in an action brought by a Vermont resident against a New York company.

🏛 RULE OF LAW

The Clean Water Act precludes a court from applying the law of an affected state against an out-of-state source.

FACTS: International Paper Company (IPC) (D) discharged effluents into Lake Champlain, which borders Vermont. Ouellette (P), a Vermont resident, sued in a Vermont court for damages and injunctive relief. The action was removed to federal district court, and the court, holding Vermont law rather than the Clean Water Act applicable, denied a motion to dismiss. IPC (D) appealed, and the Second Circuit affirmed. The U.S. Supreme Court granted certiorari.

ISSUE: Does the Clean Water Act preclude a court from applying the law of an affected state against an out-of-state source?

HOLDING AND DECISION: (Powell, J.) Yes. The Clean Water Act precludes a court from applying the law of an affected state against an out-of-state source. The Clean Water Act constituted a far-reaching attempt at solving the national problem of water pollution and, in the absence of language specifically permitting states to regulate effluents discharged into their own waters, would completely preempt the field. Congress did give states the right to restrict flows into their own waters, but it would be reaching too far to permit affected states to regulate out-of-state sources. This would in effect negate the uniformity and comprehensiveness Congress hoped for in the Environmental Protection Agency's handling of pollution problems, and, therefore, the Clean Water Act, not Vermont law, was the proper law here. Reversed.

▶ ANALYSIS

By the time of this case's decision, it was well established that the Clean Water Act largely preempted the field. This was decided in *Illinois v. Milwaukee*, 406 U.S. 91 (1972). In a subsequent hearing on the same case, the Court decided that federal common law was also preempted by the Act. *Milwaukee v. Illinois*, 451 U.S. 304 (1981).

Quicknotes

CERTIORARI A discretionary writ issued by a superior court to an inferior court in order to review the lower court's decisions; the Supreme Court's writ ordering such review.

CLEAN WATER ACT Federal statute regulating water pollution.

INJUNCTION A remedy imposed by the court ordering a party to cease the conduct of a specific activity.

NUISANCE An unlawful use of property that interferes with the lawful use of another's property.

Sierra Club v. Morton

Environmental group (P) v. Secretary of the Interior (D)

405 U.S. 727 (1972).

NATURE OF CASE: Action to enjoin agency approval of a development plan.

FACT SUMMARY: The lower court concluded that the Sierra Club (P) did not have standing to sue to enjoin approval of a proposed resort development because it had not alleged any direct injury.

▥ RULE OF LAW
Mere interest in a problem is not sufficient by itself to give an organization or person standing to seek judicial review of an agency action related thereto.

FACTS: Suing as a membership corporation with "a special interest in the conservation and the sound maintenance of the national parks, game refuges and forests of the country," the Sierra Club (P) sought to enjoin approval by Morton (D), Secretary of the Interior, of a plan which Walt Disney Enterprises had to construct a $35 million resort in the Mineral King Valley (part of the Sierra Nevada Mountains). The lower court, which held the Sierra Club (P) had no standing, specifically pointed out that there was "no allegation in the complaint that members of the Sierra Club (P) would be affected by the actions . . . other than the fact that the actions are personally displeasing or distasteful to them." Its conclusion was that such concern could not, without a showing of more direct interest, constitute standing sufficient to challenge Forest Service approval of the plan.

ISSUE: Is a person's or organization's mere interest in a problem sufficient to give standing to seek judicial review of an agency action related to that problem?

HOLDING AND DECISION: (Stewart, J.) No. Section 10 of the Administrative Procedure Act (APA) provides that "[a] person suffering legal wrong because of agency action, or adversely affected or aggrieved by agency action . . . is entitled to judicial review thereof." A party or organization which, like the Sierra Club (P), has a mere interest in a problem simply is not within the class of those "adversely affected" or "aggrieved" within the meaning of the APA and thus has no standing to bring suit for review of the related agency action. Affirmed.

DISSENT: (Douglas, J.) A federal rule should be fashioned allowing environmental issues to be litigated in the name of the inanimate object about to be despoiled.

▶ ANALYSIS

The courts have recognized that the "injury in fact" required for standing may be to interests that "reflect 'aesthetic, conservational, and recreational' as well as economic values." However, the alleged injury must be to an interest "arguably within the zone of interests to be protected or regulated" by the statutes that the agencies are claimed to have violated.

■━■

Quicknotes

STANDING Whether a party possesses the right to commence suit against another party by having a personal stake in the resolution of the controversy.

■━■

Massachusetts v. EPA

State (P) v. Federal agency (D)

549 U.S. 497 (2007).

NATURE OF CASE: Appeal from lower court's decision that state lacked standing to bring claim.

FACT SUMMARY: Massachusetts (P) challenged the Environmental Protection Agency's (the EPA's) (D) decision not to regulate greenhouse gas emissions from new motor vehicles.

🏛 RULE OF LAW

A state has standing to sue an agency for action unlawfully withheld when the state can demonstrate actual or imminent harm, that the harm is traceable to the agency's lack of action, and that there is a substantial likelihood that the judicial relief requested will prompt the agency to reconsider its decision not to take action.

FACTS: Congress ordered the EPA (D) to promulgate new regulations for the emission of "any air pollutant from any class or classes of new motor vehicle engines, which in the [Administrator's] judgment cause, or contribute to, air pollution which may reasonably be anticipated to endanger public health or welfare." The EPA (D) refused to regulate the greenhouse emissions. Massachusetts (P) brought suit to force the EPA (D) to do so. The lower court found Massachusetts (P) did not have standing.

ISSUE: Does a state have standing to sue an agency for action unlawfully withheld when the state can demonstrate actual or imminent harm, that the harm is traceable to the agency's lack of action, and that there is a substantial likelihood the judicial relief requested will prompt the agency to reconsider its decision not to take action?

HOLDING AND DECISION: (Stevens, J.) Yes. A state has standing to sue an agency for action unlawfully withheld when the state can demonstrate actual or imminent harm, that the harm is traceable to the agency's lack of action, and that there is a substantial likelihood the judicial relief requested will prompt the agency to reconsider its decision not to take action. In this matter, Congress has granted litigants a procedural right to challenge the EPA's (D) denial of Massachusetts' (P) request for a rule making petition. When a litigant is vested with such a procedural right, the litigant will have standing if there is "some possibility" that judicial relief will prompt the agency to reconsider its position on a state's petition for redress. Here, the unchallenged affidavits from Massachusetts (P) show an actual harm. That harm is the rise in sea levels that has already affected Massachusetts' (P) shores. There is causation between that harm and the EPA's (D) failure to regulate greenhouse emissions. Reducing emissions from the

U.S. transportation sector would reduce or remove massive amounts of carbon dioxide each year, even if that amount is only a small percentage of the worldwide emissions. Agencies, like legislatures, are free to regulate in incremental steps. Lastly, regarding a possible remedy, the risk of harm from greenhouse gases is real, and Massachusetts' (P) alleged harm would be addressed if a court were to order the EPA (D) to regulate the emissions. Accordingly, Massachusetts (P) has standing to bring suit.

DISSENT: The text does not include any portion of the dissent from Justices Scalia, Thomas, Alito and Chief Justice Roberts. However, the text briefly states their position that Massachusetts (P) should not have standing because the harm from climate change is too speculative to be remedied in the judicial forum. The Chief Justice wrote that this issue was one better suited for the legislative and executive branches of government.

▶ ANALYSIS

This decision is a fine example of the justices' political positions being presented through a particular legal issue. Here, the legal issue was standing, but clearly the argument between the Court's liberal and conservative justices (with Justice Kennedy in the middle) concerned the severity of the threat of climate change. As the text states in notes following the decision, Chief Justice Roberts thought the threat of harm was "pure conjecture." In addition, the case highlights another important distinction between the liberal and conservative wings of the Supreme Court. The current conservative justices view the judiciary's role in such issues much more narrowly than the liberal wing. In this case, however, Justice Kennedy joined the four liberal justices to find that Massachusetts (P) had demonstrated an actual harm.

■=∎

Quicknotes

STANDING The right to commence suit against another party because of a personal stake in the resolution of the controversy.

STANDING TO SUE Plaintiff must allege that he has a legally protectable interest at stake in the litigation.

■=∎

New York v. United States

State (P) v. Federal government (D)

505 U.S. 144 (1992).

NATURE OF CASE: Challenge to federal law regulating radioactive-waste disposal.

FACT SUMMARY: Congress enacted a law mandating that if states did not provide for disposal of radioactive waste, they would take title thereto.

🏛 RULE OF LAW
Congress cannot mandate that a state either dispose of an undesirable substance or take title to it.

FACTS: In 1986, Congress amended the 1980 low-level Radioactive Waste Policy Act (the Act). The 1980 Act had mandated that states formulate their own methods for disposal of low-level radioactive waste. The 1986 amendments provided, among other things, that if a state did not formulate a plan to dispose of such waste, it would by operation of law take title to the waste and become liable for all damages if it does not do so promptly. The State of New York (P) challenged the constitutionality of the law. The Second Circuit rejected the challenge, and the Supreme Court granted review.

ISSUE: Can Congress mandate that a state either dispose of an undesirable substance or take title to it?

HOLDING AND DECISION: (O'Connor, J.) No. Congress cannot mandate that a state either dispose of an undesirable substance or take title to it. Under principles of federalism embodied in the U.S. Constitution, states are not administrative units of the federal government; rather, they are sovereign entities retaining all powers not specifically delegated to the federal government. Under its Commerce Clause and spending powers, Congress has broad power to regulate matters between the states. Where a basis for federal jurisdiction exists, Congress can create legislation to be implemented by the Executive. However, Congress cannot, consistent with the Tenth Amendment, compel state governments to implement federal legislation. Here, Congress has given states the choice between implementing federal law or taking title to a category of material, a thing Congress cannot force upon a state. It follows that since neither option by itself can be forced upon a state by Congress, a choice between the two cannot be mandated. Consequently, the "take title" with the governmental structure established by the Constitution is inconsistent. Reversed.

▶ ANALYSIS

For much of the twentieth century, the Tenth Amendment has been all but forgotten in the post–New Deal swelling of federal power. In the last few years, however, a backlash against perceived federal encroachment on state and local powers has emerged with the Tenth Amendment as its legal cornerstone. Several significant pieces of federal legislation, such as the Brady Bill (a handgun control law) prior to its passage, unexpectedly ran into trouble with the Tenth Amendment.

■■■

Quicknotes

COMMERCE CLAUSE Article 1, section 8, clause 3 of the United States Constitution, granting Congress the power to regulate commerce with foreign countries and between the states.

LOW-LEVEL RADIOACTIVE WASTE POLICY ACT Federal act mandating that states that failed to make arrangements to dispose of low-level radioactive wastes must "take title" to such waste within their borders.

SPENDING POWER The power delegated to Congress by the Constitution to spend money in providing for the nation's welfare.

■■■

Sierra Club v. Costle

Conservation club (P) v. Government agency (D)

657 F.2d 298 (D.C. Cir. 1981).

NATURE OF CASE: Challenge to an Environmental Protection Agency (EPA) standard.

FACT SUMMARY: An undocketed meeting between Environmental Protection Agency (EPA) (D) officials, the President, and the White House staff was held during the post-comment period of the EPA rulemaking process.

> ### 🏛 RULE OF LAW
> Informal meetings with the President during the rulemaking process need not be documented.

FACTS: The EPA (D) met with the President and his staff in order to discuss the issues raised by a performance standards rule the EPA (D) intended to promulgate. The meeting occurred in the post-comment period and was undocketed. The Sierra Club (P) maintained that because the President's involvement weakened the standards of the rule, the meeting had to be documented in accordance with § 307(d) of the Clean Air Act.

ISSUE: Must informal meetings with the President during the rule-making process be documented?

HOLDING AND DECISION: (Wald, J.) No. Informal meetings with the President during the rulemaking process need not be documented. Section 307(d) of the Clean Air Act (the Act) establishes procedural rules for documenting the rulemaking process under the Act. This section of the Act insures the proper documentation of the decision-making process. The requirement, however, should not interfere with the executive branch's ability to function effectively. The EPA (D) is an agency of the executive branch. Under the Constitution, the executive branch has the authority to engage in such informal communications without violating the commands of Congress. Here, the rulemaking process was adequately documented without the inclusion of this one meeting in the docket.

▶ ANALYSIS

In a later case, the court struck down an agency decision to delete an exposure limit from a regulation at the behest of the Office of Management and Budget. Rather than address the constitutional issues of delegated powers, the court based its decision on the fact that the decision to strike the language was not supported by the record. *Public Citizen Health Research Group v. Tyson*, 796 F.2d 1479 (D.C. Cir. 1986).

Quicknotes

CLEAN AIR ACT, § 307 Makes specific provision for including "written comments" in the rulemaking docket.

Chevron U.S.A. v. Natural Resources Defense Council

Company (D) v. Environmental organization (P)

467 U.S. 837 (1984).

NATURE OF CASE: Review of agency construction of a statute.

FACT SUMMARY: The National Resources Defense Council (the NRDC) (P) appealed a court of appeals decision rejecting the Environmental Protection Agency's (the EPA's) construction of the term "stationary source," which allowed states to treat all of the pollution-emitting devices within the same industrial grouping as if they were encased in a "bubble."

RULE OF LAW
When a court reviews an agency's construction of a statute, its review is limited to whether the agency's construction of the statute in the context of its particular program was a reasonable one.

FACTS: The EPA construed the term "stationary source" as used in the nonattainment provisions of the Clean Air Act to allow states to treat all of the pollutant-emitting devices within the same industrial grouping as if they were encased in a "bubble" for the purpose of setting state (SIP) emissions limitations. Chevron U.S.A. (D) and the NRDC (P) became involved in litigation over the issuance of permits under a state's SIP. Chevron (D) challenged the EPA's construction of the term "stationary source." The court of appeal, in its own view, felt that the "bubble" concept was inappropriate in the general context of a program designed to improve air quality. From this decision, the NRDC (P) appealed.

ISSUE: When a court reviews an agency's construction of a statute, is its review limited to whether the agency's construction of the statute, in the context of its particular program, was a reasonable one?

HOLDING AND DECISION: (Stevens, J.) Yes. When a court reviews an agency's construction of a statute, its review is limited to whether the agency's construction of the statute, in the context of its particular program, was a reasonable one. Initially, a court should look for a clear expression of congressional intent with respect to the statute in question. Absent this expression of intent, however, the court should defer to any reasonable agency construction of the statute; it should not substitute its own views for the views of the agency. In the present case, the language of the statute compels no particular interpretation of the term "stationary source," but the interplay of the particular provisions relevant to the agency's construction indicate the intent to expand the scope of the agency's power to regulate sources of air pollutants. Contrary to Chevron's (D) arguments, the legislative history is likewise unilluminating as to the statute's construction. When the construction is viewed in light of the EPA's environmental policies, it must be concluded that the EPA has made a reasonable construction of the statute to effectuate these policies. The arguments over policy have already been waged in front of the Agency, which has adopted the "bubble" concept, and such arguments are not properly addressed to the judiciary. Since the Agency's construction of the statute employing the use of the "bubble" concept was not contrary to congressional intent and reasonable in light of EPA policy, the court of appeals erred in substituting its own "reasonable" views for those of the EPA. Reversed.

ANALYSIS

Since the standard involved in the present case is only whether the construction is reasonable in light of the Agency's policies, it appears that the use of the "bubble" concept may not be permanent. More than one reasonable construction may be acceptable under any given policy, and as circumstances change, agency policy may change to reflect these circumstances.

■=■

Quicknotes

SIP State implementation plan.

■=■

CHAPTER 3

Preventing Harm in the Face of Uncertainty

Quick Reference Rules of Law

Reserve Mining Company v. EPA

Mining company (D) v. Federal regulatory agency (P)

514 F.2d 492, *en banc* (8th Cir. 1975).

NATURE OF CASE: Appeal from injunction against further discharges of waste.

FACT SUMMARY: The Environmental Protection Agency (the EPA) (P) obtained an injunction preventing Reserve Mining Company (Reserve) (D) from any further dumping of mining byproducts containing asbestos into Lake Superior.

🏛 RULE OF LAW
In authorizing the United States to bring action to secure abatement of water discharges that "endanger the health or welfare of persons," the Federal Water Pollution Control Act covers instances where there is evidence of potential harm as well as those where there is evidence of actual harm.

FACTS: Although there was substantial evidence that inhalation of asbestos caused cancer, the scientific evidence as to whether ingestion of asbestos (through incorporation in drinking water, etc.) also caused cancer was uncertain at best. Yet, there was enough evidence thereof to prompt the EPA (P) to bring suit to enjoin Reserve (D) from continuing to discharge mining byproducts containing asbestos into Lake Superior. In addition to the health risk which it concluded was posed by Reserve's (D) discharges, the district court premised its issuance of an injunction to the discharges upon Reserve's (D) persistent refusal to implement a reasonable alternative plan for on-land disposal of the byproducts at issue.

ISSUE: Can the federal government seek abatement of water discharges on the grounds that they "endanger the health or welfare of persons" where there is evidence of potential harm?

HOLDING AND DECISION: (Bright, J.) Yes. The Federal Water Pollution Control Act authorizes the federal government to bring action to secure abatement of water discharges into interstate waters where the discharges violate state water quality standards and "endanger . . . the health or welfare of persons." In this context, Congress used the term "endanger" in a precautionary or preventive sense, and, therefore, evidence of potential harm as well as actual harm comes within the purview of that term. In this case, the best that can be said is that the existence of asbestos in air and water gives rise to a reasonable medical concern for the public health. The public's exposure to asbestos fibers in air and water creates some health risk. Such a contaminant should be removed. During these appeal proceedings, Reserve (D) has indicated its willingness to deposit its byproducts on land and to properly filter its air emissions. It is willing to spend $243 million in plant alterations and construction to halt its pollution of air and water. This offer, when viewed in conjunction with the uncertain quality of the health risk created by discharges of asbestos into the water supply, weighs heavily against a ruling which closes Reserve's (D) plant immediately. The district court abused its discretion by immediately closing this major industrial plant. Here, the risk of harm to the public is potential, not imminent or certain. Furthermore, Reserve (D) says it earnestly seeks a practical way to abate the pollution. A remedy should be fashioned which will serve the ultimate public weal by ensuring clean air, clean water, and continued jobs in an industry vital to the nation's welfare. Assuming agreement and designation of an appropriate disposal site, Reserve (D) is entitled to a reasonable turnaround time to construct the necessary facilities and accomplish a changeover in the means of disposing of its problematic wastes.

▶ ANALYSIS

Regulation of toxic waste is particularly complex and troublesome because such regulation often takes place at or beyond the edge of scientific knowledge. Thus, the courts are faced with the problem of engaging in judicial review in an area in which even the leading experts in the field are in disagreement as to the benefits and drawbacks of a disputed substance or method. As the authors note, "How can a cost-benefit analysis be conducted when the substance being regulated is possibly deadly, but no one knows the odds?"

■=■

Quicknotes

ABATEMENT A decrease or lessening of something; in equity, a suspension or dismissal of a cause of action.

INJUNCTION A court order requiring a person to do or prohibiting that person from doing a specific act.

■=■

Ethyl Corp. v. EPA

Petroleum company (P) v. Federal regulatory agency (D)

541 F.2d 1, *en banc* (D.C. Cir. 1976).

NATURE OF CASE: Appeal from a judgment striking down federal regulations.

FACT SUMMARY: After the Environmental Protection Agency Administrator (D) promulgated regulations to control lead emissions on the ground that such emissions presented a risk of harm to the public health, Ethyl Corp. (P) argued that the Administrator (D) could not order limits on lead emissions without proof of actual harm.

🏛 RULE OF LAW
Where a statute allows for regulation in the face of danger, regulatory action may be taken based on a probable risk of harm.

FACTS: Section 211(c)(1)(A) of the Clean Air Act authorized the Administrator of the Environmental Protection Agency (EPA) (D) to regulate gasoline additives if their emissions "will endanger the public health or welfare." Concluding that lead in gasoline presented "a substantial risk of harm," the EPA Administrator (D) ordered reductions in the lead content of gasoline. Ethyl Corp. (P) sought judicial review of the EPA (D) regulations of lead emissions, arguing that the Administrator (D) must decide that such emissions "will endanger" the public health solely on "facts" or by a chain of scientific facts or reasoning leading him ineluctably to this conclusion. The regulations were struck down by a three-judge panel of the D.C. Circuit. The EPA (D) then sought this rehearing en banc.

ISSUE: Where a statute allows for regulation in the face of danger, may regulatory action be taken based on a probable risk of harm?

HOLDING AND DECISION: (Wright, J.) Yes. Where a statute allows for regulation in the face of danger, regulatory action may be taken based on a probable risk of harm. Where evidence is difficult to come by, uncertain, or conflicting because it is on the frontiers of scientific knowledge, the Administrator (D) may assess risks. He may apply his expertise to draw conclusions from suspected, but not completely substantiated, relationships between facts, from trends among facts, and the like. A conclusion so drawn may, if rational, form the basis for health-related regulations under the "will endanger the public health" language of § 211 of the Clean Air Act. The certainty demanded by Ethyl Corp. (P) has never characterized the judicial or the administrative process. Furthermore, the standard of ordinary civil litigation, a preponderance of the evidence, demands only 51% certainty. Reversed.

▶ ANALYSIS

The holding in this case and in *Reserve Mining Co. v. EPA*, 514 F.2d 492 (8th Cir. 1975), (the public health may properly be found "endangered" both by a lesser risk of a greater harm and by a greater risk of a lesser harm) have influenced judicial interpretation of all regulatory statutes that seek to proactively protect health and the environment. In fact, when Congress authorized regulations of pollutants that "endanger" the public in the Clean Air Act, it explicitly endorsed the *Reserve Mining-Ethyl* approach to risk management.

Quicknotes

CLEAN AIR ACT Required certain states to establish a permit program for stationary sources of air pollution.

Industrial Union Dept., AFL-CIO v. American Petroleum Institute
(The *Benzene* Decision)

Safety Administration (D) v. Petroleum institute (P)

448 U.S. 607 (1980).

NATURE OF CASE: Appeal from the invalidation of a regulation promulgated by a federal agency in accord with federal law.

FACT SUMMARY: After the Occupational Health and Safety Administration (OSHA) (D) promulgated a standard lowering the amount of benzene in the workplace from 10 ppm to 1 ppm, the American Petroleum Institute (P) challenged the standard.

🏛 RULE OF LAW
Before promulgating a standard to control the use of toxic substances in the workplace, a threshold determination must be made that such standard is reasonably necessary and appropriate to provide safe or healthful places of employment.

FACTS: OSHA (D) reduced the exposure limit on airborne concentrations of benzene in the workplace from 10 ppm to 1 ppm, after determining that there was a causal connection between benzene and leukemia. OSHA (D) then determined that compliance with that level was technologically feasible and would not threaten the financial welfare of the affected firms or the general economy. Although OSHA (D) could not construct an accurate dose-response curve to predict the number of leukemias at the prior or current levels, it nevertheless determined that the benefits of the proposed standard were likely to be appreciable. The American Petroleum Institute (P) challenged the standard. The court of appeals found the regulation invalid, holding that OSHA (D) had not demonstrated that the costs of the standard bore a reasonable relationship to its benefits. OSHA (D) appealed.

ISSUE: Before promulgating a standard to control the use of toxic substances in the workplace, must a threshold determination be made that such standard is reasonably necessary and appropriate to provide safe or healthful places of employment?

HOLDING AND DECISION: (Stevens, J.) Yes. Before promulgating a standard to control the use of toxic substances in the workplace, a threshold determination must be made that such standard is reasonably necessary and appropriate to provide safe or healthful places of employment. Although OSHA (D) has no duty to calculate the exact probability of harm, it does have an obligation to find that a significant risk is present before it can characterize a place of employment as unsafe. In this case, OSHA (D) did not even attempt to carry its burden of proof. Its finding that the benefits to be derived from lowering the permissible exposure level from 10 ppm to 1 ppm were likely to be appreciable was not supported by substantial evidence. Only after the

threshold determination has been made, would it be necessary to decide whether the statute requires that the most protective standard consistent with economic and technological feasibility be selected or whether the benefits of the regulation must be weighed against the costs of its implementation. Because the threshold determination was not made here, there is no need to decide those issues. Affirmed.

CONCURRENCE: (Rehnquist, J.) Congress has improperly delegated the choice confronting us here to the Secretary of Labor (D) and, derivatively, to this Court. In the case of a hazardous substance for which a "safe" level is either unknown or impractical, the language of § 6(b)(5) gives the Secretary (D) absolutely no indication where on the continuum of relative safety he should draw his line. It is the hard choices, and not the filling in of the blanks, which must be made by the elected representatives of the people.

DISSENT: (Marshall, J.) The plurality's "threshold finding" requirement is nowhere to be found in the Act and is antithetical to its basic purposes. In reducing the permissible level of exposure to benzene, the Secretary (D) applied proper legal standards. His determinations were supported by substantial evidence. Thus, his decision was one which the governing legislation authorized him to make. OSHA (D) must decide whether to take regulatory action against possible substantial risks or to wait until more definitive information becomes available—a judgment which by its very nature cannot be based solely on determinations of fact.

▶ ANALYSIS

Prior to this case, the Fifth Circuit Court of Appeals had invalidated the standard for failure of OSHA (D) to demonstrate a reasonable cost-benefit relationship. See *American Petroleum Institute v. OSHA*, 581 F.2d 493 (5th Cir. 1978). OSHA (D) sought Supreme Court review as to whether the OSH Act required such cost-benefit balancing. The parties were surprised when the Supreme Court decided the case on other grounds. In examining §§ 3(8) and 6(b)(5), the plurality thought it clear that both the language and structure of the Act, as well as its legislative history, indicated that it intended to require the elimination, so far as feasible, of "significant" risks of harm.

■══■

Quicknotes

OSHA The Occupational Health and Safety Commission, a federal agency which oversees job safety and health regulation.

■══■

Chlorine Chemistry Council v. EPA

Trade association of chlorine manufacturers (P) v. Federal regulatory agency (D)

206 F.3d 1286 (D.C. Cir. 2000).

NATURE OF CASE: Petition for review of an Environmental Protection Agency (the EPA) (D) rule.

FACT SUMMARY: Chlorine Chemistry Council (Chlorine) (P) petitioned the court to review the standard set by the EPA (D) regarding chloroform.

🏛 RULE OF LAW
When implementing the provisions of the Safe Drinking Water Act, the EPA is required to use the best evidence available at the time of the rulemaking.

FACTS: Pursuant to the Safe Drinking Water Act (the Act), the EPA (D) set the maximum contaminant level goal (MCLG) for chloroform at zero. The MCLG is defined as the level at which no known or anticipated adverse effects on the health of persons will occur. Setting it at zero assumes there is no safe threshold. However, exposure to chloroform below some threshold level poses no risk of cancer. The EPA's (D) Notice of Data Availability discussed the findings of a panel of experts organized by the International Life Sciences Institute which concluded that chloroform was unlikely to be a carcinogen below a certain dose range. The EPA (D) agreed with the panel that the nonlinear approach was the preferred approach in quantifying the cancer risk associated with chloroform exposure. The EPA (D) then proposed an MGLA of 300 ppb, but when it promulgated its final rule, its MGLA was zero. The EPA (D) based its standard on the need to consult the report of the Science Advisory Board (SAB), which would not be available until after the deadline for rulemaking had expired. Chlorine (P) petitioned the court for review of the standard. Subsequently, the SAB's report indicated that chloroform's mode of action involves no carcinogenic effects at low doses, thus a nonlinear approach is scientifically reasonable.

ISSUE: When implementing the provisions of the Safe Drinking Water Act, must the EPA use the best evidence available at the time of the rulemaking?

HOLDING AND DECISION: (Williams, J.) Yes. When implementing the provisions of the Safe Drinking Water Act, the EPA is required to use the best evidence available at the time of the rulemaking. Here, the EPA (D) violated its mandate to use the best available evidence when implementing the provisions of the Safe Drinking Water Act. The evidence available to the EPA (D) at the time of rulemaking was that there was a certain dose range below which chloroform was unlikely to be a carcinogen. The EPA (D) did not act on its own scientific findings to create an appropriate MGLA, but rather set the MGLA at zero

pending the evidence that the SAB would later reveal. This is a violation of their mandate because the EPA (D) cannot reject the best available evidence at the time of the rulemaking based on the possibility that the future might reveal some other evidence. Although adopting a nonzero MCLG is a step which departs from previous practice, the rules require the EPA (D) to set the MCLG at the level at which no known or anticipated adverse effect on the health of persons would occur as determined on the basis of the best available evidence. Furthermore, the EPA's (D) own guidelines state that when adequate data on mode of action show that linearity is not the most reasonable working judgment and provide sufficient evidence to support a nonlinear mode of action the default assumption of linearity should not be used. Moreover, the EPA (D) is still required to fulfill its statutory obligation, even if the results may be new or politically charged. Vacated.

▶ ANALYSIS

It is unusual for a court to reverse, as it did in this case, an EPA choice among different scientific conclusions.

■=■

Corrosion Proof Fittings v. EPA

Building company (P) v. Federal regulatory agency (D)

947 F.2d 1201 (5th Cir. 1991).

NATURE OF CASE: Appeal from petition to review an Environmental Protection Agency regulation.

FACT SUMMARY: The Environmental Protection Agency (the EPA) (D) passed a regulation banning nearly all uses of asbestos.

🏛 RULE OF LAW
The EPA, prior to imposing regulation, must consider the cost and benefits of various regulatory options, commencing with the least burdensome.

FACTS: The EPA (D) passed a regulation prohibiting almost all present and future uses of asbestos. Pursuant to the Toxic Substances Control Act (the TSCA), the EPA (D) determined that the best way to lower the risk from asbestos was a total ban. This measure would cost in the range of $128–227 million to save approximately three lives. Corrosion Proof Fittings (Corrosion) (P) used asbestos in its business, and there was no substitute product it could use. Corrosion (P) contested the EPA (D) regulation.

ISSUE: Must the EPA, prior to imposing regulation, consider the cost and benefits of various regulatory options, commencing with the least burdensome?

HOLDING AND DECISION: (Smith, J.) Yes. The EPA (D), prior to imposing regulation, must consider the cost and benefits of various regulatory options, commencing with the least burdensome. The TSCA requires that, after the EPA (D) determines the appropriate level of risk, it must examine all options to determine the least burdensome option. In this case, the EPA (D) dismissed all options short of a total ban, which was the most drastic option open to it. Its failure to scrutinize other options is especially egregious in light of the fact that there currently are no substitutes for asbestos. The cost per life saved does not justify, as reasonable, the total ban on the use of asbestos. Vacated and remanded.

▶ ANALYSIS

The TSCA was promulgated to allow the EPA (D) to regulate the use of toxic substances in various industries simultaneously. As such, the EPA (D) is in a stronger position to enforce toxics regulation than OSHA since it can regulate a greater scope of activity.

■■■

Quicknotes

OSHA The Occupational Health and Safety Commission, a federal agency which oversees job safety and health regulation.

■■■

Natural Resources Defense Council v. EPA

Advocacy group (P) v. Federal agency (D)

489 F.3d 1364 (D.C. Cir. 2007).

NATURE OF CASE: Consolidated appeal of two petitions to the Environmental Protection Agency (the EPA) (D) to regulate hazardous air pollution.

FACT SUMMARY: The EPA (D) created a new low risk subcategory of sources that would allow plywood and other wood products to be processed at a lower regulatory compliance level than other pollutant sources.

RULE OF LAW
The EPA has no authority to create a new low risk subcategory providing for the release of harmful emissions that is contrary to Congress's statutory scheme.

FACTS: This decision involved two consolidated appeals from the EPA (D) action to create a new subcategory of pollutant sources that essentially would have no regulations for release of emissions. It was called the low risk subcategory. The specific pollutant source in this case was the process to create plywood and other wood products. The process releases six harmful pollutants into the air. The EPA (D) found, among other things, that the carcinogens released were not in levels higher than the statutory ceilings. The National Resources Defense Council (P) challenged the EPA's (D) statutory authority to create such subcategories.

ISSUE: Does the EPA have authority to create a new low risk subcategory providing for the release of harmful emissions that is contrary to Congress's statutory scheme?

HOLDING AND DECISION: (Rogers, J.) No. The EPA has no authority to create a new low risk subcategory providing for the release of harmful emissions that is contrary to Congress's statutory scheme. The creation of the low risk subcategory is inconsistent with § 112 of the Clean Air Act. Specifically, § 112(c)(2) requires that the EPA (D) create emissions standards even for the low risk subcategory. While the EPA (D) is correct that Congress used "category" and "subcategory" interchangeably in the Clean Air Act, § 112 (c)(2) states that the EPA (D) may remove a category, not a subcategory from its source list of polluters. In short, the EPA (D) cannot create a subcategory of sources without creating emissions standards. That action plainly contravenes the purpose of the Clean Air Act. Therefore, EPA's (D) interpretation fails part one of the *Chevron* test, because the statute is unambiguous.

ANALYSIS

In *Chevron U.S.A., Inc. v. Natural Resources Defense Council, Inc.,* 467 U.S. 837 (1984), the Supreme Court created a two-part examination for testing the sufficiency of an agency's ruling of its own enabling statute. First, a court should review the agency's enabling statute and determine if it is ambiguous as the facts apply to it. Second, the court determines if the agency's interpretation of the statute was reasonable. If the interpretation was reasonable, a reviewing court should not disturb the agency's ruling. Here, the court found that the EPA's (D) ruling was in conflict with an unambiguous portion of the Clean Air Act. Therefore, the EPA (D) could not get by stage one of the *Chevron* test.

■■▬■

Quicknotes

CLEAN AIR ACT Required certain states to establish a permit program for stationary sources of air pollution.

■■▬■

Natural Resources Defense Council v. EPA

Advocacy group (P) v. Federal agency (D)

529 F.3d 1077 (D.C. Cir. 2008).

NATURE OF CASE: Appeal of petition to the Environmental Protection Agency (the EPA) (D) to regulate synthetic organic chemicals.

FACT SUMMARY: The EPA (D) determined that under the technology-based standard for the industry, no individual would face a cancer risk greater than one hundred in one million.

🏛 RULE OF LAW

Section 112(f)(2)(A) of the Clean Air Act mandates that the EPA "promulgate standards," but it does not specify the contents of such standards.

FACTS: The EPA (D) determined that under the technology based standard for the synthetic organic chemical industry, no individual would face a cancer risk greater than one hundred in one million. The Natural Resources Defense Council (NRDC) (P) argues that the applicable provision of Section 112 of the Clean Air Act mandates that the standard for the industry involved should be a cancer risk of one in one million.

ISSUE: Section 112(f)(2)(A) of the Clean Air Act mandates that the EPA "promulgate standards," but does it specify the contents of such standards?

HOLDING AND DECISION: (Silberman, J.) No. Section 112(f)(2)(A) of the Clean Air Act mandates that the EPA (D) "promulgate standards," but it does not specify the contents of such standards. The specific provision at issue is 42 U.S.C. § 7412(f)(2)(A). The provision's third sentence states in pertinent part, "If standards promulgated pursuant to subsection (d) of this section . . . do not reduce lifetime excess cancer risks to the individuals most exposed to emissions from a source in the category or subcategory to less than one in one million, the Administrator shall promulgate standards under this subsection for such source category." The NRDC (P) reads this provision to state that the EPA's (D) standards for the industry involved must be one in one million. However, the statute does not say that. Instead, it says the EPA (D) must "promulgate standards," but it does specify what those standards must be. Therefore, EPA's (D) construction of the statute is a reasonable one and passes the *Chevron* test.

▶ ANALYSIS

This case, as with many appellate decisions involving the EPA (D), is mainly an exercise in statutory interpretation. The NRDC (P) wanted the court to find that EPA (D) must mandate the higher one in one million threshold for this industry. In response, the EPA (D) felt the lower one hun-dred in one million risk was more appropriate. The third sentence, as the decision notes, is essentially a compromise position. Where the standards for an industry do not reduce the risk to the one in one million threshold, the EPA (D) should proceed through another round of regulation for the industry. The statute does not specify what the standards shall be for that second round, only that the EPA (D) shall promulgate standards.

Quicknotes

CLEAN AIR ACT Required certain states to establish a permit program for stationary sources of air pollution.

Waste Management and Pollution Prevention

Quick Reference Rules of Law

American Mining Congress v. EPA
Mining group (P) v. Government agency (D)
824 F.2d 1177 (D.C. Cir. 1987).

NATURE OF CASE: Petition for review of Environmental Protection Agency (EPA) final rule.

FACT SUMMARY: The American Mining Congress (P) contended that the Resource Conservation and Recovery Act did not cover materials destined to be recycled.

🏛 RULE OF LAW
The term "solid waste," as used in the Resource Conservation and Recovery Act (RCRA), applies only to materials actually disposed of, and not to those materials which will be reused.

FACTS: The EPA (D) passed a rule defining solid wastes to include material destined to be recycled. The new rule gave the EPA (D) the authority to regulate material that was not yet disposed of. The American Mining Congress (AMC) (P) petitioned for review, claiming that the rule extended the EPA's (D) power to regulate beyond statutory jurisdiction.

ISSUE: Does the term "solid waste," as used in the RCRA, only apply to materials actually disposed of, and not to those materials that will be reused?

HOLDING AND DECISION: (Starr, J.) Yes. The term "solid waste," as used in the RCRA, applies only to materials actually disposed of, and not to those materials that will be reused. The RCRA empowers the EPA (D) to regulate the management of hazardous waste. The definition of hazardous waste limits the EPA's (D) jurisdiction to materials that constitute "solid waste." The statutory definition of "solid waste" uses the term "discarded material." The plain meaning of that phrase can only mean materials that are thrown away or abandoned. Materials being stored for a secondary use or recycling are not abandoned. Congressional intent supports the clear meaning of the statutory language. The EPA (D) exceeded its jurisdiction in trying to regulate materials intended for recycling. Petition for review granted.

DISSENT: (Mikva, J.) Congressional intent supports a definition of "discarded material" that encompasses all materials put in contact with the environment in a manner that could potentially cause harm. The EPA (D) rule should be upheld.

▶ ANALYSIS

The EPA (D) must be careful in regulating waste so as not to interfere with and, in effect, regulate the manufacturing process. A subsequent *AMC* case rejected the industry's claim that sludge residue from waste water was not hazardous waste because it was to be reused at some future date for mineral recovery. The court concluded that once the sludge was impounded it had entered the waste stream and was therefore subject to EPA (D) oversight. *American Mining Congress v. EPA*, 907 F.2d 1179 (D.C. Cir. 1990).

■═■

City of Chicago v. Environmental Defense Fund

City (D) v. Environmental group (P)

511 U.S. 328 (1994).

NATURE OF CASE: Grant of certiorari for appeal from Seventh Circuit ruling interpreting Hazardous and Solid Waste amendments.

FACT SUMMARY: Municipalities brought suit over judicial interpretation of a 1984 Congressional "clarification" that held that although household and nonhazardous waste incineration does not fall under Resource Conservation and Recovery Act of 1976 Subtitle C regulations for hazardous waste, the ash produced from such waste does.

🏛 RULE OF LAW
Ash generated by a resource recovery facility's incineration of municipal solid waste is not exempt from regulation as a hazardous waste.

FACTS: The Resource Conservation and Recovery Act of 1976 (RCRA) empowered the Environmental Protection Agency (EPA) to designate hazardous and nonhazardous wastes for regulation under the Act. Under RCRA Subtitle C, the EPA set standards for hazardous waste transporters and generators, as well as for owners of facilities that treat, store, and dispose of hazardous waste (TSDFs). When the EPA standards appeared in 1980, they excluded household waste from the ambit of Subtitle C despite the fact that some household waste, such as cleaning fluids and batteries, would be defined as hazardous. Instead, household waste was placed with nonhazardous wastes in the infinitely less restricted ambit of Subtitle D. Also, under the preamble to the EPA regulations, facilities disposing solely of household waste would not have their residues (i.e., incinerator ash) subject to Subtitle C, and incinerators that burned only household waste would not be classified as Subtitle C TSDFs. If the facility burned anything in addition to household waste, however, even nonhazardous waste, then the exemption for ash did not apply if the ash (which can be more hazardous than its original substance) proved to be in hazardous concentrations. In 1984, Congress enacted § 3001(I), the "Clarification of Household Waste Exclusion," which indicated that facilities that receive and burn only household and nonhazardous waste are not deemed to be "treating, storing, disposing of, or otherwise managing hazardous wastes" under Subtitle C. No explicit mention of the ash produced by such burning was made. The Environmental Defense Fund (P) sued to require Subtitle C regulation of ash that qualified as hazardous waste, even if it was the product of combined household and non-hazardous burning. Municipal incinerator representatives of the City of Chicago (the City) (D) argued that the phrase "or otherwise managing" included the disposal of ash produced from incineration and that, if this was not the case, then § 3001(I) did nothing but codify previously existing law as

promulgated by the EPA. The Seventh Circuit disagreed and ruled that the cost-saving waste stream exemption of combined household and nonhazardous waste ash was not in the statute. The City (D) appealed and the Supreme Court granted review, in part because cases debating this subject were occurring in every circuit in the country.

ISSUE: Is the ash generated by incineration of municipal solid waste exempt from regulation as a hazardous waste?

HOLDING AND DECISION: (Scalia, J.) No. The ash generated by incineration of municipal solid waste is not exempt from regulation as a hazardous waste. The plain meaning of the language of § 3001(I), the Clarification of Household Waste Exclusion, is that while the ash produced in a facility burning household waste alone is exempt, there is no such exception for combined household and nonhazardous waste. If this ash is hazardous, it must be disposed of according to Subtitle C and not disposed of in ordinary landfills. The City's (D) argument, that by exempting the facility you exempt the ash produced, is erroneous. The City's (D) other argument that if the codification by Congress does not include combined waste facilities' ash then the amendment is a nullity, is also inaccurate. RCRA has twin goals of encouraging resource recovery and protecting the environment against contamination; sometimes these two purposes will conflict. In this situation, the Seventh Circuit ruling that § 3001(I) does not create an exception for combined facilities' hazardous ash is affirmed.

DISSENT: (Stevens, J.) The apparent tension between the broad definition of the term "hazardous waste generation" in the 1976 Act and the more specific exclusion for the activity of burning household and nonhazardous wastes in the 1984 amendment should be resolved by giving effect to the latter. The amendment should be interpreted as stating that mixing nonhazardous waste does not extinguish the household exception. There is no legislative history to indicate the intent to impose significant new burdens on municipal incinerators. While the majority would give the reader the impression that the pure household ash exemption is still intact, the Court acknowledges that its construction of the statute effectively withholds all waste-stream exceptions, even from exclusively household waste facilities. This is due to its erroneous reading of the definition of "waste generation." The EPA household waste exemption was the result of weighing the balance between protecting the environment and the conservation of landfill space and recovery of energy through incineration. This balance has been directed by Congress for the EPA to

Continued on next page.

answer, even though the majority decision may represent sound policy.

▶ *ANALYSIS*

Readers may be suspicious of an opinion authored by Justice Scalia that purports to advance the cause of environmental concerns, but from which both Justices O'Connor and Stevens dissent. Scalia's insistence that he merely reads the plain meaning of the language, in opposition to the Solicitor General's plea to adopt the EPA interpretation of the amendment, appears to this editor to be an act of thumbing his nose at Congress's ability to write a clear statute. Naturally, environmental organizations will bring suit to force municipalities to dispose of hazardous ash according to Subtitle C, as they never liked the household exemption to begin with. But Subtitle C ash disposal does not make the entire operation "Subtitle C-controlled," and many would see this as a reasonable compromise. Yet the purposes of the EPA exclusion and the congressional amendment were not at odds.

■■■

Quicknotes

CERTIORARI A discretionary writ issued by a superior court to an inferior court in order to review the lower court's decisions; the Supreme Court's writ ordering such review.

HAZARDOUS WASTE Substances that present a danger to human health or the environment.

■■■

United States v. Olin Corp.

Federal government (P) v. Chemical company (D)

107 F.3d 1506 (11th Cir. 1997).

NATURE OF CASE: Review of the constitutionality of the Comprehensive Environmental Response, Compensation, and Liability Act (CERCLA).

FACT SUMMARY: Olin Corp. (D) and the United States (P) entered into a consent decree assigning Olin (D) financial responsibility for cleanup from disposal activity that occurred prior to CERCLA's effective date.

🏛 RULE OF LAW
A statute is constitutional under the Commerce Clause if it regulates an activity that arises out of or is connected with a commercial transaction, which, viewed as a whole, substantially affects interstate commerce.

FACTS: Olin Corp. (D) and the United States (P) entered into a consent decree. Under the decree, Olin (D) agreed to pay for all response costs associated with site OU-1 and was assigned financial responsibility for cleanup from disposal activity that occurred prior to CERCLA. When the parties presented the consent decree to the district court, it sua sponte ordered them to address the impact of the Supreme Court's decision in *United States v. Lopez,* 514 U.S. 549 (1995), on the legality of their proposal. Olin (D) then answered the United States' (P) original complaint and asserted that the Court's construction of the Commerce Clause in *Lopez* precluded constitutional application of CERCLA in this case. Olin (D) further contended that CERCLA was not intended to impose liability for conduct predating the statute's enactment. The district court agreed with Olin (D) on both counts, denied the motion to enter the consent decree, and dismissed the United States' (P) complaint. The United States (P) appealed.

ISSUE: Are CERCLA's cleanup provisions constitutional under the Commerce Clause?

HOLDING AND DECISION: (Kravitch, J.) Yes. A statute is constitutional under the Commerce Clause if it regulates an activity that arises out of or is connected with a commercial transaction, which, viewed as a whole, substantially affects interstate commerce. The statute remains valid as applied in this case because it regulates a class of activities that substantially affects interstate commerce. Because the legislative history of CERCLA documents how the unregulated management of hazardous substances, even strictly within individual states, significantly impacts interstate commerce, we conclude the statute can be applied constitutionally in this case. To the extent a chemical plant can dispose of its waste on-site free of regulation, it would have a market advantage over chemical companies that lack on-site disposal options; Olin's (D) actions, therefore, have an economic character. For these reasons, CERCLA constitutes a permissible exercise of Congress's authority under the Commerce Clause. Reversed.

▶ ANALYSIS

In the years after CERCLA's enactment, litigants attacked the legislation on constitutional grounds, mainly because it imposed tough liability standards for cleaning up hazardous wastes that had been deposited many years before the statute's enactment. CERCLA thus raised the issue of impermissible retroactive legislation. However, after a string of unsuccessful constitutional challenges, litigation turned its focus to questions of statutory interpretation.

■=■

Quicknotes

COMMERCE CLAUSE Article 1, section 8, clause 3 of the United States Constitution, granting Congress the power to regulate commerce with foreign countries and between the states.

DE NOVO The review of a lower court decision by an appellate court, which is hearing the case as if it had not been previously heard and as if no judgment had been rendered.

■=■

New York v. Shore Realty Corp.

State (P) v. Land developer (D)

759 F.2d 1032 (2d Cir. 1985).

NATURE OF CASE: Appeal from a determination of liability for the cleanup of a hazardous waste disposal site.

FACT SUMMARY: After LeoGrande (D) incorporated Shore Realty Corp. (Shore) (D) to acquire, for development, land which had been used to dump hazardous waste, New York (P) brought suit against Shore (D) and LeoGrande (D) for cleanup of the site.

🏛 RULE OF LAW
The Comprehensive Environmental Response, Compensation, and Liability Act (CERCLA) unequivocally imposes strict liability on the current owners of a facility where hazardous wastes have been deposited, whether or not they owned the site at the time of disposal.

FACTS: LeoGrande (D) incorporated Shore (D) to acquire a site for land development. He knew that hazardous waste was stored on the site and that cleanup would be expensive. However, neither he nor Shore (D) had participated in the generation or transportation of the large amount of hazardous waste on the premises. Before closing the purchase, Shore (D) was aware of the prior tenants' activities and could have foreseen that they would continue to dump hazardous waste at the site. The State of New York (P) brought suit against Shore (D) and LeoGrande (D) for cleanup of the hazardous waste at the site. The trial court found Shore (D) and LeoGrande (D) liable, and they appealed.

ISSUE: Does CERCLA unequivocably impose strict liability on the current owners of a facility?

HOLDING AND DECISION: (Oakes, J.) Yes. CERCLA unequivocably imposes strict liability on the current owners of a facility. Under CERCLA, the owner and operator of a facility is liable for all costs of removal or remedial action incurred by the U.S. government or a state if there is a threatened release of a hazardous substance from the facility, without regard to causation. However, strict liability under CERCLA is not absolute. There are defenses for an act of God, an act of war, or acts or omissions of a third party other than an employee or agent of the defendant, or one whose act or omission occurs in connection with a contractual relationship with the defendant. Shore (D) and LeoGrande (D), however, are not covered by any of these defenses and are therefore responsible for the State's (P) response costs. Affirmed.

▶ ANALYSIS

As the court above stated, if the current owner of a site could avoid liability merely by having purchased the site after chemical dumping had ceased, waste sites would be sold

to new owners who could avoid the liability otherwise required by CERCLA. However, CERCLA was amended in 1986 to add a new defense for "innocent landowners." Under § 101(35), those who acquire property without "reason to know" of hazardous substance disposal there are not liable as owners or operators under § 107, so long as they have undertaken all appropriate inquiry into the previous uses of the property in an effort to minimize liability. Since LeoGrande (D) knew that containers at the site held hazardous substances, he could have availed himself of this defense had it been available a year earlier.

■■■

Quicknotes

AFFIRMATIVE DEFENSE A manner of defending oneself against a claim not by denying the truth of the charge but by the introduction of some evidence challenging the plaintiff's right to bring the claim.

STRICT LIABILITY Liability for all injuries proximately caused by a party's conducting of certain inherently dangerous activities without regard to negligence or fault.

■■■

United States v. Bestfoods

Federal government (P) v. Company (D)

524 U.S. 51 (1998).

NATURE OF CASE: Appeal from a decision that, under the Comprehensive Environmental Response, Compensation, and Liability Act (CERCLA), a parent corporation was responsible for the costs of cleaning up industrial waste generated by its subsidiary.

FACT SUMMARY: When CPC International's (CPC) (D) former subsidiary corporation caused substantial industrial contamination, the Government (P) brought suit against CPC (D) for CERCLA clean-up costs, contending that CPC (D), as the subsidiary's parent corporation, was responsible for its subsidiary's contamination.

🏛 RULE OF LAW
A parent corporation that actively participated in, and exercised control over, the operations of a facility itself may be held directly liable as an operator of the facility.

FACTS: During a 30-year period, a chemical plant (Ott II) was owned by several different companies, including CPC International (CPC) (D), which subsequently spun it off. Ott II had caused a substantial amount of contamination. The Government (P) brought suit against CPC (D) for the costs of cleaning up Ott II's industrial wastes, arguing that as Ott II's parent corporation, CPC (D) was liable under CERCLA as a former "owner or operator" of the subsidiary's plant because, in part, the parent had appointed its employees as officers and directors of the subsidiary. The district court found the parent corporation liable under CERCLA. On appeal, the Sixth Circuit reversed, concluding that where a parent corporation was not directly involved in the operation of a subsidiary's facility as a joint-venturer or co-operator, it could not be held liable under CERCLA as an "owner or operator" simply because it exercised corporate oversight of a subsidiary's affairs. The Government (P) appealed.

ISSUE: May a parent corporation be an "operator" of a polluting facility which is owned and operated by its subsidiary for the purposes of CERCLA liability?

HOLDING AND DECISION: (Souter, J.) Yes. A parent corporation that actively participated in, and exercised control over, the operations of a facility itself may be held directly liable as an operator of the facility. Under CERCLA, an operator must manage, direct, or conduct operations specifically related to pollution, operations having to do with the leakage or disposal of hazardous waste, or make decisions about compliance with environmental regulations. The question is not whether the parent operates the subsidiary, but rather whether it operates the facility, and that operation is evidenced by participation in the activities of the facility, not the subsidiary. The critical question is whether, in degree and detail, actions directed to the facility by an agent of the parent alone are eccentric under accepted norms of parental oversight of a subsidiary's facility. Remanded.

▌ ANALYSIS

In holding that a parent corporation could be held liable for its subsidiary's acts under ordinary rules for piercing the corporate veil, the Supreme Court declined to decide whether the state law standard or federal standard applied because the issue had not been argued by the parties. The court of appeals below was split on this issue.

■=■

Burlington Northern & Santa Fe Railway Co. v. United States

Railroad companies (D) v. Federal government (P)

129 S. Ct. 1870 (2009).

NATURE OF CASE: Appeal from lower court decision that Shell Oil Company was an "arranger" as defined by the Comprehensive Environmental Response, Compensation, and Liability Act (CERCLA).

FACT SUMMARY: Shell Oil Company (Shell) (D) sold chemicals for use by an agricultural company. Shell (D) was aware of continuous leaks and spills occurring at the site where the chemicals were delivered.

🏛 RULE OF LAW

Under CERCLA, in order to qualify as an arranger of the disposal of hazardous products, an entity must enter into a transaction for the sale of a hazardous product with the intention that at least a portion of the product will be disposed of during the transfer process by one of the methods described in the statute.

FACTS: An entity, Brown and Bryant, Inc., opened an agricultural chemical distributing business on a piece of land in California. Later, the entity leased an adjacent parcel, owned by Burlington Northern (D) and Santa Fe Railway Co. (D). As part of its operations, Brown and Bryant purchased a chemical pesticide, D-D, from Shell (D). Brown and Bryant originally purchased the pesticide from Shell (D) in 55-gallon drums. However, Shell (D) began selling the product in bulk, so that a tanker truck full of the pesticide would have to offload the product to a bulk container at Brown and Bryant's place of business. During this transfer process, many spills and leaks occurred. The site and groundwater around the site became contaminated. Shell (D) took steps to institute a safety and training program for its vendors regarding safe transfer of the product. The Environmental Protection Agency (EPA) and the state of California investigated the site and incurred $8 million of costs during the cleanup. The state and federal governments brought actions against the railroad companies and Shell (D) to recoup their costs. The trial court and the Ninth Circuit found that Shell (D) was an "arranger" of the disposal of hazardous waste because Shell (D) knew its product was being spilled at the Brown and Bryant site. Shell (D) appealed to the Supreme Court on the grounds that it did not enter into an agreement with Brown and Bryant to "dispose" of the pesticide.

ISSUE: Under CERCLA, in order to qualify as an arranger of the disposal of hazardous products, must an entity enter into a transaction for the sale of a hazardous product with the intention that at least a portion of the product will be disposed of during the transfer process by one of the methods described in the statute?

HOLDING AND DECISION: (Stevens, J.) Yes. Under CERCLA, in order to qualify as an arranger of the disposal of hazardous products, an entity must enter into a transaction for the sale of a hazardous product with the intention that at least a portion of the product will be disposed of during the transfer process by one of the methods described in the statute. Section 9607(a)(3) of CERCLA lists those parties that may be liable for contamination of a site. Specifically, the provision states that an entity that contracts or "arrange[s] for" the disposal of hazardous material may be liable if contamination occurs thereafter. CERCLA does not precisely define the phrase "arrange for." Therefore, we give the phrase its usual and ordinary meaning. To "arrange" means to take some action directed to a specific purpose. A level of intent is involved. Here, even though there is evidence Shell (D) was aware that minor spills were occurring, there was no evidence to show that Shell (D) entered into an agreement with Brown and Bryant with the intent that the product being sold was to be disposed of. The Government (P) argues that § 6903(3)'s definition of disposal includes "spills" and "leaks." However, it was also evident that Shell (D) took steps to prevent such spills and leaks. Mere knowledge that such minor spills were occurring, particularly where the transaction was for a product to be used rather than disposed, will not give rise to liability under CERCLA. Shell (D) therefore is not an arranger under CERCLA's statutory definition.

DISSENT: (Ginsburg, J.) Under CERCLA, Shell (D) qualifies as an arranger for the disposal of hazardous products. Shell (D) was the party that modified its delivery method of the pesticide, from 55-gallon drums to tankers. This in turn led to more spills of the product. Moreover, Shell (D) was fully aware of the frequency of the spills, which occurred every time there was a transfer of the product. Based upon the record at trial, Shell (D) should be found liable under CERCLA as an arranger.

▌ ANALYSIS

This was an eight to one decision by the Supreme Court, with only Justice Ginsburg dissenting. The decision clearly restricts the government's ability to use CERCLA as a vehicle to force entities that handle hazardous materials to cover the remediation costs of contaminated sites. It remains to be seen precisely what level of intent must be reached for an entity to qualify as an arranger.

■=■

Continued on next page.

Quicknotes

CERCLA Enacted to fill gaps in environmental cleanup efforts left by Resource Conservation and Recovery Act of 1976. Permits both the government and private plaintiffs to recover cleanup costs.

■=■

Burlington Northern & Santa Fe Railway Co. v. United States

Railroad companies (D) v. Federal government (P)

129 S. Ct. 1870 (2009).

NATURE OF CASE: Appeal from Ninth Circuit's decision that remediation costs could not be apportioned between the railroad companies.

FACT SUMMARY: Two railroad companies owned a portion of land leased to an entity that operated an agricultural chemical distributing business. Three different pesticides seeped into the ground and the groundwater over the course of a number of years.

🏛 RULE OF LAW
Apportionment of liability under the Comprehensive Environmental Response, Compensation, and Liability Act (CERCLA) is appropriate when there is a reasonable basis for determining the contribution of each party to a single harm.

FACTS: An entity, Brown and Bryant, Inc., opened an agricultural chemical distributing business on a piece of land in California. Later, the entity leased an adjacent parcel, owned by Burlington Northern (D) and Santa Fe Railway Co. (D), for a period of 13 years. Three different pesticides seeped into the ground. The site and groundwater around the site became contaminated. The Environmental Protection Agency (EPA) and the state of California investigated the site and incurred $8 million of costs during the cleanup. The state and federal governments brought actions against the railroad companies and Shell Oil Company to recoup their costs. The trial court found that the railroad companies were liable for 9% of the costs of the remediation of the site. The district court based came to that conclusion for three reasons. First, the railroad companies owned only 19% of the surface area of the contaminated site. Second, Brown and Bryant operated the business for many more years than just the 13-year lease period. Third, there were releases of hazardous materials on the other part of the site ten times greater than releases on the railroad companies' property. The district court also found spills of two pesticides originated from the railroad-owned property and that those pesticides accounted for two-thirds of the total amount of pesticides released into the site. The district court then multiplied 19% (the surface area) by 45% (the period of the lease as a percentage of Brown and Bryant's 30-year operation) by 66% (the percentage of the two pesticides spilled at the site). This came to 6%, but the District Court allowed for a 50% chance of error in the calculation of amount of pesticides released, and increased the percentage of liability to 9%. The Ninth Circuit disagreed that the railroad companies' liability was capable of apportionment. Rather, the Ninth Circuit found there was not enough evidence to divide the entities' amount of fault for the contamination. Under that scenario, the railroad companies were therefore jointly and severally liable for the entire cost of the remediation. The railroad companies appealed this portion of the Ninth Circuit's ruling.

ISSUE: Is apportionment of liability under CERCLA appropriate when there is a reasonable basis for determining the contribution of each party to a single harm?

HOLDING AND DECISION: (Stevens, J.) Yes. Apportionment of liability under CERCLA is appropriate when there is a reasonable basis for determining the contribution of each party to a single harm. Under *United States v. Chem-Dyne Corp.*, 572 F. Supp. 802 (S.D. Ohio 1983), CERCLA has been held to impose strict liability, but not necessarily joint and several liability in every case. Rather, a party's liability under CERCLA depends on traditional common law tort concepts. Specifically, courts should look to § 433A of the Restatement (Second) of Torts. This section essentially says that where there is a reasonable basis for division according to the contributory acts of each tortfeasor, the tortfeasor shall only be liable for that portion of the total harm caused by it. Defendants charged with CERCLA violations bear the burden to show that apportionment is proper rather than imposition of joint and several liability. We find the district court had sufficient evidence to apportion the cost of the remediation in this case, based on the facts as discussed above. The Ninth Circuit's decision on this issue is reversed and the district court's decision is reinstated.

DISSENT: (Ginsburg, J.) The parties in this appeal took extreme positions on the issue of apportionment that were entirely unhelpful to the court. The Government's (P) position was that the railroad companies were entirely liable for the remediation costs. The railroad companies argued that they had no liability whatsoever. The district court judge was left to analyze the issue of apportionment entirely on his own. Because the parties did not brief the possibility of apportionment, the case should be remanded to the district court for further exploration of the issue.

▶ ANALYSIS

The significance of this portion of the decision is that the Supreme Court affirmed the *Chem-Dyne Corp.* analysis regarding apportionment of liability under CERCLA. In that sense, this portion of the decision did not change the legal analysis for CERCLA liability. Here, the facts were not very complex and there were only two parties involved. Where

Continued on next page.

additional parties are involved, which is usually the case, apportionment becomes more difficult.

■━■

Quicknotes

CERCLA Enacted to fill gaps in environmental cleanup efforts left by Resource Conservation and Recovery Act of 1976. Permits both the government and private plaintiffs to recover cleanup costs.

■━■

United States v. Atlantic Research Corp.

Federal government (D) v. Business (P)

551 U.S. 128 (2007).

NATURE OF CASE: Appeal from Eighth Circuit's decision in favor of Atlantic Research (P).

FACT SUMMARY: After incurring cleanup costs at a site that Atlantic Research Corp. (P) leased from the United States (D), Atlantic Research Corp. (P) sought to recover some of its costs from the government.

🏛 RULE OF LAW
Section 107(a) of the Comprehensive Environmental Response, Compensation, and Liability Act (CERCLA) provides potentially responsible parties with a cause of action to recover costs against other potentially responsible parties.

FACTS: Atlantic Research Corp. (P) leased property from the United States (D). At the site, Atlantic Research (P) retrofitted rocket motors for use by the United States (D). Atlantic Research (P) used a high pressure water spray to remove pieces of propellant from the motors. Some of the propellant and water contaminated the soil at the site. Atlantic Research (P) paid for the remediation costs and sued the United States (D), as owner of the property, to recoup a portion of the costs. Atlantic Research (P) brought its claims under both §§ 107(a) and 113(f) of CERCLA. In *Cooper Industries, Inc. v. Aviall Services, Inc.*, 543 U.S. 157 (2004), the Supreme Court previously barred use of § 113(f) for recovery claims by the moving party unless the government had previously brought an enforcement action against it under § 106 or § 107 of CERCLA. The district court therefore dismissed the Section 113 claim based on that prior Supreme Court decision because Atlantic Research (P) had not been the subject of a prior enforcement action. The district court also dismissed the § 107 claim on the grounds that § 107 did not allow recovery claims by private, nongovernmental parties. The Eighth Circuit reversed, stating that § 107's language supports an interpretation that allows for causes of action by one potentially responsible private party against another. The United States (D) appealed.

ISSUE: Does § 107(a) of CERCLA provide potentially responsible parties with a cause of action to recover costs against other potentially responsible parties?

HOLDING AND DECISION: (Thomas, J.) Yes. Section 107(a) of CERCLA provides potentially responsible parties with a cause of action to recover costs against other potentially responsible parties. Section 107(a)(4)(A) & (B) makes potentially responsible parties liable, in part, for the following: "(A) all costs of removal or remedial action incurred by the United States Government or a State or an Indian tribe not inconsistent with the national contingency plan; [and] "(B) any other necessary costs of response

incurred by any other person consistent with the national contingency plan." § 9607(a)(4)(A) & (B). In *Cooper Industries*, we held that § 113 could only be used for a contribution claim after the government brought an enforcement action against the moving party under § 107(a). We now hold that parties that incur their own cleanup costs, without the existence of an enforcement action against them, may use § 107(a) to recoup costs against other potentially responsible parties. The language of § 107(a)(4)(B) clearly states that potentially responsible parties (here, the United States) may be liable for costs incurred "by any other person." That language provides Atlantic Research (P) and other private parties similarly situated with the right to bring a civil action against other parties responsible for contamination of the site. Section 113 will still be used by parties that are initially the subject of enforcement action by the federal government. Our holding will not create friction between §§ 107 and 113. Rather, the two sections will complement each other. The sections will be used depending on the procedural posture of a case. Use of § 107 by private litigants will also not eviscerate § 113's provision that provides an incentive to settle. Section 113 includes a provision that bars further suits against a party that settles an enforcement action. Section 107 does not include such a provision. However, district courts will likely take note of the fact that any party sued under § 107 had previously been the subject of an enforcement action. The Eighth Circuit's opinion is affirmed.

▶ ANALYSIS

This unanimous decision cleared up a question left open in the *Cooper Industries* case, namely, whether private parties, not subject to a prior enforcement action, could sue to recoup their costs. By answering that question in the affirmative, the Court made CERCLA a much more effective vehicle for distributing the costs of remediation.

■=■

Quicknotes

CERCLA Enacted to fill gaps in environmental cleanup efforts left by Resource Conservation and Recovery Act of 1976. Permits both the government and private plaintiffs to recover cleanup costs.

■=■

United States v. Vertac Chemical Corp.

Federal government (P) v. Chemical company (D)

79 F. Supp. 2d 1034 (E.D. Ark. 1999).

NATURE OF CASE: Hearing to determine allocation of response costs.

FACT SUMMARY: Several parties were found responsible for the cost of having to clean up a contaminated site. The allocation of response costs for two of those parties, Hercules (D) and Uniroyal (D), is analyzed.

🏛 RULE OF LAW
Response costs can be allocated based on the volume of waste produced by each party, whether a party's actions were a necessary condition of the cleanup, and the party's cooperation with government officials.

FACTS: Hercules (D) owned or operated a chemical plant from 1961 to 1976 and was deeply involved in the daily operations of the plant. During that time, the hazardous waste generated by the plant contaminated the soil, groundwater, equipment, tanks, sewer lines, sewage treatment plants, and sediments and flood plains through leaks, spills, and drum burial. Hercules (D) produced about 33,231,400 pounds of 2,4-D, 2,4,5-T, and 2,4,5-TP. When Transvaal leased the site from Hercules (D), it produced 43,004,255 pounds of the same chemical. Uniroyal (D) was an arranger and its involvement with the plant was indirect and for a limited time. Vertac Chemical Corp. (Vertac) (D) produced 1,344,000 pounds of 2,4,5-T for sale to Uniroyal (D). Vertac (D) was ordered by the state to shut down the plant in 1979. At that time there were 2700 drums of 2,4,5-T still bottoms stored on-site. Workers placed those drums and the contaminated soil in larger drums. When Vertac (D) resumed operation, it produced only 2,4-D waste and Hercules (D) was not involved with the site during this time. Uniroyal (D) was also not involved with the management of the drummed waste. Hercules (D) responded to Environmental Protection Agency (EPA) Orders, but Uniroyal (D) did not. Hercules (D) and Uniroyal (D) were held jointly and severally liable, with other parties, for the cleanup effort, which was almost $90 million.

ISSUE: How should the response costs be allocated between Hercules (D) and Uniroyal (D)?

HOLDING AND DECISION: (Howard Jr., J.) The response costs are to be allocated based on the volume of waste produced by each party, whether their actions were a necessary condition of the cleanup and by whether they cooperated with the EPA. The court is given broad discretion to allocate costs among the parties when it is resolving contribution claims under the Comprehensive Environmental Response, Compensation, and Liability Act (CERCLA). To that end, several factors regarding the type of hazardous waste at issue and the extent of each party's involvement with it can be considered. Although the court may consider the different harms caused by different parties; in this case there was a commingling of the wastes and, therefore, the site cannot be divided into various harms attributable to a certain party. Different responsibility should be placed on Hercules (D), as owner and operator, than on Uniroyal (D), whose involvement was indirect and for a limited time. Volumetrics is how we began to assess each party's contribution because it takes into account each party's involvement at the site and their contribution to the harm created. The amount of Uniroyal's (D) share of volumes of product produced at the plant in comparison to Hercules (D) is 1.76%. Since, however, Uniroyal (D) arranged for the production of hazardous materials, it was aware of the production and it benefited from the production. Thus a larger percentage of costs can be placed on Uniroyal (D) than just what the difference in volume would indicate. Uniroyal's (D) actions were a necessary condition of the cleanup in that, but for the production of 2,4,5-T for Uniroyal (D), there would not be a certain amount of wastes left and stored in the drums that had to be incinerated. In addition, the allocation of costs is also based on the parties' cooperation with the EPA. Hercules (D) responded to EPA Orders and undertook extensive remediation thus reducing the costs. Uniroyal (D), however, disregarded the Orders and is, therefore, responsible for more than 1.76%. Uniroyal (D) is thus liable for 2.6% of the costs.

▷ ANALYSIS

This case was initiated by the United States (P) under the Resource Conservation and Recovery Act and the Clean Water Act prior to CERCLA's enactment. The decision was ultimately vacated because the court of appeals ruled the district judge had ignored the law regarding divisibility of harm.

■=■

Quicknotes

HAZARDOUS WASTE Substances that present a danger to human health or the environment.

JOINT AND SEVERAL LIABILITY Liability amongst tortfeasors allowing the injured party to bring suit against any of the defendants, individually or collectively, and to recover from each up to the total amount of damages awarded.

■=■

Akzo Nobel Coatings, Inc. v. Aigner Corp.

Polluter (P) v. Polluter (D)

197 F.3d 302 (7th Cir. 1999).

NATURE OF CASE: Appeal from a contribution action.

FACT SUMMARY: Akzo Nobel Coatings, Inc. (Akzo) (P) appealed a contribution liability determination requiring it to pay 13% of the costs that Aigner Corp. (Aigner) (D) will expend for a cleanup, because Akzo (P) generated only approximately 9% by volume of the hazardous waste at issue.

🏛 RULE OF LAW
In a contribution suit, payment a party recovers from a third party in settlement is to be deducted from the total cleanup costs, and the parties to the contribution suit are to bear the remaining costs equally.

FACTS: Akzo (P) brought a contribution action against Aigner (D). The district court divided liability among the parties on the basis of the volume of waste disposed of at the site, with all gallons of solvent being weighted equally. Basing its decision on the Uniform Comparative Fault Act (UCFA), the district court ordered Akzo (P) to pay one-third more than equal-weighting would require. Akzo (P) generated only approximately 9% by volume of the solvents but had to reimburse Aigner (D) for 13% of the costs that Aigner (D) will expend for the cleanup. Aigner (D) sent about 71% of the total volume of solvents to the site. Akzo's (P) shipments are thus 13% of the Akzo (P) and Aigner (D) total. Other shippers were ignored because they are not a party to this action.

ISSUE: Is Akzo (P) required to pay one-third more than equal-weighting requires?

HOLDING AND DECISION: (Easterbrook, J.) No. Akzo (P) is not required to pay one-third more than equal-weighting requires. Section 113(f)(1) requires claims for contribution to be brought in accordance with § 113(f)(1), Federal Rules of Civil Procedure and Federal Law. However, the UCFA is not federal law. The law of admiralty's reduction *pro tanto* approach to settling parties and contribution issues is the appropriate federal law to apply. It requires that payments Aigner (D) recovers from a third party in settlement be deducted from the total cleanup costs, and then for Akzo (P) and Aigner (D) to bear the remaining costs equally. Akzo (P), therefore, is to pay 12.56% of the costs net of what Aigner (D) has collected from its settlements. Not only must Aigner's (D) collections to date be calculated, but also what future third-party payments might be. If some of the settlements are percentage-of-cost payments, they are to be excluded from the pool. Akzo (P) is also not free to bring its own contribution actions against these parties, but rather needs to intervene in Aigner's (D) suit or challenge the bona fides of the settlements. Even though federal law is required, state law can be used if it tends to demonstrate a uniform acceptance among the states. The UCFA, however, has been adopted by only two states. Furthermore, adopting it as a federal rule would undermine the aim of § 113(f)(2), which provides that when a settlement occurs any potentially liable person is not to be discharged, and the liability of the others is to be reduced by the amount of the settlement. The district court's use of the UCFA, therefore, produces disparity in liability when third parties have settled. If Akzo (P) and Aigner (D) were the only sound parties responsible for the pollution, the 13% would stand for Akzo (P) because it reflects their relative responsibility. Aigner (D), however, has settled with other entities who polluted the site and has claims pending against potentially responsible parties. Therefore, it is unlikely that 13% is an accurate estimate of Akzo's (P) share among the entities that will eventually chip in. The district court should have applied reduction *pro tanto* where payments Aigner (D) would recover from a party in settlement would be deducted from the total cleanup costs, and Aigner (D) and Akzo (P) would then bear the remaining costs equally. This allows the court to avoid a potentially complex and unproductive inquiry into the responsibility of missing parties. Vacated and remanded.

▶ *ANALYSIS*

This case recognizes that justice requires all parties at fault, or the parties that are substantively liable, to be taken into consideration, not just those parties that are before the court in form.

■■■

Quicknotes

HAZARDOUS WASTE Substances that present a danger to human health or the environment.

PRO TANTO For so much, as far as it goes.

■■■

Philadelphia v. New Jersey

City (P) V. State (D)

437 U.S. 617 (1978).

NATURE OF CASE: Action challenging the constitutionality of a state statute.

FACT SUMMARY: Philadelphia (P) challenged the constitutionality under the Commerce Clause of a New Jersey (D) statute prohibiting the import of most out-of-state waste.

🏛 RULE OF LAW
Whatever a state's ultimate purpose, it may not be accomplished by discriminating against articles of commerce coming from outside the state unless there is some reason, apart from their origin, to treat them differently.

FACTS: Faced with the problem of conserving its remaining landfill space, New Jersey (D) passed a law prohibiting the import of most waste originating outside the state. Philadelphia (P) challenged the constitutionality of this scheme under the Commerce Clause. The New Jersey Supreme Court upheld the statute.

ISSUE: Does the Commerce Clause prohibit a state from accomplishing its ultimate purpose by discriminating against articles of commerce coming from outside the state unless there is some reason, apart from their origin, to treat them differently?

HOLDING AND DECISION: (Stewart, J.) Yes. Whatever New Jersey's (D) ultimate purpose, the Commerce Clause prohibits its being accomplished by discriminating against articles of commerce coming from outside the state unless there is some reason, apart from their origin, to treat them differently. The law at issue here falls squarely within the area that the clause puts off-limits to state regulation in that it imposed on out-of-state commercial interests the full burden of conserving New Jersey's (D) remaining landfill space. It attempts to isolate a state from a problem common to many by erecting an unconstitutional barrier against the movement of interstate trade. This is unconstitutional. Reversed.

DISSENT: (Rehnquist, J.) New Jersey (D) must, out of sheer necessity, treat its solid waste in some fashion, just as it must treat New Jersey (D) cattle suffering from hoof-and-mouth disease. It does not follow that it must, under the Commerce Clause, accept solid waste or diseased cattle from outside its borders and thereby exacerbate its problems.

▌ ANALYSIS

The New Jersey Supreme Court had questioned whether "waste" was even "commerce" at all within the meaning of the Commerce Clause. The Supreme Court answered definitively that "all objects of interstate trade merit Commerce Clause protection; none is excluded by definition at the outset."

■=■

Quicknotes

COMMERCE CLAUSE Article 1, section 8, clause 3 of the United States Constitution, granting Congress the power to regulate commerce with foreign countries and between the states.

■=■

C & A Carbone, Inc. v. Town of Clarkstown

Waste processor (P) v. Town (D)

511 U.S. 383 (1994).

NATURE OF CASE: Review of decision rejecting challenge to local waste control ordinance.

FACT SUMMARY: The Town of Clarkstown (Clarkstown) (D) mandated that all solid waste be processed at a designated processing station.

RULE OF LAW
The Commerce Clause invalidates local laws that impose commercial barriers or discriminate against an article of commerce by reason of its out-of-state origin.

FACTS: Clarkstown (D), New York, entered into an arrangement with a private company to construct and operate a solid waste processing station. Part of the agreement called for Clarkstown (D) to guarantee a certain amount of refuse per year. To accomplish this, Clarkstown (D) mandated that all waste generated with the town be processed at this station. Under the ordinance, C & A Carbone, Inc. (P), another waste processor, would be required to send its nonrecyclable waste to the new processing station at an additional cost. C & A Carbone (P) therefore challenged the ordinance as a Commerce Clause violation. The lower courts upheld the ordinance, and the Supreme Court granted review.

ISSUE: Does the Commerce Clause invalidate local laws that impose commercial barriers or discriminate against an article of commerce by reason of its out-of-state origin?

HOLDING AND DECISION: (Kennedy, J.) Yes. The Commerce Clause invalidates local laws that impose commercial barriers or discriminate against an article of commerce by reason of its out-of-state origin. A regulation that requires waste to be channeled through a designated facility impacts the Commerce Clause, not because waste itself is being regulated, but rather because nonlocal providers of the processing service are being shut out of the market. A state or city may not enact laws or ordinances that favor local interests at the expense of interstate commerce, even if, as here, local economic players are also adversely affected. A state may not, as Clarkstown (D) has done here, bar the import of a good or service. The service at issue here is waste processing; since only one company is allowed to perform the service, importation is effectively prohibited. This cannot be done in accordance with the Commerce Clause. Reversed and remanded.

DISSENT: (Souter, J.) Clarkstown's (D) ordinance does not bestow any benefit on a class of local private actors, because it only differentiates between one entity responsible for the job of processing trash and all other enterprises, regardless of their location. Therefore, it does not implicate the dormant Commerce Clause because it does not discrim-

inate against out-of-town processors, it merely forces local residents to pay more for reliable trash processing.

▶ ANALYSIS

There are two basic modes of analysis in Commerce Clause jurisprudence. The first approach, shown in the majority opinion here, occurs when a law discriminates against interstate commerce in favor of local interests. Such a law is presumptively invalid. The other mode, represented in Justice Souter's dissent, balances local benefits against the burden on interstate commerce.

Quicknotes

COMMERCE CLAUSE Article 1, section 8, clause 3 of the United States Constitution, granting Congress the power to regulate commerce with foreign countries and between the states.

United Haulers Ass'n, Inc. v. Oneida-Herkimer Solid Waste Management Authority

Solid waste hauler (P) v. Municipal entity (D)

550 U.S. 330 (2007).

NATURE OF CASE: Appeal from Second Circuit's decision in favor of municipal entity.

FACT SUMMARY: Two counties created a solid waste management authority and passed an ordinance mandating that all solid waste be delivered to the authority's processing plants.

🏛 RULE OF LAW
A law mandating that all solid waste be conveyed to processing centers operated by a government entity does not discriminate against interstate commerce for purposes of the Commerce Clause because the law treats every private business, whether in-state or out-of-state, exactly the same.

FACTS: The New York state legislature passed a law creating the Oneida-Herkimer Solid Waste Management Authority (the Authority) (D) to manage the handling and processing of all solid waste within the two counties, Oneida and Herkimer. Private waste haulers could pick up trash in the counties, but had to bring it to processing facilities operated by the Authority (D). The Authority (D) charged haulers $86 to $172 per ton. United Haulers Ass'n, Inc. (P) challenged the law on the grounds it discriminated against interstate commerce. The District Court agreed, but the Second Circuit reversed. It did so on the grounds that local governments traditionally can operate solid waste disposal and that all private companies are treated the same by the law. United Haulers Ass'n, Inc. (P) appealed.

ISSUE: Does a law mandating that all solid waste be conveyed to processing centers operated by a government entity discriminate against interstate commerce for purposes of the Commerce Clause when the law treats every private business, whether in-state or out-of-state, exactly the same?

HOLDING AND DECISION: (Robert, C.J.) No. A law mandating that all solid waste be conveyed to processing centers operated by a government entity does not discriminate against interstate commerce for purposes of the Commerce Clause because the law treats every private business, whether in-state or out-of-state, exactly the same. As opposed to private entities, local governments are responsible for the public health and safety of their residents. Because of that distinction, laws favoring local governments are not analyzed the same way as are laws favoring private entities. Laws protecting private entities may lead to economic protectionism, which the dormant Commerce Clause forbids. There is no such fear when a law is set up to favor a public entity. An opposite holding would wreak havoc on many municipal operations created by ordinance or statute that benefit the residents thereof. We therefore find that the law at issue creating the Authority (D) does not discriminate against interstate commerce. We also find that the law is not clearly excessive in relation to the benefits to the municipality. The law allows the municipality to enforce recycling laws and encourages its residents to recycle. Affirmed.

▶ ANALYSIS

The decision is significant for municipalities around the country because the Court upheld a flow control statute for the first time. The Court also answered in the affirmative the question of whether laws in favor of public entities will be given more deference than those laws favoring private entities. Public entities will likely look to this decision as support for all types of regulations that favor the municipality, even if the regulations have some impact on interstate commerce.

Quicknotes

COMMERCE CLAUSE Article 1, section 8, clause 3 of the Constitution, granting Congress the power to regulate commerce with foreign countries and among the states.

DORMANT COMMERCE CLAUSE The regulatory effect of the Commerce Clause on state activity affecting interstate commerce, where Congress itself has not acted to control the activity; a provision inferred from, but not expressly present in, the language of the Commerce Clause.

In the Matter of Louisiana Energy Services, L.P.

Decision of the Nuclear Regulatory Commission
Atomic Safety and Licensing Board

May 1, 1997

NATURE OF CASE: Opinion of Atomic Safety and Licensing Board regarding the Nuclear Regulatory Commission's (NRC) compliance with Executive Order 12,898.

FACT SUMMARY: The Atomic Safety and Licensing Board found insufficient attention had been paid to compliance with Executive Order 12,898 in the NRC Staff evaluation of a uranium enrichment plant proposed to be sited near predominantly minority communities in Louisiana.

🏛 RULE OF LAW
The nondiscrimination component of Executive Order 12,898 requires that the Nuclear Regulatory Commission Staff conduct an objective, thorough, and professional investigation of site selection processes to ensure its licensing activities do not have the effect of subjecting any persons or populations to racial discrimination.

FACTS: The Louisiana Energy Services (LES) sought a 30-year materials license to possess and use byproduct, source, and special nuclear material in order to enrich uranium using a gas centrifuge process at the Claiborne Enrichment Center (CEC). The Applicant planned to build the CEC on a site in Claiborne Parish, Lousiana, that is immediately adjacent to and between the African-American communities of Center Springs and Forest Grove. LES contends that the CEC site selection process was not racially biased nor based on racial considerations. The Intervenor contended that the site selection process was racially and socioeconomically biased. The NRC Staff's investigation concluded that there was no specific evidence to support the charge of racial or socioeconomic bias in the site selection process, based on its review of public comments and the LES description of the process in its environmental report. The Licensing Board reviewed the case.

ISSUE: Is the Nuclear Regulatory Commission's facial review of an applicant's environmental report regarding site selection sufficient to comply with the nondiscrimination component of Executive Order 12,898?

HOLDING AND DECISION: (Moore, Cole, and Shon, JJ.) No. The non-discrimination component of Executive Order 12,898 requires that the NRC Staff conduct an objective, thorough, and professional investigation of site selection processes to ensure its licensing activities do not have the effect of subjecting any persons or populations to racial discrimination. In the circumstances presented in this licensing action, the Staff failed to comply with the President's directive by limiting its consideration to a facial review of the information in the applicant's environmental report. Racial discrimination in the facility site selection process cannot be uncovered with only a cursory review of the description of that process appearing in an applicant's environmenal report. If it were so easily detected, racial discrimination would not be such a persistent and enduring problem in American society. Racial discrimination is often rationalized under some other seemingly racially neutral guise, making it difficult to ferret out. Moreover, direct evidence of racial discrimination is seldom found. The Intervenor's statistical evidence and its evidence concerning the application of the low population criterion stand as significant probative evidence in the current record that racial considerations played a part in the site selection process. This evidence demonstrates that a thorough Staff investigation of the site selection process is needed in order to comply with the President's nondiscrimination directive in Executive Order 12,898.

▶ ANALYSIS

Controversy attends the question of whether the pattern of locally undesirable land uses presently located in largely poor, minority communities is more attributable to decisions made in the site-selection process or to the subsequent movement of populations to communities neighboring such facilities because of low-cost housing associated with the property-value-depressing effects of locally undesirable land use. Concerns raised by the environmental justice movement have produced much more sensitivity to the distributional justice issues posed by such siting decisions at present and in the future.

■═■

Air Pollution Control

Quick Reference Rules of Law

Massachusetts v. EPA

State (P) v. Federal agency (D)

549 U.S. 497 (2007).

NATURE OF CASE: Appeal from D.C. Circuit's decision in favor of the defendant.

FACT SUMMARY: Environmental Protection Agency (the EPA) (D) refused to regulate greenhouse gases, include carbon dioxide, from new automobiles.

🏛 RULE OF LAW
Because greenhouse gases fit well within the Clean Air Act's broad definition of an air pollutant, the EPA has statutory authority to regulate emission of such gases from new motor vehicles.

FACTS: After several private entities petitioned the EPA (D) to regulate greenhouse gases from new automobiles, the EPA (D) denied the petition. Specifically, the EPA (D) stated that the Clean Air Act did not authorize the EPA (D) to issue regulations to address global climate change. The EPA (D) also felt that the causal link between greenhouse gas emissions and climate change was not established unequivocally. Massachusetts and other states intervened and joined the petition. The D.C. Circuit of Appeals decided in favor of the EPA (D). Massachusetts and the other plaintiffs appealed.

ISSUE: Because greenhouse gases fit well within the Clean Air Act's broad definition of an air pollutant, does the EPA have the statutory authority to regulate emission of such gases from new motor vehicles?

HOLDING AND DECISION: (Stevens, J.) Yes. Because greenhouse gases fit well within the Clean Air Act's broad definition of an air pollutant, the EPA has statutory authority to regulate emission of such gases from new motor vehicles. Section 202 of the Clean Air Act is extremely broad. It allows the EPA (D) to regulate "any air pollution agent," including "any" physical or chemical substance released into the air. Carbon dioxide and other greenhouse gases qualify as physical or chemical substances. The EPA's (D) reliance on our prior decision that tobacco was not subject to regulation by the Food and Drug Administration (the FDA) is unavailing. In that matter, the FDA and Congress had repeatedly stated that tobacco was not a drug to be regulated by the FDA. Here, Congress made no similar pronouncements that greenhouse gases were not to be regulated by the EPA (D). The EPA (D) regulation of greenhouse gases would not conflict with the Department of Transportation's fuel mileage regulations, which relate only to the need to promote energy efficiency, not clean air. Furthermore, the EPA's (D) second reason for inaction, that it would be unwise to regulate the gases at this time, is not statutorily authorized. If the EPA (D) makes a finding that greenhouse gases endanger human life, the EPA (D) must regulate the gases. Under the Clean Air Act, the EPA (D) can only decide not to take action if it makes a determination that greenhouse gases do not contribute to climate change. The EPA (D) may also provide a reasonable justification as to why it will not exercise its discretion to make the endangerment determination. The EPA (D) has refused to comply with its statutory obligations. Instead, it has provided unsupported reasons why it will not regulate the gases. The EPA (D) has also not provided a reasonable justification for its refusal to determine if the greenhouse gases contribute to climate change. On remand, we state only that the EPA (D) must ground its refusal in the statute. We do not reach the question of whether the EPA (D) must actually make an endangerment finding regarding greenhouse gases. Reversed.

▶ ANALYSIS

The Court, divided five to four, sided against the Bush Administration's policy not to regulate the greenhouse emissions. The decision was significant because it essentially ordered the federal government to begin examining climate change and the possible reasons for climate change.

■══■

Quicknotes

CLEAN AIR ACT Required certain states to establish a permit program for stationary sources of air pollution.

■══■

Engine Manufacturers Association v. South Coast Air Quality Management District

Manufacturers association (P) v. State subdivision (D)

541 U.S. 246 (2004).

NATURE OF CASE: Appeal from affirmance of judgment upholding rules issued by a state subdivision as not preempted by the Clean Air Act.

FACT SUMMARY: The Engine Manufacturers Association (P) contended that "Fleet Rules" issued by South Coast Air Quality Management District (the District) (D), a state's subdivision, governing operators of fleets of various types of vehicles and requiring the purchase or lease of certain types of vehicles, were preempted by the Clean Air Act, which prohibits the adoption or attempted enforcement of any state or local "standard relating to the control of emissions from new motor vehicles or new motor vehicle engines."

🏛 RULE OF LAW
Rules enacted by a state's subdivision that regulate the purchase of vehicles, rather than their manufacture or sale, are preempted by Clean Air Act provisions prohibiting states or localities from adopting or enforcing a standard relating to the control of emissions from new motor vehicles or motor vehicle engines.

FACTS: The District (D), a state subdivision, enacted six Fleet Rules prohibiting the purchase or lease by various public and private fleet operators of vehicles that did not comply with requirements in the Rules. The Engine Manufacturers Association (P) sued the District (D) and its officials, claiming that the Fleet Rules were preempted by § 209 of the federal Clean Air Act, which prohibits the adoption or attempted enforcement of any state or local "standard relating to the control of emissions from new motor vehicles or new motor vehicle engines." In upholding the Fleet Rules, the district court found that they were not "standards" under § 209 because: "Where a state regulation does not compel manufacturers to meet a new emissions limit, but rather affects the purchase of vehicles, as the Fleet Rules do, that regulation is not a standard." The court of appeals affirmed, and the Supreme Court granted certiorari.

ISSUE: Are rules enacted by a state's subdivision that regulate the purchase of vehicles, rather than their manufacture or sale, preempted by Clean Air Act provisions prohibiting states or localities from adopting or enforcing a standard relating to the control of emissions from new motor vehicles or motor vehicle engines?

HOLDING AND DECISION: (Scalia, J.) Yes. Rules enacted by a state's subdivision that regulate the purchase of vehicles, rather than their manufacture or sale, are preempted by Clean Air Act provisions prohibiting states or localities from adopting or enforcing a standard relating to the control of emissions from new motor vehicles or motor vehicle engines. The Fleet Rules do not escape preemption just because they address the purchase of vehicles, rather than their manufacture or sale. Neither the district court's interpretation of "standard" to include only regulations that compel manufacturers to meet specified emission limits nor its resulting distinction between purchase and sales restrictions finds support in § 209(a)'s text or the Clean Air Act's structure. The ordinary meaning of language employed by Congress is assumed accurately to express its legislative purpose. Today, as when § 209(a) became law, "standard" means that which "is established by authority, custom, or general consent, as a model or example; criterion; test." The criteria referred to in § 209 relate to the emission characteristics of a vehicle or engine. This interpretation is consistent with the use of "standard" throughout Title II of the Clean Air Act. Defining "standard" to encompass only production mandates confuses standards with methods of enforcing standards. Manufacturers (or purchasers) can be made responsible for ensuring that vehicles comply with emission standards, but the standards themselves are separate from enforcement techniques. While standards target vehicles and engines, standard-enforcement efforts can be directed toward manufacturers or purchasers. This distinction is borne out in the enforcement provisions immediately following Clean Air Act § 202. A purchase/sale distinction also makes no sense, since a manufacturer's right to sell federally approved vehicles is meaningless absent a purchaser's right to buy them. A command, accompanied by sanctions that certain purchasers may buy only vehicles with particular emission characteristics is as much an "attempt to enforce" a "standard" as a command accompanied by sanctions that a certain percentage of a manufacturer's sales volume must consist of such vehicles. In light of these principles, it is likely that at least certain aspects of the Fleet Rules are preempted, but it does not necessarily follow that they are preempted in toto. To determine the extent to which they are preempted, the lower courts must address questions that were not presented below. Vacated and remanded.

▶ ANALYSIS

On remand, the district court ruled that as directed at governmental fleets, the Fleet Rules constituted propriety actions (regarding how public monies will be spent). Such actions fall within the market participation doctrine, which

Continued on next page.

requires that Congress's intent to preempt such actions must be "clear and manifest." Applying this doctrine, the court held that the Clean Air Act lacked the "clear and manifest" desire to preempt the Fleet Rules.

■══■

Quicknotes

CLEAN AIR ACT (CAA) Required certain states to establish a permit program for stationary sources of air pollution.

PREEMPTION Doctrine holding that matters of national interest take precedence over matters of local interest; the federal law takes precedence over state law.

■══■

Central Valley Chrysler-Jeep, Inc. v. Goldstene

Automobile dealers (P) v. State (D)

529 F. Supp. 2d 1151 (E.D. Cal. 2007).

NATURE OF CASE: Trial court decision on plaintiff's motion for summary judgment.

FACT SUMMARY: California (D) passed a law requiring the California Air Resources Board (CARB) to issue regulations for the emissions of greenhouse gases from automobiles. Automobile dealers and manufacturers sued to block implementation of the law.

> ## 🏛 RULE OF LAW
> California's law requiring CARB to promulgate emissions regulations does not conflict with the provisions of the federal Energy Policy and Conservation Act (EPCA) regarding fuel efficiency standards for new vehicles.

FACTS: California (D) passed a state law, AB 1493, requiring CARB to issue regulations for four greenhouse gases from automobiles: carbon dioxide, methane, nitrous oxide and hydrofluorocarbons. Typically, Section 209 of the federal Clean Air act preempts state regulations of emissions. However, the Clean Air Act also provided an exception for any state that regulated emissions prior to 1966. California (D) was the only state with such preexisting regulations. The Clean Air Act also provides California (D) the ability to file a waiver request with the Environmental Protection Agency (the EPA) if the state wants to promulgate emissions standards more stringent than the federal standards. The EPCA mandates the Department of Transportation (DOT) to issue regulations regarding fuel economy standards for new automobiles. The court accepts as true the premise that AB 1493 will require increased motor vehicle fuel efficiency. In addition, it is undisputed compliance with AB 1493 may be achieved in manners other than increased fuel efficiency in motor vehicles. The plaintiffs move for summary judgment on the ground that the EPCA essentially preempts state law regarding fuel efficiency.

ISSUE: Does California's law requiring CARB to promulgate emissions regulations conflict with the provisions of the federal EPCA regarding fuel efficiency standards for new vehicles?

HOLDING AND DECISION: (Ishii, J.) No. California's (D) law requiring CARB to promulgate emissions regulations does not conflict with the provisions of the federal EPCA regarding fuel efficiency standards for new vehicles. We reach that conclusion for three reasons. First, under the Supreme Court's 2007 *Massachusetts v. EPA* decision, it is clear Congress intended the EPA to regulate emissions even though the regulation may affect fuel economy standards governed by the EPCA. Second, the National Highway Traffic Safety Administration (NHTSA) must take into account the EPA's emissions standards when setting its own fuel economy standards. Under the Clean Air Act, the EPA has the broader scope of authority to regulate vehicle exhaust emissions to protect the public's health. Third, after the EPA grants a waiver for a state regulation, that regulation is treated no differently than an EPA regulation for preemption purposes. On the issue of preemption generally under the EPCA, the court holds that the EPCA does not expressly or impliedly preempt AB 1493. In fact, the EPCA includes a provision that the NHTSA must consider standards promulgated pursuant to § 209 waivers. In addition, DOT's mandate to promote fuel efficiency and the EPA's mandate to protect the public health generally are not inconsistent. Summary judgment motion denied.

▶ ANALYSIS

Following this decision, the EPA denied California's (D) waiver request in December of 2007. However, the EPA, under the Obama administration, granted the waiver on June 30, 2009. The new administration had previously passed more stringent standards that conformed to California's (D) standards set out in AB 1493.

■■■■

Quicknotes

CLEAN AIR ACT Required certain states to establish a permit program for stationary sources of air pollution.

■■■■

Lead Industries Association v. EPA

Industry association (P) v. Federal regulatory agency (D)

647 F.2d 1130 (D.C. Cir. 1980).

NATURE OF CASE: Appeal from judgment in an action challenging the validity of the national ambient air quality standard for lead.

FACT SUMMARY: The Lead Industries Association (P) challenged the validity of the national ambient air quality standard for lead adopted by the Environmental Protection Agency (the EPA) (D) in its interpretation of §§ 108 and 109 of the Clean Air Act.

🏛 RULE OF LAW
Economic issues are not considered in the promulgation of ambient air quality standards under the Clean Air Act.

FACTS: The EPA (D), in interpreting §§ 108 and 109 of the Clean Air Act, set the air quality standards for lead without considering the issues of economic and technological feasibility. The Lead Industries Association (P) and St. Joe Minerals Corporation (St. Joe) (P) brought suit, challenging the validity of the regulations. St. Joe (P) argued that the Administrator (D) abused his discretion by refusing to consider economic and technological feasibility in determining the appropriate margin of safety for the lead standards. St. Joe (P) maintained that the lead air quality standards would have a disastrous economic impact on industrial sources of lead emissions.

ISSUE: May economic issues play a part in the promulgation of ambient air quality standards under the Clean Air Act?

HOLDING AND DECISION: (Wright, C.J.) No. Economic issues are not considered in the promulgation of ambient air quality standards under the Clean Air Act. Congress expressly provided in which sections it intended the Administrator (D) to consider economic and technological feasibility. Congress specifically directed the Administrator (D) to allow an adequate margin of safety to protect against effects that have not yet been uncovered by research and effects whose medical significance is a matter of disagreement. Moreover, Congress has recently acknowledged that more often than not the margins of safety that are incorporated into air quality standards turn out to be very modest or nonexistent, as new information reveals adverse health effects at pollution levels once thought to be harmless. Congress's directive to the Administrator (D) to allow an adequate margin of safety plainly refutes any suggestion that the Administrator (D) is only authorized to set primary air quality standards that are designed to protect against health effects that are known to be clearly harmful.

▶ ANALYSIS

Exasperated by the lack of significant progress toward dealing with the problem of air pollution under the Air Quality Act of 1967, Congress abandoned the approach of offering suggestions and setting goals in favor of taking a stick to the states in the form of the Clean Air Amendments of 1970. Congress was well aware that, together with §§ 108 and 110, § 109 imposed requirements of a technology-forcing character. Furthermore, § 109(b) speaks only of protecting the public health and welfare.

Quicknotes

CLEAN AIR ACT Required certain states to establish a permit program for stationary sources of air pollution.

Whitman v. American Trucking Ass'ns

Federal agency (D) v. Trucking association (P)

531 U.S. 457 (2001).

NATURE OF CASE: Appeal of certain determinations regarding the extent of the Environmental Protection Agency's (the EPA's) (D) power under the Clean Air Act (the Act).

FACT SUMMARY: Challenges were made regarding whether costs are to be considered when the EPA (D) promulgates national ambient air quality standards (NAAQS) under the Clean Air Act, and whether the nondelegation doctrine was violated by the power given to the EPA (D) under the Act.

RULE OF LAW
(1) The Administrator of the EPA (D) may not consider the costs of implementation in setting NAAQS.
(2) The Act does not delegate legislative power to the Administrator.

FACTS: The Act instructs the EPA (D) to set NAAQS, the attainment and maintenance of which are requisite to protect the public health with an adequate margin of safety. The court of appeals decided that the Administrator (D) may not consider the costs of implementation in setting NAAQS under the Act. The court of appeals also found that the Act did not provide an intelligible principle to guide the EPA's (D) exercise of authority in setting NAAQS and, therefore, the EPA's (D) interpretation violated the nondelegation doctrine.

ISSUE:
(1) May the Administrator (D) consider the costs of implementation in setting NAAQS under the Act?
(2) Does the Act delegate legislative power to the Administrator of the EPA (D)?

HOLDING AND DECISION: (Scalia, J.)
(1) No. The Administrator (D) may not consider the costs of implementation in setting NAAQS under the Act. Economic considerations may not play a part in the promulgation of NAAQS under the Act. The EPA (D), based on information about health effects, is to identify maximum airborne concentrations of a pollutant that the public can tolerate, decrease the concentration to provide an adequate margin of safety, and set the standard at that level. The term "public health" as contained in the Act means the health of the public and not the ways and means of conserving the health of the members of a community, as by preventative medicine and organized care of the sick. Furthermore, Congress was aware that compliance costs could injure the public health so the Act permits the Administrator (D) to

waive the compliance deadline for stationary sources if sufficient control measures were unavailable and the continued operation of such sources is essential to the public heath or welfare. In addition, other provisions require economic costs to be taken into account when implementing the air quality standards. Since a consideration of costs has been expressly granted in certain sections of the Act, it need not be implicit in other sections that there be an authorization to consider costs. Moreover, respondents are unable to show a textual commitment of authority to the EPA (D) to consider costs in setting NAAQS under the Act. The Act's two terms "adequate margin" and "requisite" do not give the power to the EPA (D) to determine whether implementation costs should moderate national air quality standards. Lastly, the provisions in the Act which do require attainment cost data to be generated enable the Administrator (D) to assist the States in carrying out their statutory role as implementers of the NAAQS. Affirmed.

(2) No. The Act does not delegate legislative power to the Administrator of the EPA (D). The text of the Act requires that for a discrete set of pollutants and based on published air quality criteria that reflect the latest scientific knowledge, the EPA (D) must establish uniform national standards at a level that is requisite to protect public health from the adverse effects of the pollutant in the ambient air. This scope of discretion is well within the outer limits of our nondelegation precedents. In addition, it is rare that the Court will second-guess Congress regarding the permissible degree of policy judgment that can be left to those applying the law. Congress must provide substantial guidance on setting air standards that affect the entire national economy. Congress does not, however, have to say how much is too much. A certain degree of discretion is inherent in most executive or judicial action. The Act, which requires the EPA (D) to set air quality standards at the level that is not lower or higher than is necessary to protect the public health with an adequate margin of safety, fits within the scope of discretion permitted by our precedent. Affirmed as to the Act barring cost considerations from the NAAQS setting process. Reversed as to the EPA's (D) interpretation violating the nondelegation doctrine and remanded.

▌ ANALYSIS

In a concurring opinion, Justice Stevens argued that the Court should acknowledge that the power delegated to the

Continued on next page.

EPA (D) is legislative, and the delegation is constitutional because it is adequately limited by the term of the authorizing statute.

■■■

Quicknotes

JURISDICTION The authority of a court to hear and declare judgment in respect to a particular matter.

■■■

Union Electric Company v. EPA

Electric company (P) v. Federal regulatory agency (D)

427 U.S. 246 (1976).

NATURE OF CASE: Appeal from judgment in an action challenging a state plan implementing the mandates of the Clean Air Act.

FACT SUMMARY: After the Environmental Protection Agency (the EPA) (D) approved a state implementation plan (SIP) that was more stringent than the standards required by federal law, Union Electric Company (P) claimed that meeting the state standards was technologically and economically infeasible.

🏛 RULE OF LAW
States may implement pollution control plans more stringent than federal law demands, without considering technological or economic factors.

FACTS: Union Electric Company (P) brought this suit, protesting the Administrator's (D) approval of an SIP. The Utility (P) argued that the standards set by the state were economically and technologically infeasible. In addition, Union Electric (P) and other power companies argued that § 110(a)(2)'s requirement that the plan contain such control devices "as may be necessary" to achieve the primary and secondary air quality standards precluded the states from submitting implementation plans more stringent than federal law required. The Utility (P) appealed the lower court ruling.

ISSUE: May states implement pollution control plans more stringent than federal law demands?

HOLDING AND DECISION: (Marshall, J.) Yes. States may implement pollution control plans more stringent than federal law demands, without considering technological or economic factors. The "as may be necessary" language of § 110(a)(2)(B) demands only that the implementation plan meet the "minimum conditions" of the amendments. That conclusion is bolstered by the recognition that the amendments do allow claims of technological and economic infeasibility to be raised in situations where consideration of such claims will not substantially interfere with the primary congressional purpose of prompt attainment of the national air quality standards. If the industry is not excepted from, or accommodated by, the original plan, it may obtain a variance. Lastly, where an industry is denied an exemption from the SIP or denied a subsequent variance, it may be able to take its claims of economic or technological infeasibility to the state courts. Thus, the state has near absolute power in allocating emissions limitations so long as the national standards are met.

▶ ANALYSIS

The 1970 Amendments to the Clean Air Act were a drastic remedy to what was perceived as a serious and otherwise unchecked problem of air pollution. The strict minimum compliance requirements are of a "technology-forcing character." Congress decided that the dangers posed by uncontrolled air pollution made the risks entailed in a technology-forcing policy worth taking.

■■■

Quicknotes

CLEAN AIR ACT (CAA) Required certain states to establish a permit program for stationary sources of air pollution.

SIP State implementation plan.

■■■

Virginia v. EPA

State (D) v. Federal regulatory agency (P)

108 F.3d 1397 (D.C. Cir. 1997).

NATURE OF CASE: Appeal from the Environmental Protection Agency's (the EPA's) state implementation plan (SIP) call which ordered 13 jurisdictions to adopt the California Low Emission Vehicle program or institute alternative measures.

FACT SUMMARY: Virginia (D) contends that the EPA's state implementation plan call effectively ordered the adoption of the California standards, because the measures required of a state choosing not to adopt it were so unreasonable and impracticable as to amount to no real alternative.

🏛 RULE OF LAW
The EPA may not condition approval of a state's implementation plan on the state's adoption of a particular control measure.

FACTS: The 1990 amendments to the Clean Air Act (the Act) recognized the significant interstate aspect of the automobile smog problem in a variety of ways, including through the creation of the Northeast Ozone Transport Commission (the NOTC). The Act authorized the NOTC to recommend control measures for the region necessary to bring any area in the region into attainment with the ozone national ambient air quality standards (NAAQS). Under that authorization, the NOTC petitioned the EPA to recognize that adoption of the California Low Emission Vehicle (LEV) program was such a necessary control measure. EPA ultimately responded to the NOTC petition by issuing an order. EPA found the California LEV program to be necessary for the 13-member jurisdictions and also found that the SIPs of these jurisdictions were substantially inadequate unless they adopted the California program or instituted other measures that were highly infeasible or more draconian than the California program.

ISSUE: Does the EPA have the authority to force particular control measures on the states?

HOLDING AND DECISION: (Randolph, J.) No. The EPA may not condition approval of a state's implementation plan on the state's adoption of a particular control measure. Under the Clean Air Act, the state is at liberty to adopt whatever mix of emission limitations it deems best suited to its particular situation so long as the ultimate effect of that choice is compliance with the national standards for ambient air. The SIP call the EPA issued with respect to each state cannot stand. Petitions for review granted. Rule vacated in its entirety.

▌ ANALYSIS

A major aspect of the SIP process is the continuing interaction between federal and state authorities. The SIP process is dynamic, as sources close down or change their emissions, new sources arrive, and models and data are developed. These events may require significant changes in the SIP. As SIP revisions require both state and EPA approval, SIPs are continually in flux.

■■■■

Quicknotes

CLEAN AIR ACT (CAA) Required certain states to establish a permit program for stationary sources of air pollution.

SIP State implementation plan.

■■■■

Alaska Department of Environmental Conservation v. EPA

State agency (P) v. Federal regulatory agency (D)

540 U.S. 461 (2004).

NATURE OF CASE: Appeal from affirmance of an Environmental Protection Agency (the EPA) order issued under the Clean Air Act.

FACT SUMMARY: The Alaska Department of Environmental Conservation (ADEC) (P) contended that the EPA's (D) oversight role as described in Clean Air Act §§ 113(a)(5) and 167 did not extend to ensuring that a state permitting authority's Best Available Control Technology (BACT) determination is reasonable in light of the statutory guidelines so as to authorize the EPA (D) to stop construction of a major pollutant emitting facility if the EPA (D) finds an authority's BACT determination is unreasonable.

RULE OF LAW

The Clean Air Act authorizes the EPA to stop construction of a major pollutant-emitting facility permitted by a state authority when the EPA finds that an authority's BACT determination is unreasonable in light of statutorily prescribed guidelines.

FACTS: Cominco Inc. (Cominco) operated Red Dog Mine (Red Dog), a zinc concentrate mine. To increase its operations in Alaska, north of the Arctic Circle, Red Dog would need to increase its electrical generating capacity, which in turn would significantly increase nitrogen oxide (NOx) emissions. The expansion therefore triggered a Prevention of Significant Deterioration (PSD) requirement that the new generating capacity come equipped with BACT. BACT is defined as an emission limitation based on maximum pollution reduction that the permitting authority [here, ADEC (P)] determines is achievable in light of energy, environmental, and economic impacts and costs. ADEC (P) determined that BACT for a proposed standby generator already in place would be selective catalytic reduction (SCR), which reduces NOx emissions by 90%. Red Dog then modified its expansion plans, proposing to install an entirely new generator, MG-17. It suggested that a BACT for this should be a technology known as Low NOx, which removes 30% of NOx emissions. ADEC (P) then issued a draft PSD permit that determined that Low NOx was BACT for both generators, even though SCR was feasible for them. ADEC (P) also accepted Red Dog's plan to apply Low NOx to all its generators, based on Red Dog's assertion that doing so would enable the plant as a whole to meet emissions reductions commensurate with applying SCR to the two generators, and would in fact result in significantly lower emissions. ADEC (P) stated that the Low NOx solution "achieve[d] a similar maximum NOx reduction as the most stringent controls; [could] potentially result in a greater NOx reduction; and is logistically and economically less onerous to

[Red Dog]." The EPA (D) and other federal agencies objected, contending that the PSD provisions requiring BACT could not be satisfied by imposing new controls on other emissions units. In response, ADEC (P) issued a new permit that indicated that Low NOx was BACT for the two generators, having concluded that SCR would impose a disproportionate cost on the mine (even though it received no evidence supporting this conclusion). The EPA (D) again objected, claiming that Red Dog had not adequately demonstrated any site-specific factors to support their claim that the installation of SCR was economically infeasible at the Red Dog Mine. Therefore, the EPA (D) concluded that elimination of SCR as BACT based on cost-effectiveness grounds was not supported by the record and was clearly erroneous. Nonetheless, ADEC (P) issued the final permit without supplementing its analysis. The EPA (D) then issued an order, under Clean Air Act § 113(a)(5) preventing Red Dog from proceeding with construction. This statute is triggered when the EPA (D) finds that a state is not acting in compliance with any requirement relating to the construction of new sources. The EPA (D) was also acting under Clean Air Act § 167 to "take such measures, including issuance of an order . . . to prevent the construction . . . of a major emitting facility which does not conform to the [PSD] requirements." The court of appeals affirmed the EPA's (D) order, and the Supreme Court granted review.

ISSUE: Does the Clean Air Act authorize the EPA to stop construction of a major pollutant emitting facility permitted by a state authority when the EPA finds that an authority's BACT determination is unreasonable in light of statutorily prescribed guidelines?

HOLDING AND DECISION: (Ginsburg, J.) Yes. The Clean Air Act authorizes the EPA (D) to stop construction of a major pollutant emitting facility permitted by a state authority when the EPA (D) finds that an authority's BACT determination is unreasonable in light of statutorily prescribed guidelines. A central issue is whether the EPA's (D) oversight role, described by Congress in Clean Air Act §§ 113(a)(5) and 167, extends to ensuring that a state permitting authority's BACT determination is reasonable in light of the statutory guides. The EPA (D) has rationally construed the Clean Air Act's BACT definition and the statute's listing of BACT as a preconstruction requirement for the PSD program to mandate a determination of BACT faithful to the statute's definition. BACT's statutory definition requires selection of an emission control technology that results in the "maximum" reduction of a pollutant "achievable for [a] facility" in view of "energy, environmental, and economic impacts, and other costs." The

Continued on next page.

EPA (D) urges that state permitting authorities' statutory discretion is constrained by the definition's strong, normative terms "maximum" and "achievable." In support of this reading, the EPA (D) emphasizes that Congress intended the PSD program to prevent significant deterioration of air quality in clean-air areas. Without a federal EPA (D) surveillance role that extends to BACT determinations, the EPA (D) maintains, this goal is unlikely to be realized. The Clean Air Act's legislative history suggests that, absent national guidelines, a state deciding to set and enforce strict clean-air standards may lose existing industrial plants to more permissive states. The legislative history further suggests that without a federal check, new plants will play one state off against another with threats to locate in whichever state adopts the most permissive pollution controls. Such an interpretation is reflected in interpretive guides the EPA (D) has published several times, and the Court normally accords particular deference to an agency interpretation of "longstanding duration." ADEC (P) argues that the Clean Air Act's BACT definition unambiguously assigns to "the permitting authority" alone the decision of the control technology qualifying as "best available." From this it reasons that the EPA's (D) enforcement role is restricted to the requirement that the permit contain a BACT limitation. The Clean Air Act entrusts state authorities with initial responsibility to make BACT determinations because they are best positioned to adjust for local circumstances that might make a technology "unavailable" in a particular area. However, according state authorities initial responsibility does not signify that there can be no unreasonable state agency BACT determinations. Congress vested the EPA (D) with explicit and sweeping authority to enforce the Clean Air Act's "requirements" relating to the construction and modification of sources under the PSD program, including BACT. Having expressly endorsed an expansive surveillance role for the EPA (D) in two independent Clean Air Act provisions, Congress would not have implicitly precluded EPA (D) from verifying a state authority's substantive compliance with the BACT requirement. Nor would Congress have limited the EPA (D) to determining whether the state permitting authority had uttered the key word "BACT." Notwithstanding the EPA's (D) oversight powers, the permitting state retains considerable leeway, since the EPA (D) may step in only when a state agency's BACT determination is not based on a reasoned analysis. Also unavailing is ADEC's (P) argument that any reasoned justification requirement for a BACT determination may be enforced only through state administrative and judicial processes in order to allow development of an adequate factual record, to ensure the EPA (D) carries the burdens of proof, and to promote certainty. The Court declines to read into the Clean Air Act's silence the unusual requirement that a federal agency's decisions enforcing federal law must be remitted solely to state court. Moreover, the court of appeals' review of the EPA's (D) order was in keeping with the Court's holding that the EPA (D) may not reduce the burden it must carry by electing to invoke its stop-construction-order authority. Because that court rested its judgment on what the EPA (D) showed from ADEC's (P) own report, its conclusion that the EPA's (D) order was justified was

neither arbitrary nor capricious. The issue ultimately, therefore, is whether ADEC's (P) BACT determination was a reasonable one. Here, the EPA (D) properly exercised its statutory authority and did not act arbitrarily or capriciously in finding that ADEC's (P) acceptance of Low NOx as BACT for MG-17 lacked evidentiary support. While the EPA's (D) three skeletal orders were not composed with ideal clarity, they properly ground the EPA's (D) BACT determination when read together with the EPA's (D) accompanying explanatory correspondence. The EPA (D) rightly concluded that ADEC's (P) switch from finding SCR economically feasible to finding SCR economically infeasible had no factual basis in the record. ADEC (P) forthrightly conceded it was disarmed from reaching a judgment on SCR's economic impact on the mine by Cominco's refusal to provide relevant financial data. No record evidence suggested that the mine, were it to use SCR, would be obliged to cut personnel or raise zinc prices. Having acknowledged that it lacked information needed to judge SCR's impact on the mine's operation, profitability, or competitiveness, ADEC (P) could not simultaneously proffer threats to the mine's operation and competitiveness as reasons for declaring SCR economically infeasible. ADEC's (P) justification that lower aggregate emissions would result from Cominco's agreement to install Low NOx on all its generators is also unpersuasive. The final PSD permit did not offset MG-17's emissions against those of the mine's six existing generators. As ADEC (P) recognized, a state may treat emissions from several pollutant sources as falling under one "bubble" for PSD permit purposes only if every pollutant source so aggregated is part of the permit action. However, only MG-17 was covered by the permit action. Affirmed.

▶ *ANALYSIS*

The dissent, written by Justice Kennedy, argued that the EPA (D), based on nothing more than its substantive disagreement with ADEC's (P) discretionary judgment, exceeded its powers in setting aside ADEC's (P) BACT determination, especially since ADEC (P) had followed procedures that complied with the Clean Air Act and accompanying regulations promulgated by the EPA (D). Thus, according to the dissent, the EPA's (D) orders were tantamount to administrative fiat.

■══■

Quicknotes

BACT Best Available Control Technology.

CLEAN AIR ACT (CAA) Required certain states to establish a permit program for stationary sources of air pollution.

■══■

Environmental Defense v. Duke Energy Corp.

Advocacy group (P) v. Corporation (D)

549 U.S. 561 (2007).

NATURE OF CASE: Appeal from Fourth Circuit Court of Appeals' decision in favor of the defendant.

FACT SUMMARY: After Duke Energy Corp. (D) updated its electricity-generating plants, Environmental Defense (P) brought suit arguing that its modifications subjected Duke Energy (D) to permit requirements under the Clean Air Act.

🏛 RULE OF LAW
Where Environmental Protection Agency (EPA) regulations for the New Source Review (NSR) program state that a change to a plant constituting a major modification requires a new permit, the EPA is free to interpret the word "modification" in a manner that is not limited by the regulation's reference to the definition of the word "modification" in another regulation, the New Source Performance Standard (the NSPS).

FACTS: Between 1988 and 2000, Duke Energy Corp. (D) updated its electricity-generating plants in order to extend the life of the plants but more importantly to allow the plants to run longer each day. Environmental Defense (P) contends that this change constituted a "modification" under the EPA's NSR regulations, requiring Duke Energy (D) to obtain a permit under the Clean Air Act for such modifications. Duke Energy (D) contended that the new NSR regulations included a reference to the definition of "modification" in the separate NSPS regulation. In the NSPS regulation, modification to emissions means an increase in the hourly rate of discharge. Because Duke Energy's (D) modifications did not increase the hourly rate of discharge, Duke Energy (D) argued it was not required to obtain a permit under the NSR regulations. The district court and the Fourth Circuit Court of Appeals agreed and dismissed the action. Environmental Defense (P) appealed.

ISSUE: Where EPA regulations for the NSR program state that a change to a plant constituting a major modification requires a new permit, is the EPA free to interpret the word "modification" in a manner that is not limited by the regulation's reference to the definition of the word "modification" in another regulation, the NSPS?

HOLDING AND DECISION: (Souter, J.) Yes. Where EPA regulations for the NSR program state that a change to a plant constituting a major modification requires a new permit, the EPA is free to interpret the word "modification" in a manner that is not limited by the regulation's reference to the definition of the word "modification" in another regulation, the NSPS. It is true that the NSR regulation specifically referred back to the section that defined "modification" for the purposes of the NSPS. However, we find nothing in the text of the statutes and legislative history suggests that Congress considered the impact of regulatory implementation of modified emissions sources, such as the Duke Energy (D) plants at issue here. We find no specific Congressional intent to bar the EPA from interpreting the word "modification" in the NSR regulation by looking to the surroundings of the term within the regulation where it resides. The NSR regulations do not limit the definition of "modification" solely to an increase in the hourly rate of emissions discharge. Therefore, the EPA may find that Duke Energy's (D) extension of operating hours per day does constitute a modification under the NSR, requiring that Duke Energy (D) proceed through a permit application process for the plant upgrade. Reversed.

▶ ANALYSIS

This unanimous decision provided a victory to environmentalists by providing the EPA with broader discretion to enforce its regulations. In short, the decision mandates that plants undergoing upgrades will likely have to proceed through a permitting process where the overall annual emissions discharge will increase. Surprisingly, after the decision, the EPA considered modification of the NSR regulation to conform to the hourly rate standard of the NSPS. The EPA has since retreated from that position.

■■■

Quicknotes

AGENCY DISCRETION The authority conferred upon a public agency by law to act reasonably in accordance with its own judgment under certain circumstances.

CLEAN AIR ACT Required certain states to establish a permit program for stationary sources of air pollution.

■■■

Alliance for Clean Coal v. Bayh

Mining alliance (P) v. Environmental agency (D)

72 F.3d 556 (7th Cir. 1995).

NATURE OF CASE: Appeal from summary judgment in an action challenging the validity of a state environmental statute.

FACT SUMMARY: The Alliance for Clean Coal (Alliance) (P) contended that the Indiana Environmental Compliance Plans Act (the ECPA) unconstitutionally burdened interstate commerce by promoting the use of Indiana's (D) high-sulfur content coal at the expense of low-sulfur western coal.

🏛 RULE OF LAW
State environmental statutes that discriminate against interstate commerce based solely upon geographic origin violate the Commerce Clause.

FACTS: Under the Clean Air Act, the Environmental Protection Agency (EPA) (D) initially provided two methods for controlling sulphur dioxide emissions: (1) the use of low-sulfur coal; and (2) the installation of a device to scrub high-sulfur coal emissions before they reached the atmosphere. Because scrubbing was costlier than using low-sulfur coal, states producing high-sulfur coal suffered competitively. Indiana (D), a high-sulfur coal-mining state, adopted its ECPA, favoring the use of high-sulfur Indiana (D) coal. The Alliance (P) brought suit, contesting the validity of the ECPA. Alliance (P) moved for summary judgment. The district court concluded that the ECPA was intended to promote high-sulfur coal at the expense of low-sulfur western coal, thus unconstitutionally burdening interstate commerce. Indiana (D) appealed.

ISSUE: Do state environmental statutes that discriminate against interstate commerce based solely upon geographic origin violate the Commerce Clause?

HOLDING AND DECISION: (Cummings, J.) Yes. State environmental statutes that discriminate against interstate commerce based solely upon geographic origin violate the Commerce Clause. The clear intent of the Indiana ECPA is to benefit Indiana (D) coal at the expense of western coal. The fact that the ECPA does not explicitly forbid the use of out-of-state coal or require the use of Indiana (D) coal does not make the ECPA any less discriminatory. Moreover, Indiana (D) did not meet its burden of proving that the discrimination was justified by a legitimate and compelling governmental interest. While a healthy Indiana (D) mining industry may aid Indiana (D) in achieving a low-cost electrical service, that is not a legitimate justification for discrimination against interstate commerce.

▮ ANALYSIS

The outcome of this case was controlled by *Alliance for Clean Coal v. Miller*, 44 F.3d 591 (7th Cir. 1995). In *Miller*, the court invalidated a similar act enacted on the heels of the Clean Air Act Amendments of 1990 by the state of Illinois. The Illinois Act was struck down for identical reasons.

■▬■

Quicknotes

CLEAN AIR ACT Required certain states to establish a permit program for stationary sources of air pollution.

SUMMARY JUDGMENT Judgment rendered by a court in response to a motion by one of the parties, claiming that the lack of a question of material fact in respect to an issue warrants disposition of the issue without consideration by the jury.

■▬■

Michigan v. EPA

State (P) v. Federal agency (D)

213 F.3d 663 (D.C. Cir. 2000).

NATURE OF CASE: Petitions for review of an Environmental Protection Agency (EPA) rule.

FACT SUMMARY: Several states and industry groups (P) challenged various aspects of the Environmental Protection Agency's (the EPA's) (D) 1998 rule mandating that certain states and the District of Columbia revise their state implementation plans (SIPs) under the Clean Air Act to mitigate the interstate transport of ozone by uniformly requiring that each state reduce nitrogen oxides (NOx—an ozone precursor) by the amount accomplishable by what the EPA (D) dubbed "highly cost-effective controls," namely, those controls the EPA (D) found capable of removing NOx at a cost of $2,000 or less per ton.

🏛 RULE OF LAW
An EPA SIP call is not impermissible where it requires revision of SIPs to mitigate the interstate transport of ozone by uniformly requiring that each state reduce nitrogen oxides (NOx) by the amount accomplishable by what the EPA determines are "highly cost-effective controls."

FACTS: In 1998, the EPA (D) promulgated a rule mandating that certain states and the District of Columbia revise their SIPs under the Clean Air Act to mitigate the interstate transport of ozone by uniformly requiring that each state reduce nitrogen oxides (NOx—an ozone precursor) by the amount accomplishable by what the EPA (D) dubbed "highly cost-effective controls," namely, those controls the EPA (D) found capable of removing NOx at a cost of $2,000 or less per ton. The reason the EPA (D) instituted this new rule was because it determined that the affected jurisdictions were "significant" contributors to downwind nonattainment. The Clean Air Act, in § 110(a)(2)(D)(i)(I), prohibits states from having emissions that "contribute significantly" to nonattainment of air pollution controls/maintenance standards of another, downwind state. In making its determination of which states were "significant" contributors, the EPA (D) drew lines based on the magnitude, frequency, and relative amount of each state's ozone contribution to a nonattainment area. Although the dividing line was a very low threshold of contribution, the EPA's (D) rule called for termination of only a subset of each state's contribution. The EPA's (D) design was to have a lot of states make what it considered modest NOx reductions, uniformly limited to ones that could be achieved (in the EPA's (D) estimate) for less than $2,000 a ton. As a result, the ultimate line of "significance," whether measured in volume of NOx emitted or arriving in nonattainment areas, would vary from state to state depending on variations in cutback costs. As part of this program, because the EPA (D)

determined that NOx reductions provide the key to addressing regional ozone problems, the EPA's (D) SIP call addressed regional ozone nonattainment through NOx emissions "budgets" established by the agency for each covered state. The budgets represented the amount of allowable NOx emissions remaining after a covered state prohibits the NOx amount contributing significantly to downwind nonattainment. Although the EPA (D) calculated the budgets using highly cost-effective emission controls, it allowed the states to choose the control measures necessary to bring their emissions within the budget requirements. As part of the states' ability to choose the set of controls that would assure achievement of the budget, each state had the option of adopting an interstate trading program that allows it to purchase NOx "allowances" from sources that have elected to over-control. States could also use "banked" allowances from prior years. Through petitions for review by the court of appeals, states and industry groups (P) challenged the EPA's (D) determination of "significance" on several grounds, including: (1) the EPA (D) acted contrary to precedent; (2) the EPA (D) considered forbidden factors, namely, costs of reduction; (3) the EPA's (D) NOx budget program impermissibly intruded on the statutory right of the states to fashion their SIP submissions in the first instance.

ISSUE: Is an EPA SIP call impermissible where it requires revision of SIPs to mitigate the interstate transport of ozone by uniformly requiring that each state reduce nitrogen oxides (NOx) by the amount accomplishable by what the EPA determines are "highly cost-effective controls"?

HOLDING AND DECISION: (Per curiam) No. An EPA SIP call is not impermissible where it requires revision of SIPs to mitigate the interstate transport of ozone by uniformly requiring that each state reduce nitrogen oxides (NOx) by the amount accomplishable by what the EPA (D) determines are "highly cost-effective controls." As to past precedent, prior to the EPA's (D) rule, and prior to the Clean Air Act's 1990 amendments, the Clean Air Act directed the EPA (D) to insist on SIP provisions adequate to prevent sources within a state from emitting air pollution that would "prevent attainment or maintenance [of primary or secondary standards] by any other State." The EPA (D) found, with approval of the courts, that various emissions of a particular state, having a proportionate impact on some downwind state greater than the impacts at issue under the new rule, did *not* meet that standard. Therefore, the states (P) argued, the EPA (D) was barred from regarding the ozone emissions here as "significant" within the meaning of § 110(a)(2)(D)(i)(I). Thus the states (P) would equate the old standard—"prevent attainment"—with

Continued on next page.

the new standard: "contribute significantly to nonattainment." However, nothing in the text of the statute spells out a criterion for classifying "emissions activity" as significant, nor did the EPA (D) bind itself to any criterion. Further, the prior decisions related to sulfur dioxide, and the EPA (D) could argue that the standards for ozone emissions are distinguishable from sulfur dioxide emissions. Finally, because the states have not shown that the EPA (D) bound itself to any concept of how much is too much, this precedent-related claim is dismissed. As to consideration of cost, the states and industry groups (P) maintain that the Clean Air Act does not permit the EPA (D) to take into consideration the cost, or cost-effectiveness, of reducing ozone. By its terms, the Clean Air Act is focused on "amounts" of "emissions activity" that "contribute significantly to non-attainment." The fundamental dispute is over the clarity of the phrase "contribute significantly." The issue is whether the EPA (D) must simply pick some flat "amount" of contribution, based exclusively on health concerns, such that any excess would put a state in the forbidden zone of "significance" or whether it may consider differences in cutback costs, so that, after reduction of all that could be cost-effectively eliminated, any remaining "contribution" would not be considered "significant." In deciding on the permissible ceiling, the EPA (D) used "significant" in the second way. The term "significant" does not in itself convey a thought that significance should be measured in only one dimension—here, in the petitioners' view, health alone. In some contexts, "significant" begs a consideration of costs. The EPA (D) has determined that ozone has some adverse health effects—however slight—at every level. Thus, without consideration of cost it is hard to see why any ozone-creating emissions should not be regarded as fatally "significant" under § 110(a)(2)(D)(i)(I). Moreover, it is settled law in this jurisdiction that only where there is clear congressional intent to preclude consideration of cost that agencies are barred from considering costs. Since there has not been such an expression of congressional intent, the EPA's (D) use of cost considerations is permissible. Regarding whether the EPA's (D) NOx budget program was permissible, under Supreme Court precedent and precedent of this court, it is clear that under Clean Air Act § 110, states have the power to initially determine which sources of pollution would be burdened by regulation and to what extent. The EPA (D) has only a secondary role in the process of determining and enforcing specific, source-by-source emission limitations. Whether the NOx budget program is barred by federalism concerns depends on whether the program constitutes an impermissible source-specific means rather than a permissible end goal. However, the program's validity also depends on whether the EPA's (D) budgets allow the covered states real choice with regard to the control measure options available to them to meet the budget requirements. Here, based on § 110's silence, the EPA (D) reasonably interpreted § 110 as providing it with the authority to determine a state's NOx significant contribution level, and its budget plan, therefore, does no more than project whether states have reduced emissions sufficiently to mitigate interstate transport. Under § 110, the EPA (D) must "approve a [SIP] submittal as a whole if it meets all of the applicable requirements of [the

Act]." While the states (P) have considerable latitude in fashioning SIPs, the Clean Air Act "nonetheless subjects the states to strict minimum compliance requirements" and gives the EPA (D) the authority to determine a state's compliance with the requirements. Given the EPA's (D) authority to ensure that submitted SIPs adequately prohibit significantly contributing emissions, the EPA (D) permissibly relied on its general rule-making authority to prospectively inform the states of the EPA's (D) significance determinations. Moreover, under its program, the EPA (D) does not dictate to states how they must achieve SIP compliance. The states have real, meaningful choices and full discretion in how they will achieve the NOx reduction levels that the EPA (D) has set for them. This is exemplified by the fact that states implementing alternative controls will not be penalized with more stringent emissions targets. With some minor exceptions, the petitions for review are denied.

▶ ANALYSIS

As part of the EPA's (D) SIP call, the subject states had the option of adopting an interstate trading program that would enable each state to purchase NOx "allowances" from sources that had elected to over-control. Such a trading program, more commonly known as a cap-and-trade program, has become the EPA's (D) preferred approach to addressing numerous air quality problems that involve multiple sources, such as in the instant case. The name cap-and-trade reflects the approach taken in this case, whereby an emissions ceiling is first established (the cap—here called the NOx Budgets), and then affected states/sources are allowed to trade allowances to comply with that cap.

■=■

Quicknotes

CLEAN AIR ACT (CAA) Required certain states to establish a permit program for stationary sources of air pollution.

SIP State implementation plan.

■=■

North Carolina v. EPA

State (P) v. Federal agency (D)

531 F.3d 896 (D.C. Cir. 2008).

NATURE OF CASE: State and other entities challenged the Environmental Protection Agency's (the EPA's) (D) new regulation, the Clean Air Interstate Rule (CAIR).

FACT SUMMARY: In 2005, the EPA (D) promulgated CAIR to regulate emissions from "upwind" states that were polluting the air of downwind states.

🏛 RULE OF LAW

To eliminate emissions that flow to downwind states, CAIR must measure each state's significant contribution to downwind nonattainment, rather than measuring emissions levels on a region-wide basis.

FACTS: In 2005, the EPA (D) promulgated CAIR. CAIR's purpose is to reduce emissions, namely smog, from upwind sources on downwind areas of nonattainment. To eliminate a state's significant contribution of smog, the EPA (D) sets an annual emissions cap on a region where the state is located. North Carolina (P) argues that CAIR does not comply with § 110(a)(2)(D)(i)(I), which prohibits emissions sources within "each state" from contributing significantly to nonattainment "in any other state."

ISSUE: To eliminate emissions that flow to downwind states, must CAIR measure each state's significant contribution to downwind nonattainment, rather than measuring emissions levels on a region-wide basis?

HOLDING AND DECISION: (Per curiam) Yes. To eliminate emissions that flow to downwind states, CAIR must measure each state's significant contribution to downwind nonattainment, rather than measuring emissions levels on a region-wide basis. Because CAIR bases its emissions requirements on region-wide levels of emissions, the EPA (D) never actually reviewed each upwind state's contributions of emissions to downwind states. This conflicts with the EPA's (D) statutory mandate under the Clean Air Act. Under § 110(a)(2)(D)(i)(I), the Act prohibits emissions sources within "each state" from contributing significantly to nonattainment "in any other state." Therefore, because CAIR is meant to serve as the regulation implementing that section, CAIR must do more than achieve emissions reductions across a region. Rather, CAIR must require elimination of emissions from sources that contribute significantly to downwind nonattainment areas. To do this, it must measure each state's emissions levels specifically, and not just a region of states. Accordingly, CAIR is vacated.

▶ ANALYSIS

This is a fairly straightforward decision, based on the clear conflict between the regulations and the statute. CAIR included a cap and trade program among states, but the decision noted that CAIR could not verify the compliance with the cap and trade system if the EPA (D) was not examining each state's contributions to smog collecting in the downwind states.

Quicknotes

CLEAN AIR ACT Required certain states to establish a permit program for stationary sources of air pollution.

Water Pollution Control

Quick Reference Rules of Law

United States v. Riverside Bayview Homes, Inc.

Federal government (P) v. Homebuilder (D)

474 U.S. 121 (1985).

NATURE OF CASE: Appeal from denial of an injunction in action to prevent discharge of fill into wetlands.

FACT SUMMARY: The United States Army Corps of Engineers (the Corps) (P) sought to enjoin Riverside Bayview Homes (Riverside) (D), a developer, from dumping landfill on wetlands adjacent to a navigable lake.

🏛 RULE OF LAW
Wetlands are "waters" under the Clean Water Act, even if they are not regularly flooded by adjacent waterways.

FACTS: Riverside (D) owned land adjacent to Lake St. Claire. In order to build homes on the land, Riverside (D) began to place fill materials on its property. The Corps (P), vested with authority to issue dredge and fill permits under § 404 of the Clean Water Act, sought an injunction to prevent Riverside (D) from proceeding without a permit. The Corps (P) claimed that Riverside's (D) land was a wetland under a 1975 regulation defining "wetlands adjacent to waterways" as "waters of the United States" and thus subject to its permit authority. The district court granted the injunction, but the court of appeals remanded for consideration of a subsequent 1977 regulation defining wetlands as an area capable of supporting vegetation adapted to soil conditions. On remand, the district court again held the property to be a wetland, but the appellate court reversed, finding that the property's saturated condition was not a result of flooding from nearby navigable waters. The Corps (P) appealed.

ISSUE: Are wetlands "waters" under the Clean Water Act?

HOLDING AND DECISION: (White, J.) Yes. Wetlands are "waters" under the Clean Water Act. The intent of Congress in passing the Clean Water Act, broadly stated, was to maintain the integrity, i.e., the aquatic ecosystems, of the nation's waters. The Corps (P) has expanded its definition of waters to include wetlands adjacent to navigable waters. The justification given for this expansion was that the regulation, to be effective, must include the entire "aquatic system." It was reasonably within the Corps' (P) discretion to determine that the condition of wetlands affects the ecosystem of the waterways they adjoin. This holds true even for wetlands that may not be inundated by the waters of adjacent lakes or streams. As such, Riverside (D) must acquire a permit before placing fill on its land. Reversed.

▶ ANALYSIS

Not surprisingly, developers have been attempting to redefine wetlands in a more restrictive fashion for the last two decades. Given the new Republican majority in Congress, their efforts may now be successful. As a means to the same end, an alternative strategy would be to reinterpret the takings doctrine to require compensation when environmental regulations cause a specific percentage—say, 10% or more—of diminution in a property's value.

Quicknotes

INJUNCTION A court order requiring a person to do, or prohibiting that person from doing, a specific act.

Solid Waste Agency of Northern Cook County v. U.S. Army Corps of Engineers

Owner of land where migratory birds inhabit (P) v. Federal agency (D)

531 U.S. 159 (2001).

NATURE OF CASE: Appeal of judgment that certain regulations as enacted by the United States Army Corps of Engineers (Corps) (D) are permitted under the Clean Water Act (CWA).

FACT SUMMARY: The Corps (D) enacted regulations that gave it jurisdiction over Solid Waste Agency of Northern Cook County's (Solid Waste) (P) land. Solid Waste (P) challenged the conclusion that the CWA gave the Corps (D) such authority to regulate.

RULE OF LAW
The United States Army Corps of Engineers has jurisdiction only over navigable waters or waters that abut navigable waters.

FACTS: The Corps (D) has the authority, under § 404(a) of the CWA, to issue permits for the discharge of filled materials into navigable waters. Pursuant to this authority, it created a Migratory Bird Rule that states that § 404(a) extends to intrastate waters which would be used by certain migratory birds or endangered species or are used to irrigate crops sold in interstate commerce. The Corps (D) determined that Solid Waste (P) lands, which include an abandoned gravel pit and isolated ponds completely located within two Illinois counties, fall under § 404(a)'s definition of navigable waters because they serve as a habitat for migratory birds. The court of appeals found that the Migratory Bird Rule should stand in part because millions of people spend over a billion dollars annually on recreational pursuits relating to migratory birds and, therefore, Congress has the power to regulate such intrastate activities that have a substantial effect on interstate commerce. Solid Waste (P) appealed.

ISSUE: Did the Corps (D) have the authority, pursuant to the CWA, to enact the Migratory Bird Rule that would give it authority over nonnavigable waters?

HOLDING AND DECISION: (Rehnquist, C.J.) No. The Migratory Bird Rule is not fairly supported under the CWA. Although Congress evidenced its intent to regulate some waters that would not be deemed navigable, such as those adjacent to navigable waters, it did not intend to allow the Corps (D) to regulate ponds that are not adjacent to navigable waters. That Congress did not pass legislation which would have overturned the Corps' (D) regulations does not mean that Congress acquiesced to the Corps' (D) interpretation of the CWA to include non-navigable, isolated, intrastate waters. A failed 1977 House bill that would have defined navigable waters as all waters that can be used as a means to transport interstate or foreign commerce does not demonstrate Congress's acquiescence to the Corps' (D)

regulations. A bill can be proposed and rejected for any number of reasons. Congressional acquiescence is also not present simply because it extended jurisdiction to the EPA in § 404(g) to waters other than traditional navigable waters. Section 404(g) could have been referring to waters adjacent to navigable waters, and thus the phrase "other . . . waters" does not necessarily mean an incorporation of the Corps' (D) regulations. Moreover, isolated ponds, including those that are just seasonal, which are completely located within two Illinois counties, do not fall under § 404(a)'s definition of navigable waters because they serve as a habitat for migratory birds. To do so would mean that the use of the word "navigable" in the statute does not have any independent significance. The term shows us that Congress wanted the CWA to cover waters that were or had been navigable, or could be made so. Just because the phrase "waters of the United States" is used within the statute does not mean that the term "navigable waters" should be read out of the statute. Furthermore, although Congress may not have addressed the exact scope of § 404(a) with regard to nonnavigable, isolated, intrastate waters, deference should not be given to the Migratory Bird Rule. This is because where an administrative interpretation of a statute, such as the Corps' (D) interpretation, invokes the outer limits of Congress's power to encroach upon a traditional state power, there should be a clear indication that Congress intended that result. In the present case, there is no such indication. Given that Congress did not make a clear statement that it intended § 404(a) to reach an abandoned sand and gravel pit, to then permit the Corps (D) to claim federal jurisdiction over ponds falling within the Migratory Bird Rule would impinge on the state's traditional power over land and water use without an intent by Congress to even do so. The constitutional issue, therefore, of whether Congress has the power to regulate such intrastate activities that may substantially affect interstate commerce under the Commerce Clause does not have to be addressed given that Congress has not expressed an intent to regulate such an area. The statute is thus written to avoid such constitutional questions and, therefore, administrative deference is denied. Reversed.

ANALYSIS

This case was decided by the same 5-4 division of judges that decided *United States v. Lopez*, 514 U.S. 549 (1995).

■■■■

Continued on next page.

Quicknotes

COMMERCE CLAUSE Article 1, section 8, clause 3 of the United States Constitution, granting Congress the power to regulate commerce with foreign countries and between the states.

Rapanos v. United States

[Party not identified] (D) v. Federal government (P)

547 U.S. 715 (2006).

NATURE OF CASE: Appeal from judgment in consolidated actions brought under the Clean Water Act (CWA).

FACT SUMMARY: Rapanos (D) contended that the term "waters of the United States" in the CWA had to be limited to a traditional definition that requires that the "waters" be navigable in fact, or susceptible of being rendered navigable, so that the CWA does not extend to wetlands that do not contain and are not adjacent to waters that are navigable in fact.

🏛 RULE OF LAW
The term "waters of the United States" in the CWA encompasses only those relatively permanent, standing or continuously flowing bodies of water "forming geographic features" that are described in ordinary parlance as "streams," "oceans," "rivers," and "lakes," and does not include channels through which water flows intermittently or ephemerally, or channels that periodically provide drainage for rainfall, so that wetlands that do not contain and are not adjacent to waters that are navigable in fact, or do not have a continuous surface connection to such waters, are not covered by the CWA.

FACTS: Rapanos (D) contended that the term "waters of the United States" in the CWA had to be limited to a traditional definition that requires that the "waters" be navigable in fact, or susceptible of being rendered navigable, so that the CWA does not extend to wetlands that do not contain and are not adjacent to waters that are navigable in fact. The Corps regulations had included such wetlands as being covered by the CWA, and, therefore, under Corps' jurisdiction. In an action by the United States (P) against Rapanos (D), the court of appeals ruled in favor of the Corps' interpretation. The Supreme Court granted certiorari.

ISSUE: Does the term "waters of the United States" in the CWA encompass only those relatively permanent, standing or continuously flowing bodies of water "forming geographic features" that are described in ordinary parlance as "streams," "oceans," "rivers," and "lakes," and does not include channels through which water flows intermittently or ephemerally, or channels that periodically provide drainage for rainfall, so that wetlands that do not contain and are not adjacent to waters that are navigable in fact, or do not have a continuous surface connection to such waters, are not covered by the CWA?

HOLDING AND DECISION: (Scalia, J.) Yes. The term "waters of the United States" in the CWA encompasses only those relatively permanent, standing or continuously flowing bodies of water "forming geographic features" that

are described in ordinary parlance as "streams," "oceans," "rivers," and "lakes," and does not include channels through which water flows intermittently or ephemerally, or channels that periodically provide drainage for rainfall, so that wetlands that do not contain and are not adjacent to waters that are navigable in fact, or do not have a continuous surface connection to such waters, are not covered by the CWA. The phrase "the waters of the United States" includes only those relatively permanent, standing or continuously flowing bodies of water "forming geographic features" that are described in ordinary parlance as "streams," "oceans, rivers, [and] lakes," Webster's New International Dictionary 2882 (2d ed.), and does not include channels through which water flows intermittently or ephemerally, or channels that periodically provide drainage for rainfall. The Corps' expansive interpretation of that phrase is thus not "based on a permissible construction of the statute." While the meaning of "navigable waters" in the CWA is broader than the traditional definition found in this Court's past decisions, the CWA authorizes federal jurisdiction only over "waters." The use of the definite article "the" and the plural number "waters" show plainly that the CWA does not refer to water in general, but more narrowly to water "as found in streams," "oceans, rivers, [and] lakes," Webster's New International Dictionary 2882 (2d ed.). Those terms all connote relatively permanent bodies of water, as opposed to ordinarily dry channels through which water occasionally or intermittently flows. The CWA's use of the traditional phrase "navigable waters" further confirms that the CWA confers jurisdiction only over relatively permanent bodies of water. Traditionally, such "waters" included only discrete bodies of water, and the term still carries some of its original substance. This Court's prior decisions interpreting "the waters of the United States" likewise confirms this limitation, and the CWA itself categorizes the channels and conduits that typically carry intermittent flows of water separately from "navigable waters," including them in the definition of "point sources." Moreover, only the foregoing definition of "waters" is consistent with CWA's stated policy "to recognize, preserve, and protect the primary responsibilities and rights of the States . . . to plan the development and use . . . of land and water resources . . . ." In addition, "the waters of the United States" hardly qualifies as the clear and manifest statement from Congress needed to authorize intrusion into such an area of traditional state authority as land-use regulation or to authorize federal action that stretches the limits of Congress's commerce power. A wetland may not be considered "adjacent to" remote "waters of the United States" based on a mere hydrologic connection.

Continued on next page.

Ecological considerations do not provide an independent basis for including entities like "wetlands" within the phrase "waters of the United States." Isolated ponds are not "waters of the United States" in their own right, and present no boundary-drawing problem justifying the invocation of such ecological factors. Thus, only those wetlands with a continuous surface connection to bodies that are "waters of the United States" in their own right, so that there is no clear demarcation between the two, are "adjacent" to such waters and covered by the CWA. Establishing coverage of the Rapanos (D) sites requires finding that the adjacent channel contains a relatively permanent "water of the United States," and that each wetland has a continuous surface connection to that water, making it difficult to determine where the water ends and the wetland begins. Because the court of appeals applied an incorrect standard to determine whether the wetlands at issue are covered "waters," and because of the paucity of the record, the cases are remanded for further proceedings. Vacated and remanded.

CONCURRENCE: (Kennedy, J.) The court of appeals correctly recognized that a water or wetland constitutes "navigable waters" under the CWA if it possesses a "significant nexus" to waters that are navigable in fact or that could reasonably be so made, but did not consider all the factors necessary to determine that the lands in question had, or did not have, the requisite nexus. The Court's prior decisions establish the framework for the inquiry here. The nexus required must be assessed in terms of the CWA's goals and purposes. Congress enacted the law to "restore and maintain the chemical, physical, and biological integrity of the Nation's waters," and it pursued that objective by restricting dumping and filling in "waters of the United States." The rationale for the CWA's wetlands regulation, as the Corps has recognized, is that wetlands can perform critical functions related to the integrity of other waters, such as pollutant trapping, flood control, and runoff storage. Accordingly, wetlands possess the requisite nexus, and thus come within the statutory phrase "navigable waters," if the wetlands, alone or in combination with similarly situated lands in the region, significantly affect the chemical, physical, and biological integrity of other covered waters understood as navigable in the traditional sense. When, in contrast, their effects on water quality are speculative or insubstantial, they fall outside the zone fairly encompassed by the term "navigable waters." Because the Corps' theory of jurisdiction in these cases—adjacency to tributaries, however remote and insubstantial—goes beyond the Court's precedent, its assertion of jurisdiction cannot rest on such a theory. The breadth of the Corps' existing standard for tributaries—which seems to leave room for regulating drains, ditches, and streams remote from any navigable-in-fact water and carrying only minor water-volumes toward it—precludes that standard's adoption as the determinative measure of whether adjacent wetlands are likely to play an important role in the integrity of an aquatic system comprising navigable waters as traditionally understood. Absent more specific regulations, the

Corps must establish a significant nexus on a case-by-case basis when seeking to regulate wetlands based on adjacency to nonnavigable tributaries, to avoid unreasonable applications of the CWA. In the instant case, the record contains evidence pointing to a possible significant nexus, but neither the Corps nor the lower courts considered the issue in these terms. Thus, the cases should be remanded for further proceedings.

DISSENT: (Stevens, J.) The plurality fails to adequately defer to the Corps and its more than 30 years of practice in this area, which has implicitly been approved by Congress. In its expertise and experience, the Corps has determined that wetlands adjacent to tributaries of traditionally navigable waters preserve the quality of United States waters by, among other things, providing habitat for aquatic animals, keeping excessive sediment and toxic pollutants out of adjacent waters, and reducing downstream flooding by absorbing water at times of high flow. The Corps' resulting decision to treat these wetlands as encompassed within the term "waters of the United States" is a quintessential example of the Executive's reasonable interpretation of a statutory provision, and, therefore, should be deferred to, and given effect.

▶ ANALYSIS

In a concurring opinion, Chief Justice Roberts bemoaned that because "no opinion commands a majority of the Court on precisely how to read Congress's limits on the reach of the Clean Water Act[, l]ower courts and regulated entities will now have to feel their way on a case-by-case basis." He suggested, however, that such a situation could have been readily avoided if the Corps had issued new regulations clarifying the statute's reach. He noted that under *Chevron,* agencies delegated rulemaking authority under a statute such as the CWA are afforded generous leeway by the courts in interpreting the statute they are entrusted to administer. According to Roberts, rather than refining its view of its authority and providing guidance meriting deference under the Court's generous standards, the Corps chose to adhere to its essentially boundless view of the scope of its power, so that the upshot of the Court's decision was another defeat for the Corps.

■■■

Quicknotes

CONSOLIDATION The joining of several causes of action into one suit pursuant to a court order if the actions involve the same parties, issue and subject matter or if there is a common issue of law.

■■■

National Mining Association v. Army Corps of Engineers

Trade association (P) v. Federal government (D)

145 F.3d 1399 (D.C. Cir. 1998).

NATURE OF CASE: Appeal from decision that fallback of dredged material does not violate the Clean Water Act.

FACT SUMMARY: The Army Corps of Engineers (Corps) (D) contends that excavation activities producing any incidental redeposition of dredge materials, however small, requires permits under the Clean Water Act if such activities would degrade or destroy wetlands.

🏛 RULE OF LAW
Incidental fallback, which returns dredged material virtually to the spot from which it came, does not constitute an addition of material, and, therefore, does not require a permit under the Clean Water Act.

FACTS: Section 404 of the Clean Water Act authorizes the Corps (D) to issue permits for the discharge of dredged or fill material into navigable waters at specified disposal sites. "Discharge" is defined as any "addition of any pollutant to navigable waters from any point source." Responding to litigation which arose in 1993, the Corps (D) issued a new rule defining the term of "discharge" to cover any addition of dredged material into, including any redeposit of dredged material within, the waters of the United States. Redeposit occurs when material removed from the water is returned to it. If it takes place in the same spot as the initial removal, it is called fallback. The new rule, known as the Tulloch Rule, effectively subjected to federal regulation virtually all excavation and dredging performed in wetlands. Under the Tulloch Rule, it is impossible to conduct mechanized land clearing, ditching, channelization or excavation in waters of the United States without causing fallback. As a result, the Tulloch Rule effectively requires a permit for all those activities, subject to a limited exception according to the Corps (D) discretion. The National Mining Association (Association) (P), whose members engage in dredging and excavation, mounted a challenge of the regulation, arguing that it exceeded the scope of the Corps' (D) regulatory authority under the Clean Water Act by regulating fallback. The district court held for the Association (P). The Corps (D) appealed.

ISSUE: Does the Tulloch Rule exceed the Corps' (D) statutory jurisdiction under the Clean Water Act?

HOLDING AND DECISION: (Williams, J.) Yes. The straightforward statutory term "addition" cannot reasonably be said to encompass the situation in which material is removed from the waters of the United States and a small portion of it happens to fall back. Because incidental fallback represents a net withdrawal, not an addition, of material, it cannot be a discharge. The Corps' (D) primary counterargument—that fallback constitutes an "addition of any pollutant" because material becomes a pollutant only upon being dredged—is ingenious but unconvincing. Regardless of any legal metamorphosis that may occur at the moment of dredging, we fail to see how there can be an addition of dredged material when there is no addition of material. By asserting jurisdiction over any redeposit, including incidental fallback, the Tulloch Rule outruns the Corps' (D) statutory authority. The Clean Water Act simply cannot accommodate the Tulloch Rule. Affirmed.

CONCURRENCE: (Silberman, J.) The Clean Water Act's language defining "discharge" is ambiguous. Discharge is defined as the "addition of any pollutant to navigable waters." The term "addition" in the definition carries with it a temporal and geographic ambiguity. However, it would be unreasonable to call incidental fallback an "addition," as this would mean that all dredging results in an addition of pollutants to navigable waters and subject to application of the Clean Water Act. Under this definition, the Rivers and Harbors Act, which purports to regulate dredging, would be totally superfluous. Because the Clean Water Act is ambiguous as to discharge, the court need not defer to the Corps' (D) interpretation of the term to include incidental fallback in dredging and excavation activities.

▎ ANALYSIS

The court also noted that the removal of material from waters of the United States, as opposed to the discharge of material into those waters, is governed by a completely independent statutory scheme under the Rivers and Harbors Act of 1899. Congress has enacted two separate statutory frameworks: the Rivers and Harbors Act covers the act of dredging, while the Clean Water Act covers the disposal of dredged material.

■■■

Quicknotes

FALLBACK When material removed from water is returned to it in the same spot.

■■■

South Florida Water Management District v. Miccosukee Tribe of Indians

State agency (D) v. State citizens (P)

541 U.S. 95 (2004).

NATURE OF CASE: Appeal from affirmance of grant of summary judgment to plaintiffs in citizens suit brought under the Clean Water Act (Act).

FACT SUMMARY: Miccosukee Tribe of Indians (the Tribe) (P) contended that under the Act, a South Florida Water Management District (the District) (D) pumping facility (S-9) that transferred water from a canal (C-11) into a reservoir (WCA-3) was required to obtain a discharge permit under the National Pollutant Discharge Elimination System (NPDES).

🏛 RULE OF LAW
For purposes of a CWA requirement that a NPDES permit be obtained for the discharge of pollutants into the nation's waters, such a discharge includes a point source that does not itself generate the pollutants.

FACTS: The District (D) operated a pumping facility (S-9) that transferred water from a canal (C-11) into a nearby reservoir (WCA-3). The Tribe (P) brought a citizens' suit contending that under the CWA, the District (D) was required to obtain a discharge permit under the NPDES because the pump station was moving phosphorous-laden water. The Act prohibits "the discharge of any pollutant by any person" unless done in compliance with some provision of the Act. The NPDES requires dischargers to obtain permits that place limits on the type and quantity of pollutants that can be released into the Nation's waters. The Act defines the phrase "discharge of a pollutant" to mean "any addition of any pollutant to navigable waters from any point source." A "point source," in turn, is defined as "any discernible, confined and discrete conveyance," such as a pipe, ditch, channel, or tunnel, "from which pollutants are or may be discharged." The District (D) did not dispute that phosphorous is a pollutant, or that C-11 and WCA-3 were "navigable waters" within the meaning of the Act. The question, it contended, was whether the operation of the S-9 pump constituted the "discharge of [a] pollutant" within the meaning of the Act. The district court agreed with the Tribe (P) that it did, and granted the Tribe (P) summary judgment. The court of appeals affirmed, and the Supreme Court granted certiorari. The federal government (Government) filed an amicus brief in favor of the District (D).

ISSUE: For purposes of a CWA requirement that a NPDES permit be obtained for the discharge of pollutants into the nation's waters, does such a discharge include a point source that does not itself generate the pollutants?

HOLDING AND DECISION: (O'Connor, J.) Yes. For purposes of a CWA requirement that a NPDES permit be obtained for the discharge of pollutants into the nation's waters, such a discharge includes a point source that does not itself generate the pollutants. First, the District's (D) argument that the pump could not be considered a point source because it did not generate the pollutants in the waters it pumped is rejected. The Government next contends that all water bodies that are navigable waters under the Act should be viewed unitarily for purposes of NPDES permitting. Because the Act requires NPDES permits only when a pollutant is added to navigable waters, the Government contends that such permits are not required when water from one navigable body is discharged, unaltered, into another navigable body—even if one body of water is polluted and the other is pristine. Under this approach, no permit would be needed for the pump. The "unitary waters" argument focuses on the Act's definition of a pollutant discharge as "any addition of any pollutant to navigable waters from any point source." The Government contends that the absence of the word "any" prior to the phrase "navigable waters" in the Act signals Congress's understanding that NPDES permits would not be required for pollution caused by the engineered transfer of one "navigable water" into another. However, the CWA does not explicitly exempt non-point pollution sources from the NPDES program if they also fall within the "point source" definition. Moreover, several NPDES provisions can be read to suggest a view contrary to the unitary waters approach. Finally, the Government and numerous amici warn that affirming the court of appeals in this case would have significant practical consequences, possibly requiring thousands of new permits, particularly in western states, whose water supply networks often rely on engineered transfers among various natural water bodies. Nonetheless, despite the relevance of the "unitary waters" approach, neither the District (D) nor the Government raised it before the court of appeals or in their briefs respecting certiorari, and this Court is unaware of any case that has examined the argument in its present form. Thus, the Court declines to resolve the argument here. However, because the judgment must be vacated in any event, the unitary waters argument will be open to the parties on remand. The District (D) and the Government believe that the C-11 canal and WCA-3 impoundment area are not distinct water bodies, but are two hydrologically

Continued on next page.

indistinguishable parts of a single water body. The Tribe (P) agrees that, if this is so, pumping water from one into the other cannot constitute an "addition" of pollutants within the meaning of the Act, but it disputes the District's (D) factual premise that C-11 and WCA-3 are one. The parties also disagree about how the relationship between S-9 and WCA-3 should be assessed. This Court does not decide here whether the district court's test, on which summary judgment was premised, is adequate for determining whether C-11 and WCA-3 are distinct, because that court applied its test prematurely. Summary judgment is appropriate only where there is no genuine issue of material fact, but some factual issues remain unresolved here. The district court correctly characterized the flow through S-9 as non-natural, and it appears that if S-9 were shut down, the water in the C-11 canal might for a brief time flow east, rather than west. But the record also suggests that if S-9 were shut down, the area drained by C-11 would flood, which might mean C-11 would no longer be a distinct body of navigable water, but instead part of a larger water body extending over WCA-3 and the C-11 basin. It also might call into question the conclusion by the court of appeals that S-9 is the cause in fact of phosphorous addition to WCA-3. Nothing in the record suggests that the district court considered these issues when it granted summary judgment. If, after further development of the record, that court concludes that C-11 and WCA-3 are not meaningfully distinct water bodies, S-9 will not need an NPDES permit. Vacated and remanded.

▶ ANALYSIS

This decision indicates that NPDES permits may be necessary for pumps that transfer polluted water from one body of water to another, even if the pollutants do not exist in either body but are introduced by stormwater runoff. However, under a "unitary waters" approach, advocated for by the federal government, a permit would not be needed if the two bodies are considered as one. After the decision in this case was handed down, the Environmental Protection Agency (EPA) concluded that water transfers—"activities that convey or connect navigable waters without subjecting the water to intervening industrial, municipal, or commercial use"—are not subject to NPDES permitting requirements.

■■■

Quicknotes

AMICUS BRIEF A brief submitted by a third party, not a party to the action, that contains information for the court's consideration in conformity with its position.

NPDES National Pollutant Discharge Elimination System, a program of the Office of Wastewater Management (a division of the Environmental Protection Agency), which regulates the discharge of pollutants into the pubic water system by industrial, municipal, and other facilities.

POINT SOURCE A stationary location or fixed facility from which pollutants are discharged or emitted such as a pipe, ditch, or ship.

SUMMARY JUDGMENT Judgment rendered by a court in response to a motion made by one of the parties, claiming that the lack of a question of material fact in respect to an issue warrants disposition of the issue without consideration by the jury.

■■■

NRDC v. Costle

Environmental organization (P) v. Federal regulatory agency (D)

568 F.2d 1369 (D.C. Cir. 1977).

NATURE OF CASE: Appeal from summary judgment in action seeking declaratory judgment that certain Environmental Protection Agency (the EPA) regulations were unlawful.

FACT SUMMARY: After the EPA (D) exempted several classes of point source polluters from the permit requirements of section 402 of the Clean Water Act, the National Resource Defense Council (the NRDC) (P) challenged the exemptions as unlawful.

RULE OF LAW
The EPA does not have the authority to exempt categories of point source polluters from the permit requirements of the Clean Water Act.

FACTS: Section 402 of the Federal Water Pollution Control Act (FWPCA) (later renamed the Clean Water Act) requires all point source polluters to have permits. The Environmental Protection Agency (EPA) (D) promulgated a regulation exempting several of the most controversial categories of point source polluters from this requirement in order to focus the resources of the agency on more serious polluters. The exempted sources included all silvicultural point sources, all confined animal feedlots, and certain irrigation return flows. The NRDC (P) brought suit for declaratory relief, arguing that the Clean Water Act did not authorize the EPA (D) to exclude any class of point sources from the permit program. The district court granted the NRDC's (P) motion for summary judgment. The EPA (D) appealed.

ISSUE: Does the EPA (D) have the authority to exempt categories of point source polluters from the permit requirement of the Clean Water Act?

HOLDING AND DECISION: (Leventhal, J.) No. The EPA (D) does not have the authority to exempt categories of point source polluters from the permit requirements of the Clean Water Act. The language of the Clean Water Act, its legislative history, and precedents are very strong and clear: the discharge of pollutants without a permit is unlawful. The Act gives the EPA (D) discretion to set the requirements and the conditions for issuing discharge permits. If the EPA (D) is overburdened by the mass of potential permits, it may resolve that problem by alternative means, such as area-wide general permits. However, the EPA (D) has no authority to exempt point source polluters from the permit program itself since Congress's clear mandate was that all point sources have permits.

► ANALYSIS

In 1977, in response to the above case, Congress alleviated some of the EPA's (D) regulatory burden by amending

§ 502(14) of the Clean Water Act to exempt "agricultural stormwater discharges and return flows from irrigated agriculture." States may still choose to take responsibility for such point sources through their own National Pollution Discharge Elimination System (NPDES) permit programs. Agricultural irrigation continues to be a major source of water pollution.

■■■

Quicknotes

POINT SOURCE A stationary location or fixed facility from which pollutants are discharged or emitted such as a pipe, ditch, or ship.

SUMMARY JUDGMENT Judgment rendered by a court in response to a motion by one of the parties, claiming that the lack of a question of material fact in respect to an issue warrants disposition of the issue without consideration by the jury.

■■■

United States v. Plaza Health Laboratories, Inc.

Federal government (P) v. Water polluter (D)

3 F.3d 643 (2d Cir. 1993).

NATURE OF CASE: Appeal from conviction on two counts of knowingly discharging pollutants into a waterway in violation of the Clean Water Act (CWA).

FACT SUMMARY: After Villegas (D) disposed of numerous blood vials from his business, Plaza Health Laboratories, Inc. (Plaza Health) (D), they were found washed up on shore in Staten Island.

🏛 RULE OF LAW
The discharge of a pollutant by an individual person is not a violation of the CWA.

FACTS: Villegas (D), co-owner and vice president of Plaza Health (D), on at least two occasions loaded containers of numerous vials of human blood generated from his business into his personal car, depositing them at low tide within a crevice below the high-water line in a bulkhead separating his condominium complex from the Hudson River. Some of the vials containing human blood washed up on the shore of Staten Island, New York. New Jersey authorities later retrieved numerous blood vials from the bulkhead. Plaza Health (D) and Villegas (D) were indicted for violating the CWA by knowingly discharging pollutants from a "point source" without a permit. The jury found Villegas (D) guilty on all four counts. Villegas (D) appealed.

ISSUE: Is the discharge of pollutant by an individual person unlawful under the Clean Water Act?

HOLDING AND DECISION: (Pratt, J.) No. The discharge of pollutant by an individual person does not violate the CWA. The CWA defines a discharge as "any addition of any pollutant to navigable waters from any point source." Human beings are not among the enumerated items that may be a "point source." The CWA generally targets industrial and municipal sources of pollutants. Moreover, the legislative history of the CWA confirms the Act's focus on industrial polluters. The CWA does not expressly recognize a human being as a "point source"; nor does the Act make structural sense when one incorporates a human being into that definition. The term "point source" as applied to a human being is at best ambiguous. In criminal prosecutions, the rule of lenity requires that ambiguities in the statute be resolved in the defendant's favor. Under the rule of lenity, therefore, the prosecutions against Villegas (D) must be dismissed.

DISSENT: (Oakes, J.) When a company chooses to use the nation's waters as a dumpsite for waste it has created and gathered in a manageable place, it should ask for a permit or face prosecution. "... [B]ecause I do not agree that a person can never be a point source, and because I

believe that Mr. Villegas's (D) actions, as the jury found them, fell well within the bounds of activity proscribed by the Clean Water Act's bar on discharge of pollutants into navigable waters, I am required to dissent." The point is that the source of the pollution was clear, and would have been easy to control. He simply chose not to use an appropriate waste disposal mechanism.

▶ ANALYSIS

The problem, according to the majority, is that the statute was never designed to address the random, individual polluter like Villegas (D). If every discharge involving humans were to be considered a "discharge from a point source," the statute's lengthy definition of "point source" would have been unnecessary. The court found no suggestion either in the Act itself or in the history of its passage that Congress intended the CWA to impose criminal liability on an individual for the myriad, random acts of human waste disposal, such as a passerby who flings a candy wrapper into the Hudson River or a urinating swimmer. The Supreme Court subsequently declined the Government's (P) request for review of this case.

■=■

Quicknotes

POINT SOURCE A discrete conveyance in municipal water management processes, e.g., pipes or man-made ditches.

RULE OF LENITY The doctrine that where a statute is ambiguous as to the term of punishment imposed, it should be construed in favor of the less severe punishment.

■=■

Chemical Manufacturers Association v. NRDC

Trade association (P) v. Environmental organization (D)

470 U.S. 116 (1985).

NATURE OF CASE: Appeal from decision setting aside an Environmental Protection Agency (EPA) regulation.

FACT SUMMARY: An Environmental Protection Agency (the EPA) (P) regulation granted variances to toxic dischargers who could show that their plants differed fundamentally from the industry norm.

🏛 RULE OF LAW
The Clean Water Act's prohibition against modifying any requirements applicable to toxic pollutants does not prohibit "fundamentally different factors" (FDF) variances.

FACTS: Under Clean Water Act § 301(l), the EPA (P) may not "modify" any toxic materials standard. The EPA (P) granted variances to certain dischargers of toxics who could show FDF from those considered by the EPA (P). The Natural Resources Defense Council (the NRDC) (D) claimed that the language should apply to all modifications in order to carry out congressional intent. In response, the EPA (P) argued that the statutory language did not prohibit granting FDF variances since the term "modifications" should be read to apply only to those modifications referred to in other provisions of § 301, i.e., economic and water quality grounds. The court of appeals found for the NRDC (D), holding that FDF variances could not be granted for toxic discharges, and the EPA (P) appealed.

ISSUE: Does the Clean Water Act's prohibition against modifying any requirements applicable to toxic pollutants prohibit FDF variances?

HOLDING AND DECISION: (White, J.) No. The Clean Water Act's prohibition against modifying any requirements applicable to toxic pollutants does not prohibit FDF variances. It makes no sense to forbid the EPA (P) to ever amend its own standards. Thus, the term "modifications" in the statute is not used in its plain, all-encompassing meaning. The EPA (P), in order to function, must be allowed to make some changes in its requirements. An FDF variance is not an exception to the standard-setting process, nor a modification, but only a tailoring of a standard to the individual situation of a particular plant. The issuance of variances does not contravene the purpose of the Clean Water Act since it merely effectuates the same result that could be reached by creating permissible classifications had the EPA (P) been able to take all relevant factors into account. Section 301(l) does not prohibit FDF variances. Reversed.

DISSENT: (Marshall, J.) There is clear congressional intent to prohibit all modifications by the EPA (P), as evidenced by the legislative history.

▶ ANALYSIS

Three years later, Congress clarified the problem addressed in this case in its 1987 Amendments to the Clean Water Act. Affected industries and the EPA (P) need no longer speculate as to permissible bases for granting FDF variances for toxic pollutants; they may now look to § 301(n) of the 1987 Clean Water Act Amendments for guidance.

■━■

Quicknotes

VARIANCE Exemption from the application of zoning laws.

■━■

Arkansas v. Oklahoma

State (P) v. State (D)

503 U.S. 91 (1992).

NATURE OF CASE: Appeal from judgment overturning issuance of a National Pollution Discharge Elimination System (NPDES) permit.

FACT SUMMARY: Oklahoma (P) challenged a permit granted by the Environmental Protection Agency's (the EPA's) allowing a plant in Arkansas (D) to discharge into a stream emptying into the Illinois River in Oklahoma (P).

🏛 **RULE OF LAW**

It is within the EPA's authority to require an upstream discharger to comply with the water pollution regulations of the downstream state.

FACTS: The EPA granted a permit to a plant in Arkansas (D) which was discharging into a waterway that ultimately emptied into the Illinois River. Oklahoma (P) petitioned the EPA for review since the Illinois River ran through its state, and the allowed discharges would, it argued, violate Oklahoma's (P) zero-tolerance water quality standards. The permit imposed specific limitations on the quantity and character of the discharge. Two administrative reviews affirmed the issuance of the permit on the basis of Oklahoma law. Arkansas (D) and Oklahoma (P) both sought judicial review. The court of appeals reversed and invalidated the permit. Arkansas (D) appealed.

ISSUE: Is it within the EPA'S authority to require an upstream discharger to comply with the water pollution regulations of the downstream state?

HOLDING AND DECISION: (Stevens, J.) Yes. It is within the EPA's authority to require an upstream discharger to comply with the water pollution regulations of the downstream state. The permit at issue here was federally issued since Arkansas (D) was not yet authorized to issue NPDES permits. The EPA has broad discretion to establish conditions for NPDES permits. The application of state water quality standards in the interstate context is consistent with the Act's purpose to restore and maintain the integrity of the nation's waters. Granting the permit will not violate Oklahoma's (P) water quality standards. Reversed.

▶ *ANALYSIS*

Again the Court gives great deference to a legislative interpretation of the EPA. Cf. *Chevron, U.S.A. v. NRDC,* 467 U.S. 837 (1984). Under the EPA's interpretation of the Clean Water Act and Oklahoma's (P) standards, what mattered was not the river's current status, but whether the proposed discharge would have a detectable effect on that status. The

Court found, therefore, that the EPA's decision to allow the new plant was not arbitrary or capricious.

■==■

Quicknotes

NPDES National Pollutant Discharge Elimination System, a program of the Office of Wastewater Management (a division of the Environmental Protection Agency), which regulates the discharge of pollutants into the public water system by industrial, municipal, and other facilities.

■==■

PUD No. 1 of Jefferson County v. Washington Department of Ecology

Utility district (P) v. State agency (D)

511 U.S. 700 (1994).

NATURE OF CASE: Appeal from judgment conditions placed on grant of a federal license.

FACT SUMMARY: PUD No. 1 of Jefferson County (P), a city and local utility district, challenged Washington state's (D) minimum stream flow requirements when seeking a federal license for a hydroelectric dam from the Federal Energy Regulatory Commission (FERC).

🏛 RULE OF LAW
A state may condition the grant of a federal license for projects discharging into navigable waters upon any limitations necessary to ensure compliance with state water quality standards.

FACTS: PUD No. 1 of Jefferson County (P) proposed to build the Elkhorn Hydroelectric Project on the Dosewallips River. The planned site was to be on federally owned land, and therefore PUD (P) had to obtain a FERC license. Because the project might result in discharges into the river, PUD (P) was also required to obtain state certification of the project pursuant to § 401 of the Clean Water Act. Section 401 requires states to provide a water quality certification before a federal license or permit can be issued for activities that may result in any discharge into intrastate navigable waters. Washington state (D) had adopted EPA approved comprehensive water quality standards and a statewide antidegradation policy requiring that beneficial uses be maintained. Because the Dosewallips River supported two species of salmon and one of trout, the state issued a § 401 water quality certification imposing a variety of conditions, including a minimum stream-flow requirement that was well above the anticipated minimum stream-flow predicted by PUD (P) for the project. A state administrative appeals board determined that the state (D) stream-flow calculations were intended to enhance, not merely maintain, the fishery and that the requirement exceeded state (D) authority. The superior court reversed, holding the calculation was to maintain, not enhance. The Washington Supreme Court agreed, concluding that § 401(d) conferred on states the power to consider all state actions related to water quality in imposing conditions on § 401 certificates. The Supreme Court granted certiorari.

ISSUE: May a state condition the grant of a federal license or permit for projects upon any limitations necessary to ensure compliance with state water quality standards?

HOLDING AND DECISION: (O'Connor, J.) Yes. A state may condition the grant of a federal license for projects discharging into navigable waters upon any limitations necessary to ensure compliance with state water quality

standards. To determine if the minimum stream flow requirement is permissible, it is necessary to determine the scope of the state's (D) authority under § 401. PUD (P) argues that § 401(a) limits the state's (D) authority to regulate the discharges in question, and that minimum stream-flow is unrelated to those discharges. Section 401(d), however, provides that any certification shall set forth any effluent limitations and other limitations necessary to ensure that any applicant will comply with the various provisions of the Clean Water Act and appropriate state law requirements. Read together, once the condition of a discharge has been satisfied as per § 401(a), § 401(d) authorizes additional conditions and limitations on the activity as a whole. Thus, PUD's (P) argument is incorrect. The EPA interprets § 401(d) to mean that activities, not just discharges, must comply with state water quality standards and the agency interpretation is entitled to deference. However, since the state (D) can condition certification on any limitations to ensure compliance, it must be determined if minimum stream flow is one of those limitations. In this case, the minimum stream flow requirement in the certification is necessary to enforce a designated use in a state water quality standard—i.e., as a fishery—and is also necessary to implement the state's (D) antidegradation policy. Affirmed.

DISSENT: (Thomas, J.) The majority makes two fundamental errors. First, its interpretation of § 401 fails to harmonize the two sections in question, as it leaves § 401(a) moot. Second, it places no meaningful limitation on a state's authority to impose conditions on certification. Combined with its expansive interpretation of § 401(d), the majority also indicates that not only criteria but uses as well can delineate the requirements. The regulations promulgated under § 303 make clear that a use is an aspirational goal to be attained through compliance with corresponding criteria. Allowing states to impose conditions on § 401 certification to protect "uses" in the abstract makes § 401(d) limitless.

▶ ANALYSIS

While Justice O'Connor does avow that § 401(d) cannot travel to some places in its spawning of limitations, Justice Thomas is correct in asserting that she sets no objective boundaries. Thomas tries to connect beneficial uses with appropriate criteria, but O'Connor sees them as separate entities, and the notion of beneficial use is as wide as the great outdoors. It would seem, from this ruling, that if a state has a beneficial use reference in their water quality standards, then a study indicating that a beneficial use would be adversely affected would win the day every time.

■■■■

Pronsolino v. Nastri

Representative of California (P) v. EPA representative (D)

291 F.3d 1123 (9th Cir. 2002).

NATURE OF CASE: Appeal of judgment that the Environmental Protection Agency (the EPA) (D) acted within its authority under the Clean Water Act (CWA).

FACT SUMMARY: The EPA (D) required California (P) to set total maximum daily loads (TMDLs) for a river the EPA (D) deemed to have insufficient pollution controls. Pronsolino (P) challenged the EPA's (D) authority to so regulate.

🏛 RULE OF LAW
Waters that are impaired only by nonpoint sources of pollution are subject to the CWA listing and TMDL requirements.

FACTS: The EPA (D), pursuant to the CWA, required California (P) to set the TMDLs for pollution entering the Garcia River so that it could attain water quality standards because it was a body of water with insufficient pollution controls. The river had insufficient controls because the effluent limitations, or restrictions on pollutants discharged from nonpoint sources, were not stringent enough to implement any water quality standard. Garcia River is polluted from nonpoint sources. Nonpoint sources of pollution are non-discrete sources, such as sediment runoff from timber harvesting. Point sources of pollution are those from a discrete conveyance, such as a pipe or tunnel. The CWA requires states to compile a list and a calculation of a TMDL for those waters for which certain effluent limitations are not stringent enough to implement any water quality standard. The lists and TMDLs are submitted to the EPA (D) for its approval or disapproval and are then incorporated into the state's continuing planning process. Those waters that must be included on the list are any segment where it is known that the water quality does not meet applicable water quality standards, or may not meet such standards after an application of the effluent limitations. States must identify those waters on the lists as still requiring TMDLs if any required effluent limitation will not bring the water into compliance with water quality standards. Pronsolino (P) challenged the EPA's (D) authority under the CWA to classify the river as having insufficient pollution controls and to require California (P) to set the TMDLs. The district court found that the EPA (D) acted appropriately, and Pronsolino (P) appealed.

ISSUE: Did the EPA exceed its authority in identifying the Garcia River pursuant to the CWA and establishing the Garcia River TMDL, even though the river is polluted only by nonpoint sources of pollution?

HOLDING AND DECISION: (Berzon, J.) No. The EPA (D) did not exceed its authority in identifying the Garcia River pursuant to the CWA and establishing the

Garcia River TMDL, even though the river is polluted only by nonpoint sources of pollution. The CWA includes in its listing and TMDL listing requirements waters impaired only by nonpoint sources of pollution. The CWA requires states to compile a list and a calculation of a TMDL for those waters for which certain effluent limitations are not stringent enough to implement any water quality standard applicable for such waters. Based on the language of the CWA alone, the list must contain any waters for which the particular effluent limitations will not be adequate to attain the statute's water quality goals. Each state has to identify those waters within its boundaries, then only those waters that will attain water quality standards after application of the source technology are excluded from the list, leaving only those waters for which that technology will not implement any water quality standard applicable to such waters. Furthermore, there is no general division throughout the CWA between the regulatory schemes applicable to point and nonpoint sources. Although point sources are treated differently from nonpoint sources for many purposes under the statute, they are not so treated for all. There is no distinction for the purpose for which the list and TMDLs are compiled, which is the attainment of state-defined water quality standards. In addition, the list requires that waters be listed if they are impaired by a combination of point sources and nonpoint sources, and then TMDLs shall be established at a level necessary to implement the applicable water quality standards. In blended waters, therefore, TMDLs are to be calculated with regard to nonpoint sources of pollutions, otherwise it would be impossible to implement the applicable water quality standards that do not differentiate sources of pollution. Moreover, the statute does not suggest that Congress wanted a distinction to be made in the lists and TMDLs between waters with one insignificant point source and substantial nonpoint source pollution, and waters with only nonpoint source pollution. To do so would require monitoring of waters to determine whether a point source had been added or removed and to adjust the list and TMDLs accordingly. Lastly, by establishing TMDLs for waters impaired only by nonpoint source pollution, the EPA (D) has not upset the balance of federal-state control over land use by a state. The TMDL expressly recognizes that implementation and monitoring are state responsibilities, and for that reason the EPA (D) did not include implementation and monitoring plans within the TMDL. In addition, the CWA requires that each state include in its continuing planning process adequate implementation for revised water quality standards. Therefore, the TMDL is an

Continued on next page.

informational tool for the creation of the state's implementation plan independently required by Congress. California (P) chose if and how it would implement the Garcia River TMDL. Affirmed.

▶ *ANALYSIS*

Agricultural interests have been opponents of including nonpoint sources in load allocations with TMDLs because § 319 should be the remedy for nonpoint source pollution. Congress addressed nonpoint sources specifically in § 319 and not in § 303(d).

■━━■

Quicknotes

POINT SOURCE A stationary location or fixed facility from which pollutants are discharged or emitted such as a pipe, ditch, or ship.

TMDL Total maximum daily load.

■━━■

Coeur Alaska, Inc. v. Southeast Alaska Conservation Council

Corporation (D) v. Advocacy group (P)

2009 WL 1738643 (2009).

NATURE OF CASE: Appeal from Court of Appeals decision for the plaintiff.

FACT SUMMARY: Coeur Alaska, Inc. (D) sought to dispose of slurry from its mines into Lower State Lake.

🏛 RULE OF LAW
Section 404(a) of the Clean Water Act gives the Army Corps of Engineers (Corps), not the EPA, the power to issue permits for the discharge of dredged or fill material, without qualification.

FACTS: Coeur Alaska, Inc. (D) is a mining company that sought to open a gold mine in Alaska. It sought to dispose of crush rock and water, or slurry, into the Lower State Lake. Coeur's (D) slurry deposits would raise the lake bed by fifty feet and increase the size of the lake from 23 to 60 acres. The Southeast Alaska Conservation Council (SEACC) (P) argued that the slurry was subject to an EPA new source performance standard, and prohibited under § 402 of the Clean Water Act. The Ninth Circuit agreed with SEACC (P) and Coeur (D) appealed.

ISSUE: Does § 404(a) of the Clean Water Act give the Corps, not the EPA, the power to issue permits for the discharge of dredged or fill material, without qualification?

HOLDING AND DECISION: (Kennedy, J.) Yes. Section 404(a) of the Clean Water Act gives the Corps, not the EPA, the power to issue permits for the discharge of dredged or fill material, without qualification. All parties concede the slurry at issue constitutes fill or dredged material. Section 402 of the Clean Water Act (the Act) gives the EPA the authority to issue permits for the discharge of any pollutant, with one significant exception that is dispositive in this matter. The EPA may not issue permits for fill or dredged material that is subject to the Corps' authority under § 404 of the Act. Section 404 refers to all fill material, without exception or qualification. Therefore, the Corps, and not the EPA, has the authority to issue permits for the discharge of fill or dredged material. In addition, SEACC (P) argues that § 306(e) of the Act regarding restrictions on emissions from new sources prohibits the slurry discharge. However, because the fill does not require an EPA issued permit under Section 402 of the Act, the performance standards for new sources (here, a gold mine) do not apply. We base our holding on this issue on an internal EPA memo, even though the memo is not compliant with *Chevron*'s requirement of formal agency procedures. The memo stated that the new source performance standards shall not apply where a § 402 permit is not required. Reversed.

CONCURRENCE: (Breyer, J.) As I understand the court's opinion, the law allows regulating agencies to classify material either as dredged or fill material under § 404 or as a pollutant under § 402. The classification of the material as one or the other must be reasonable.

CONCURRENCE: (Scalia, J.) I concur, but dispute the Court's protestation that the internal memo should not be accorded *Chevron* deference.

DISSENT: (Ginsburg, J.) The issue in the case is straightforward. Is a pollutant discharge from a new source, specifically prohibited by § 306, eligible for a Corps-issued permit under § 404? I would answer "no." Section 404, regarding dredged or fill material, does not contain an exception for pollutants from new sources that qualify under § 306. Here, the slurry at issue is a pollutant from a new source. Therefore, § 306 should apply.

▶ ANALYSIS

Perhaps the most interesting opinion is that of Justice Breyer, regarding the agencies' ability to classify material either as a pollutant or fill material. The concurring opinion will provide both sides of the debate over the discharge of pollutants from new sources with support for their relative positions.

■≡■

Quicknotes

CLEAN WATER ACT Federal statute regulating water pollution that imposes a maximum penalty of $10,000 per day for placement of fill in navigable water.

CLEAN WATER ACT § 404 Requires property owners to obtain a permit prior to filling the property.

■≡■

CHAPTER 7

Land Use Regulation and Regulatory Takings

Quick Reference Rules of Law

Village of Euclid v. Ambler Realty Co.

Ohio municipality (P) v. Real estate company (D)

272 U.S. 365 (1926).

NATURE OF CASE: Appeal from decision concerning the constitutionality of a zoning ordinance.

FACT SUMMARY: Ambler Realty Co. (Ambler) (D) contends that the Village of Euclid's (P) zoning ordinance is unconstitutional.

🏛 RULE OF LAW
The question of whether the power exists to forbid the erection of a building of a particular kind or use is to be determined by considering it in connection with the circumstances and the locality.

FACTS: The Village of Euclid (P), an Ohio municipality, adopted a comprehensive zoning plan. Ambler (D) owned 68 acres of vacant land that had been zoned residential. Ambler (D) alleged that it had held the land for years in anticipation of selling and developing it for industrial uses for which it would have a market value of $10,000 per acre, but that the residential zoning would reduce the market value to less than $2,500 per acre.

ISSUE: Are zoning ordinances constitutional?

HOLDING AND DECISION: (Sutherland, J.) Yes. The question of whether the power exists to forbid the erection of a building of a particular kind or use is to be determined by considering it in connection with the circumstances and the locality. The ordinance now under review must find its justification in some aspect of the police power, asserted for the public welfare. The line which in this field separates the legitimate from the illegitimate assumption of power is not capable of precise delimitation. It varies with circumstances and conditions. A regulatory zoning ordinance, which would be clearly valid as applied to the great cities, might be clearly invalid as applied to rural communities. In solving doubts, the maxim "one should use their property in such a manner as not to injure that of another" will furnish a helpful clue. The matter of zoning has received much attention at the hands of commissions and experts, and the results of their investigations have been set forth in comprehensive reports. These reports concur in the view that the segregation of residential, business, and industrial buildings will make it easier to provide fire apparatus suitable for the character and intensity of the development in each section; that it will increase the safety and security of home life; greatly tend to prevent street accidents, especially to children, by reducing the traffic and resulting confusion in residential sections; decrease noise and other conditions which produce or intensify nervous disorders; and preserve a more favorable environment in which to rear children. The reasons are sufficiently cogent to preclude us from saying that the ordinance can be declared unconstitutional, being clearly arbitrary and unreasonable, having no substantial relation to the public health, safety, morals, or general welfare.

▌ *ANALYSIS*

This was a landmark ruling by the Supreme Court on the constitutionality of zoning. Following this decision, the use of zoning by municipalities spread quickly. By 1930, nearly one thousand cities encompassing more than two-thirds of the nation's urban population had adopted zoning ordinances.

■■■

Quicknotes

ZONING Municipal statutory scheme dividing an area into districts in order to regulate the use or building of structures within those districts.

■■■

Penn Central Transportation Co. v. City of New York

Land owner (P) v. Local government (D)

438 U.S. 104 (1978).

NATURE OF CASE: Appeal from decision that the application of New York City's Landmarks Law did not effect a "taking" of Penn Central Transportation Company's (Penn Central's) (P) property.

FACT SUMMARY: Penn Central (P) challenged New York City's (D) Landmarks Law as effecting a taking for which Penn Central (P) deserves just compensation.

> ## 🏛 RULE OF LAW
> The economic impact of a regulation on a claimant and the extent to which the regulation has interfered with distinct investment-backed expectations are relevant considerations in determining whether the government has effected a taking.

FACTS: Penn Central (P) challenged New York City's (D) Landmarks Law because it prohibited Penn Central (P) from building a 55-story office building above Grand Central Terminal (Terminal), a landmark designated under the law. Under the legislation, owners of historic structures who were denied permission to build received transferable development rights that could be sold to permit development elsewhere. The court below found for New York City (D). Penn Central (P) appealed.

ISSUE: Does the New York City (D) Landmarks Law effect a taking for which historic landmark owners deserve just compensation?

HOLDING AND DECISION: (Brennan, J.) No. The New York City (D) Landmarks Law does not effect a taking for which historic landmark owners deserve just compensation. Economic impact of a regulation on a claimant and the extent to which the regulation has interfered with distinct investment-backed expectations are relevant considerations in determining whether the government has effected a taking. First, the submission that Penn Central (P) may establish a taking simply by showing that they have been denied the ability to exploit a property interest that they heretofore had believed was available for development is simply untenable. Second, Penn Central (P) holds the position that the only means of ensuring that selected owners are not singled out to endure financial hardship for no reason is to hold that any restriction imposed on individual landmarks pursuant to the New York City (D) scheme is a taking requiring the payment of just compensation. Agreement with this argument would invalidate not just New York City's (D) law, but all comparable landmark legislation in the nation. We find no merit in it. Furthermore, Penn Central (P) exaggerates the effect of the law on their ability to make use of the air rights above the Terminal in two respects. First, it cannot be maintained that Penn Central (P) has been prohibited from occupying any portion of the airspace above the Terminal. Since Penn Central (P) has not sought approval for the construction of a smaller structure, we do not know that they will be denied any use of any portion of the airspace above the Terminal. Second, Penn Central (P) has not been denied all use of preexisting air rights. Their ability to use these rights are made transferable to at least eight parcels in the vicinity of the Terminal, one or two of which have been found suitable for the construction of new office buildings. The transferable development rights afforded are valuable and mitigate whatever financial burdens the law has imposed on Penn Central (P). This must be taken into account in considering the impact of regulation. Therefore, the application of New York City's (D) Landmarks Law has not effected a taking of Penn Central's (P) property. The restrictions imposed are substantially related to the promotion of the general welfare, and not only permit reasonable beneficial use of the landmark site, but also afford Penn Central (P) opportunities further to enhance not only the Terminal site proper but also other properties. Affirmed.

▶ ANALYSIS

Justice Rehnquist, along with Chief Justice Burger and Justice Stevens, dissented. Rehnquist argued that the historic landmark unfairly singled out one-tenth of 1% of all buildings in New York City (D) without providing them the reciprocity of advantage that zoning ordinances typically provide. The majority rejected the notion that Penn Central (P) had been singled out, commenting that the Landmarks Law was part of a comprehensive plan to preserve historic structures wherever they might be found in the city, and that it had applied to 400 structures and 31 historic districts.

■=■

Quicknotes

TAKINGS CLAUSE Provision of the Fifth Amendment to the United States Constitution prohibiting the government from taking private property for public use without providing just compensation therefor.

■=■

Lucas v. South Carolina Coastal Council

Beach property owner (P) v. State agency (D)

505 U.S. 1003 (1992).

NATURE OF CASE: Consideration on remand from the Supreme Court of a regulatory taking of private property.

FACT SUMMARY: After Lucas's (P) allegations of a compensatory regulatory taking of his property were heard by the Supreme Court, the Court remanded the case to the state court to decide whether Lucas's (P) development of his beachfront property was prohibited by state nuisance or property law.

🏛 **RULE OF LAW**
A plaintiff is entitled to a cause of action for the temporary deprivation of the use of his property, unless it can be shown that his intended use of his land is not part of the bundle of rights inhering in his title.

FACTS: Lucas (P) had filed suit against South Carolina (D), alleging a regulatory taking of his beach property as the result of state legislation prohibiting the building of any habitable structure on his land. After the Supreme Court heard Lucas's (P) appeal, it determined that he must be compensated unless South Carolina (D) could identify background principles of nuisance or property law that would prohibit Lucas's (P) proposed development. The case was remanded to the state courts for consideration in light of the Court's ruling.

ISSUE: Is the plaintiff entitled to a cause of action for the temporary deprivation of the use of his property, unless it can be shown that his intended use of his land is not part of the bundle of rights inhering in his title?

HOLDING AND DECISION: (Scalia, J.) Yes. A plaintiff is entitled to a cause of action for the temporary deprivation of the use of his property, unless it can be shown that his intended use of his land is not part of the bundle of rights inhering in his title. No common law basis exists to restrain Lucas's (P) desired use of his land. Pursuant to the 1990 amendment of the Act, Lucas (P) may apply for a special permit to build seaward of the baseline. Clearly, Lucas has been only temporarily deprived of the use of his land if he can now obtain a special permit to construct habitable structures on his lots. Thus, the sole issue on remand to the circuit level is a determination of the actual damages Lucas (P) has sustained as the result of his being temporarily deprived of the use of his property. Vacated and remanded.

CONCURRENCE: (Kennedy, J.) The majority defined "reasonable expectation" too narrowly in reviewing a finding of "no value" under the Takings Clause. In determining whether a regulation deprives a landowner of all value in her real property, the landowner's reasonable expectations must be understood in light of the whole of our legal tradition. The common law of nuisance is too narrow a confine for the exercise of regulatory power. Nevertheless, because the state did not act until after the property had been zoned for individual lot development, the owner here could not reasonably have expected the instant regulation.

DISSENT: (Blackmun, J.) The majority has ignored its jurisdictional limits, remade its traditional rules of review, and created a new categorical rule, plus an exception, not rooted in prior case law or common law. Until now, the court has rejected the contention that the government's power to act without paying compensation turns on whether the prohibited activity is a common law nuisance. Therefore, there is no historical justification for the court's new taking doctrine.

▶ **ANALYSIS**

The state supreme court found that Lucas (P) had suffered a temporary taking deserving of compensation beginning with the 1988 Act and continuing through the date of the Court's order here. The court's ruling was without prejudice to the right of the parties to litigate any subsequent deprivations which might arise if the Coastal Council (D) denied Lucas's (P) request for a special permit. After Lucas (P) applied for and was granted permission to develop his lots, the Council (D) negotiated a lump-sum settlement with him, including the purchase of his two lots, which the state later resold at market value for residential construction.

Quicknotes

TAKINGS CLAUSE Provision of the Fifth Amendment to the United States Constitution prohibiting the government from taking private property for public use without providing just compensation therefor.

Palazzolo v. Rhode Island

Landowner (P) v. State (D)

533 U.S. 606 (2001).

NATURE OF CASE: Appeal of state court's barring of a takings claim.

FACT SUMMARY: Palazzolo (P) sought compensation under the Takings Clause for the wetlands on his property.

🏛 RULE OF LAW

(1) A takings claim is ripe for review if a landowner first follows the necessary steps to allow a regulatory agency to exercise its full discretion in considering development plans for the property.

(2) A state cannot by prospective legislation define property rights and reasonable investment-backed expectations so that subsequent owners cannot claim any injury from lost value.

(3) If all economically beneficial use is not deprived from a property when a taking occurs, compensation is not required.

FACTS: Palazzolo (P) sought compensation under the Takings Clause for the wetlands on his property. When the Council (D) promulgated its wetlands regulations, the parcel at issue was owned not by Palazzolo (P) but by the corporation of which he was the sole shareholder. When title was transferred to him, the wetlands regulations were in force. The state court barred Palazzolo's (P) takings claim on the basis of it being unripe for review. The court noted he acquired the property after the regulations took effect, therefore the post-regulation acquisition of title was fatal to the claim for deprivation of all economic use. Palazzolo (P) appealed.

ISSUE:

(1) Is Palazzolo's (P) takings claim ripe for review?

(2) Does his acquisition after the regulations took effect bar his claim?

(3) Was all economically beneficial use not deprived because the uplands portion of the property can still be improved?

HOLDING AND DECISION: (Kennedy, J.)

(1) Yes. Palazzolo's (P) taking claim is ripe for review. A landowner must first follow the necessary steps to allow a regulatory agency to exercise their full discretion in considering development plans for the property, including the opportunity to grant any variances or waivers allowed by law. In the present case, Palazzolo (P) has done just that. The Council (D) interpreted its regulations to bar Palazzolo (P) from engaging in any filling or development activity on the wetlands. Further permit applications were not necessary to establish this point. The upland portion of Palazzolo's (P) property, however, can consensually be developed.

(2) No. Palazzolo's (P) acquisition after the regulations took effect does not bar his claim. Rhode Island (D) cannot by prospective legislation define property rights and reasonable investment-backed expectations so that subsequent owners cannot claim any injury from lost value. States can restrict, through zoning and land use restrictions, the right to improve property. However, the Takings Clause enables a landowner to assert that a certain exercise of that power is unreasonable so as to compel compensation. Such a rule as given by Rhode Island (D)—that the passing of title after regulations take effect bars a takings claim—would absolve Rhode Island (D) from having to defend any action restricting land use, no matter how extreme or unreasonable. Furthermore, owners who own the property at the time the regulations take effect are prejudiced as well because they will be unable to transfer the interest in property that they had prior to the regulation until a successful challenge is made, which may take years, if at all. A regulation that otherwise would be unconstitutional absent compensation is not transformed into a background principle of the state's law by mere virtue of the passage of title.

(3) Yes. All economically beneficial use was not deprived because the uplands portion of the property can still be improved. A government's actions constitute a regulatory taking and will require compensation under the Takings Clause if (1) the regulation denies all economically beneficial or productive use of land or (2) certain factors make it a taking such as the regulations economic effect on the landowner, the extent to which the regulation interferes with reasonable investment-backed expectation, and the character of the government action. Palazzolo's (P) property retains $200,000 in development value and, therefore, he has not suffered a total taking. Palazzolo (P) can build a substantial residence on an 18-acre parcel. Since the case before us is based on the premise that Palazzolo's (P) entire parcel serves as the basis for his takings claim, the total deprivation argument fails. Reversed as to the state supreme court's ripeness and acquisition of title baring claim rulings. Affirmed as to the finding that Palazzolo (P) failed to establish a deprivation of all economic value. Affirmed in part, reversed in part, and remanded.

CONCURRENCE: (O'Connor, J.) Interference with investment-backed expectations is one of a number of factors that a court must examine. The regulatory structure in place at the time Palazzolo (P) acquired the property

Continued on next page.

shapes the reasonableness of those expectations. Other factors to consider are the economic impact of the regulation on Palazzolo (P) and the character of the government action.

CONCURRENCE: (Scalia, J.) The fact that a restriction existed at the time Palazzolo (P) took title should have no bearing on the determination of whether the restriction is so substantial as to constitute a taking. It will not be unfair to allow in some circumstances a subsequent purchaser to nullify an unconstitutional partial taking by the government.

▶ ANALYSIS

Regulations usually cannot be shown to deprive real estate of all of its economic value.

■━■

Quicknotes

TAKINGS CLAUSE Provision of the Fifth Amendment to the United States Constitution prohibiting the government from taking private property for public use without providing just compensation therefor.

■━■

Tahoe-Sierra Preservation Council, Inc. v. Tahoe Regional Planning Agency

Landowners (P) v. Government agency (D)

535 U.S. 302 (2002).

NATURE OF CASE: Appeal of judgment that a taking had not occurred.

FACT SUMMARY: Moratoria were put in place by the Tahoe Regional Planning Agency (the TRPA) (D) while it considered a land-use plan. Tahoe-Sierra Preservation Council, Inc. (TSPC) (P) alleged that a taking had occurred on its land during that time.

🏛 RULE OF LAW
When deciding whether a moratorium on development, which was imposed during the process of devising a comprehensive land-use plan, constitutes a taking of property requiring compensation under the Takings Clause, a per se rule cannot be used, but rather the analysis requires an evaluation of many factors specific to each individual case.

FACTS: The TRPA (D) ordered two moratoria, Ordinance 81-5 and Resolution 83-21, to maintain the status quo while it studied the impact of development on Lake Tahoe and designed a strategy for environmentally sound growth. All development on a portion of property subject to TRPA's (D) jurisdiction was prohibited during the moratoria. The district court broke apart TSPC (P) property into temporal segments corresponding to the regulations at issue and then analyzed whether they were deprived of all economically viable use during each period. The district court held that the ordinances and resolutions did, in fact, deny TSPC (P) all economically viable use of their land. The court of appeals reversed, and TSPC (P) appealed.

ISSUE: Does a moratorium on development which was imposed during the process of devising a comprehensive land-use plan constitute a per se taking of property requiring compensation under the Takings Clause?

HOLDING AND DECISION: (Stevens, J.) No. When deciding whether a moratorium on development constitutes a taking of property requiring compensation under the Takings Clause, a per se rule cannot be used, but rather the analysis requires an evaluation of many factors specific to each individual case. Regulatory jurisprudence is characterized by ad hoc factual inquiries that examine and weigh the relevant circumstances of each case. Therefore, a per se rule cannot be used. Moreover, the concepts of fairness and justice that underlie the Takings Clause will be better served by an inquiry into all of the relevant circumstances in particular cases and not by a categorical rule. A categorical rule that states that any deprivation of all economic use, no matter how brief,

constitutes a compensable taking cannot be sustained because it would apply to numerous normal delays and such a change in the law should be the product of legislative rulemaking rather than adjudication. Furthermore, precedent rejects TSPC's (P) argument that the mere enactment of a temporary regulation, that while in effect denies a property owner of all viable economic use of her property, gives rise to an unqualified constitutional obligation to compensate her for the value of its use during that period. TSPC's (P) reliance on *First English Evangelical Lutheran Church v. County of Los Angeles*, 482 U.S. 304 (1987), is misplaced because it did not address whether the temporary regulation at issue did in fact constitute a taking. *Lucas v. South Carolina Coastal Council*, 505 U.S. 1003 (1992), also is not dispositive of the present issue because *Lucas* was decided based on a permanent takings claim. The *Lucas* rule is that compensation is required when a regulation deprives an owner of all economically beneficial uses of his land. The issue in this case, however, is whether a regulation prohibiting any economic use of land for a 32-month period is a taking. You cannot sever a 32-month segment from the remainder of each landowner's fee simple estate, and then ask whether that segment has been taken in its entirety by the moratoria. To do so would mean that every delay would become a total ban, and therefore the moratorium and the normal permit process alike would constitute categorical takings. The parcel as a whole must be focused on and not just a denominator. Moreover, a regulation temporarily denying an owner of all use of his property may not constitute a taking because a state has the authority to institute safety regulations or normal delays, such as those due to obtaining building permits, changes in zoning ordinances, and the like. In addition, a fee simple estate cannot be rendered valueless by a temporary prohibition on economic use because the property will recover value as soon as the prohibition is lifted. A narrower rule would still impose serious financial constraints on the planning process and would cause officials to rush through the planning process or abandon the practice altogether, creating ill-conceived growth. Interest in protecting the planning process is stronger when an agency is developing a regional plan than when it is considering a permit for a single parcel. By considering comments and criticisms from interested parties the process attempts to protect the interests of all landowners against immediate construction that might be inconsistent with provisions of the plan that is ultimately adopted. Lastly, moratoria often result in property value increases. A rule, therefore, that assumes moratoria will always force indi-

Continued on next page.

viduals to bear a special burden that should be shared by the public as a whole should not be adopted because in some cases a one-year moratorium may not impose a burden at all. Formulating a general rule that every delay of over one year is constitutionally unacceptable, and formulating such a rule is for the legislature to decide. Affirmed.

DISSENT: (Rehnquist, C.J.) TSPC (P) was prevented from building any structures on its land for over five years. A ban lasting this long does not resemble a traditional land-use planning device, and the government is required to pay compensation when it deprives an owner of all economically viable uses of their land pursuant to the Takings Clause. A distinction between this case as a temporary prohibition and the *Lucas* case, where the taking was only for two years, is tenuous. Time frames given to regulations often change and temporary prohibitions can be extended into long-term bans. Furthermore, *First English* makes no distinction between temporary and permanent takings when a landowner is completely deprived of all economic beneficial use of his land. The total deprivation of use is equivalent to a physical appropriation requiring compensation. In addition, applying *Lucas* here would not compel a finding that an array of traditional, short-term, land-use planning devices are takings. Property rights are enjoyed under an implied limitation of state property law including valid zoning and land-use restrictions. A moratorium prohibiting all economic use for six years is not an implied limitation of state property law.

▶ ANALYSIS

The majority in this case opts for a *Penn Central*, 438 U.S. 104 (1978), analysis rather than a per se rule.

■══■

Quicknotes

TAKINGS CLAUSE Provision of the Fifth Amendment to the United States Constitution prohibiting the government from taking private property for public use without providing just compensation therefor.

■══■

Dolan v. City of Tigard

Business owner (P) v. City (D)

512 U.S. 374 (1994).

NATURE OF CASE: Appeal from judgment approving conditions to a building permit imposed by a city.

FACT SUMMARY: Dolan (P), a business owner, appealed the City of Tigard's (the City) (D) conditioning of a building permit on her dedicating a percentage of her property on a flood plain to the City (D) for a flood control greenway and a bike path.

⚖ RULE OF LAW
In determining if a condition to a building permit requiring an exaction survives the Takings Clause, the conditioning government body bears the burden of showing a rough proportionality between the harm caused by the new land use and the benefit obtained by the condition.

FACTS: Dolan (P) requested a permit to double the size of her downtown plumbing and electric supply store and to pave over the gravel parking lot. The City (D) conditioned the permit based on requirements in their downtown plan for flood control and traffic congestion. The two conditions were that Dolan (P) dedicate the unusable portion of her property in the flood plain along Fanno Creek to the City (D) so that it could improve the storm drainage system with a greenway and also dedicate a fifteen-foot strip next to the flood plain for a bike path. Dolan's (P) paving and building would impact storm drainage in the area by covering over permeable ground and result in increased traffic congestion downtown. Dolan (P) appealed to the Land Use Board of Appeals (LUBA) on the ground that the City's (D) dedication requirements were not related to the proposed development and constituted an uncompensated taking under the Fifth Amendment. LUBA found a reasonable relationship between the proposed developmental impacts and the requirements. The Oregon Court of Appeals affirmed, rejecting Dolan's (P) claim that in *Nollan v. California Coastal Commission*, 483 U.S. 825 (1987), the Supreme Court had abandoned the reasonable relationship test for a stricter "essential nexus" test. The Oregon Supreme Court affirmed. The U.S. Supreme Court granted certiorari.

ISSUE: In determining if a condition to a building permit requiring an exaction survives the Takings Clause, must the conditioning government body bear the burden of showing a rough proportionality between the harm caused by the new land use and the benefit obtained by the condition?

HOLDING AND DECISION: (Rehnquist, C.J.) Yes. In *Nollan*, the court rejected the California Coastal Commission's requirement of a dedication of an easement on the beach for coastal access between public beaches as a condition to remodeling a bungalow. It held that there was no nexus between the requirement and the state interest. In this case, however, the required nexus is present. The prevention of flooding and the reduction of traffic congestion are logically connected to limiting the impacts of development in the flood plain and providing alternative access downtown. The degree to which these exactions must correspond to the projected impacts of the project must be roughly proportional. No mathematical precision is required, but the City (D) must make some sort of individualized determination that the required dedication is related both in nature and extent to the impact of the proposed development. The City (D) has failed to meet its burden for both dedications. The findings that the city relies on do not show the required reasonable relationship between the flood plain easement and the proposed development. Nor has the city met its burden of showing that the additional number of vehicle trips to the site reasonably relates to the dedication of the bike path easement. The city must make some effort to quantify its findings beyond the conclusory statement that the path could help alleviate traffic. Reversed.

DISSENT: (Stevens, J.) It is not in dispute that the enlarged hardware store will have an adverse impact on the city's legitimate interests in traffic and storm drainage. That impact is sufficient to justify an outright denial of Dolan's (P) permit. While the majority is correct that the City (D) may not attach arbitrary conditions to a permit even when it can deny it outright, their description of the doctrinal underpinnings, the phrasing of their "rough proportionality" test, and the application of that test to this case run contrary to traditional treatment of these cases and break unpropitious new ground. The majority has saddled state governments with an entirely novel burden of proof where previously a party challenging state action had to overcome a presumption of constitutionality.

DISSENT: (Souter, J.) *Nollan* should not be applied here because the Court has placed the burden of producing evidence of relationship on the City (D). The City (D), however, has provided enough necessary evidence between bicycle paths and reduced street traffic congestion to satisfy *Nollan*, and, therefore, the City (D) should not lose.

▶ ANALYSIS

The linguistic niceties, the mathematical requirement giving with one hand and taking with the other and the new burden of proof in Rehnquist's decision are all unsound

Continued on next page.

means to an end. A prominent part of the Republican Contract with America is legislation designed to compensate property owners for partial takings by the government. Claiming that the single requirement of public access to a retail store over unusable land is a taking is a dangerous precedent in takings analysis.

■■■

Quicknotes

TAKINGS CLAUSE Provision of the Fifth Amendment to the United States Constitution prohibiting the government from taking private property for public use without providing just compensation therefor.

■■■

Lingle v. Chevron, U.S.A., Inc.

State official (D) v. Private property owner (P)

544 U.S. 528 (2005).

NATURE OF CASE: Appeal from affirmance of judgment that a regulation constituted an unconstitutional uncompensated taking.

FACT SUMMARY: Lingle (D), on behalf of the state, argued that the state's regulation did not amount to an unconstitutional uncompensated taking of Chevron, U.S.A., Inc.'s (Chevron) (P) property.

🏛 RULE OF LAW
An owner of private property seeking to challenge a government regulation as an unconstitutional uncompensated taking of private property may not rely on a "substantially advances" test, under which a regulation works as an uncompensated taking if it does not substantially advance a legitimate governmental interest.

FACTS: Chevron (P) brought suit claiming that a state regulation constituted an unconstitutional uncompensated taking of Chevron's (P) property because the regulation did not substantially advance a legitimate government interest. The district court agreed with Chevron (P), and the court of appeals affirmed. The Supreme Court granted certiorari.

ISSUE: May an owner of private property seeking to challenge a government regulation as an unconstitutional uncompensated taking of private property rely on a "substantially advances" test, under which a regulation works as an uncompensated taking if it does not substantially advance a legitimate governmental interest?

HOLDING AND DECISION: (O'Connor, J.) No. An owner of private property seeking to challenge a government regulation as an unconstitutional uncompensated taking of private property may not rely on a "substantially advances" test, under which a regulation works as an uncompensated taking if it does not substantially advance a legitimate governmental interest. Regulatory actions generally will be deemed per se takings for Fifth Amendment purposes (1) where government requires an owner to suffer a permanent physical invasion of her property, see *Loretto v. Teleprompter Manhattan CATV Corp.*, 458 U.S. 419 (1982), or (2) where regulations completely deprive an owner of "*all economically beneficial use*" of her property, *Lucas v. South Carolina Coastal Council*, 505 U.S. 1003 (1992). Outside these two categories, regulatory takings challenges are governed by *Penn Central Transportation Co. v. New York City*, 438 U.S. 104 (1978). *Penn Central* identified several factors—including the regulation's economic impact on the claimant, the extent to which it interferes with distinct investment-backed expectations, and the character of the government action—that are particularly significant in determining whether a regulation effects a taking. Because the three inquiries reflected in *Loretto*, *Lucas*, and *Penn Central* all aim to identify regulatory actions that are functionally equivalent to a direct appropriation of or ouster from private property, each of them focuses upon the severity of the burden that government imposes upon property rights. In stark contrast to these three regulatory takings tests, the "substantially advances" inquiry reveals nothing about the magnitude or character of the burden a particular regulation imposes upon private property rights or how any regulatory burden is distributed among property owners. Thus, this test does not help to identify those regulations whose effects are functionally comparable to government appropriation or invasion of private property; it is tethered neither to the text of the Takings Clause nor to the basic justification for allowing regulatory actions to be challenged under the Clause. Although the Court drew on the language of the "substantially advances" test in its prior takings decisions, it never actually applied that test to decide those cases. Although *Nollan v. California Coastal Commission*, 483 U.S. 825 (1987), and *Dolan v. City of Tigard*, 512 U.S. 374 (1994), drew upon the "substantially advances" language, the rule those cases established is entirely distinct from the "substantially advances" test. Those cases involved a special application of the "doctrine of unconstitutional conditions," which provides that the government may not require a person to give up the constitutional right to receive just compensation when property is taken for a public use in exchange for a discretionary benefit that has little or no relationship to the property. The "substantially advances" formula is not a valid takings test, and has no proper place in regulatory takings jurisprudence. Therefore, a plaintiff seeking to challenge a government regulation as an uncompensated taking of private property may proceed under one of the three theories discussed above. Reversed and remanded.

▶ ANALYSIS

The majority opinion indicated that the "substantially advances" formula is not a valid method of identifying compensable regulatory takings because it prescribes an inquiry in the nature of a due process test, which, the Court concluded, has no proper place in the Court's takings jurisprudence. The Court emphasized that the formula, which unquestionably was derived from due process precedents, is too imprecise. In his concurrence, Justice Kennedy observed that the Court's decision did not foreclose the possibility that a regulation might be so arbitrary or irrational as to violate due process—and could, theoretically, be stricken on due process grounds.

■=■

Continued on next page.

Quicknotes

DUE PROCESS The constitutional mandate requiring the courts to protect and enforce individuals' rights and liberties consistent with prevailing principles of fairness and justice and prohibiting the federal and state governments from such activities that deprive its citizens of life, liberty, or property interest.

TAKING A governmental action that substantially deprives an owner of the use and enjoyment of his property, requiring compensation.

■═■

Environmental Impact Assessment

Quick Reference Rules of Law

Calvert Cliffs Coordinating Committee v. United States Atomic Energy Commission

Environmental group (P) v. Federal agency (D)

449 F.2d 1109 (D.C. Cir. 1971).

NATURE OF CASE: Action challenging agency rulemaking pursuant to the National Environmental Policy Act of 1969 (NEPA).

FACT SUMMARY: In an attempt to comply with NEPA, the United States Atomic Energy Commission (Commission) (D) required that a detailed statement on the environmental impact of a proposed power plant accompany any application but need not be considered by the hearing board which decides the application.

🏛 RULE OF LAW
NEPA requires an agency to take environmental factors into consideration at every important stage of its decision-making process.

FACTS: NEPA requires all federal agencies to consider values of environmental preservation in their spheres of activities, and it prescribes certain procedural measures, including the preparation of a "detailed statement," to ensure full respect for those values. The Commission (D) implemented a policy that would require all applicants seeking to build a nuclear power plant to submit a report assessing environmental impact, which the Commission (D) would then use to prepare its own detailed statement, as required by the NEPA. However, the Commission (D) required that the detailed statement merely "accompany" the proposal through the review process; the hearing board need not actually review the environmental issues unless a party to the proceeding raised an objection. Calvert Cliffs Coordinating Committee (P), an environmental group, challenged the Commission's (D) rule as a violation of NEPA.

ISSUE: Does NEPA require an agency to take environmental factors into consideration at every important stage of its decision-making process?

HOLDING AND DECISION: (Wright, J.) Yes. NEPA requires an agency to take environmental factors into consideration at every important stage of its decision-making process. The language of NEPA gives the agencies broad discretion to weigh the various competing interests. However, its mandate is equally clear that the agency must give serious consideration to environmental factors. The Commission's (D) crabbed interpretation of NEPA makes a mockery of NEPA. What possible purpose could there be in requiring the detailed statement to be passed along, unopened, if the hearing board is free to ignore it? Congressional intent was not to have agencies make pro forma examinations but to actively consider alternatives to its actions that would reduce environmental damage.

▶ ANALYSIS

This case actively illustrates the hostility with which administrators initially received NEPA and the reluctant manner in which they chose to administer it. Beginning with this influential decision, reviewing courts have enthusiastically enforced § 102's procedural provisions. Strict compliance with the environmental impact statement provisions is mandatory, unless a relevant statute is in direct conflict.

■■■

Quicknotes

RULEMAKING The promulgation of a rule governing a particular activity by an administrative agency, acting within the scope of its power pursuant to statute.

■■■

Strycker's Bay Neighborhood Council, Inc. v. Karlen

Government agency (D) v. Opponent of housing project (P)

444 U.S. 223 (1980).

NATURE OF CASE: Appeal from decision reversing judgment in a National Environmental Policy Act of 1969 (NEPA) action case.

FACT SUMMARY: Strycker's Bay Neighborhood Council, Inc. (Strycker) (D) appealed from a decision reversing a judgment entered in its favor in Karlen's (P) action under NEPA to enjoin construction of low-income housing, contending that the U.S. Department of Housing and Urban Development (HUD) had sufficiently considered the environmental consequences of its acts in compliance with NEPA.

🏛 **RULE OF LAW**

Once an agency, in selecting a course of action, renders a decision in compliance with NEPA's procedural requirements, the court's function on review is to ensure that the agency has adequately considered the environmental consequences of the course of action.

FACTS: As part of a program to renew a certain portion of Manhattan's Upper West Side, HUD (D), along with others, designated a certain area for low-income housing. Suit was brought by Trinity (P), under NEPA, to enjoin the construction of the low-income housing, and Karlen (P) intervened in that action. Eventually that matter was remanded, the court of appeals determining that HUD had failed to comply with a NEPA requirement to study, develop, and describe appropriate alternatives to recommended courses of action in any proposal which involves unresolved conflicts concerning alternative uses of available resources. HUD (D) generated a new report, which incorporated a study of nine alternative sites for the low-income housing, all of which were determined to be unacceptable. HUD (D) further concluded that any relocation of the units at this time would result in an unacceptable delay of two years. The district court determined that the decision to use that site for low-income housing was not in violation of NEPA, but the court of appeals vacated that decision and remanded again, holding that the delay could not be an overriding factor in HUD's (D) decision to proceed with the development. Strycker (D) had intervened in the action. From the court of appeals decision, HUD (D) and Strycker (D) appealed.

ISSUE: Once an agency, in selecting a course of action, renders a decision in compliance with NEPA's procedural requirements, is the court's function on review to ensure that the agency has adequately considered the environmental consequences of the course of action?

HOLDING AND DECISION: (Per curiam) Yes. Once an agency, in selecting a course of action, renders a decision in compliance with NEPA's procedural requirements, the court's function on review is to ensure that the agency has adequately considered the environmental consequences of the course of action. There is no requirement that those environmental concerns be elevated over other appropriate considerations. In the present case there is no doubt that HUD (D) considered the environmental consequences of its decision to redesignate the proposed site for low-income housing. NEPA requires no more. Reversed.

DISSENT: (Marshall, J.) The present decision misstates the issue, which was whether HUD (D) was free under NEPA to reject an alternative solely on the grounds of an unacceptable delay. The arbitrary and capricious standard of review contemplates a searching and careful inquiry designed to ensure that the agency's decision was not an unreasonable exercise of discretion and merits a plenary hearing.

▶ *ANALYSIS*

It is clear that the decision in the present case takes some of the teeth out of the court's ability to enforce NEPA's broad mandate. Although it is clear that the courts may still be able to compel the agency to consider certain environmentally preferable alternatives, the court cannot substitute its own judgment for that of the agency, and if the appropriate factors are considered, the agency's decision will stand. See *Ocoee River Council v. TVA*, 540 F. Supp. 788 (E.D. Tenn. 1981).

■══■

Quicknotes

ENJOIN The ordering of a party to cease the conduct of a specific activity.

■══■

Kleppe v. Sierra Club

Environmental agency (D) v. Environmental group (P)

427 U.S. 390 (1976).

NATURE OF CASE: Action for declaratory and injunctive relief.

FACT SUMMARY: The Sierra Club (P) maintained that federal officials could not allow further development of coal mining in the Northern Great Plains Region without preparing a comprehensive, environmental impact statement on the entire region.

🏛 RULE OF LAW

A court cannot require the preparation of an environmental impact statement to begin prior to the formal recommendation or report on a proposal for federal action.

FACTS: The Sierra Club (P) claimed an interest by its members in the enjoyment of the environment of the Northern Great Plains Region and sought both injunctive and declaratory relief against an alleged threat thereto from coal-related operations which federal agencies were authorizing. It argued that federal officials could not allow further development without preparing a comprehensive environmental impact statement on the entire region, although all the federal actions involved were either local or national in scope rather than regional. The district court found that there was no existing or proposed plan or program on the part of the federal government for the regional development of the area described in the complaint. However, the court of appeals concluded that a regional plan or program was contemplated and reversed a decision denying the requested relief.

ISSUE: Can a court require the preparation of an environmental impact statement to begin before there has been a formal recommendation or report on a proposal for federal action?

HOLDING AND DECISION: (Powell, J.) No. The language of the pertinent statute leads to the conclusion that a court cannot require the preparation of an environmental impact statement to begin prior to the formal recommendation or report on a proposal for federal action. Mere "contemplation" of federal action, as in this case, is not sufficient to require an impact statement under said statute and a court has no authority to depart from statutory language and determine a point during the germination process of a potential proposal at which an impact statement should be prepared. Even if one were required, the determination of the region, if any, with respect to which it would be necessary, is properly left to the informed discretion of the responsible federal agencies and would not be disturbed absent a showing that it was arbitrarily made. No such showing has been made here. Reversed.

CONCURRENCE AND DISSENT: (Marshall, J.) Preventing courts from addressing violations of the National Environmental Policy Act of 1969 (NEPA) prior to the end of the decision-making process fails to make use of an effective remedy. Requiring an agency to comply with the mandate of NEPA prior to its final decision avoids the inadequate remedy of setting aside finished plans or rationalizing decisions based on after-the-fact environmental impact studies.

▶ ANALYSIS

Regulations of the Council on Environmental Quality attempt to delineate precisely when a proposal "exists" and thus requires preparation of a statement. It exists "at that stage in the development of an action when an agency . . . has a goal and is actively preparing to make a decision on one or more alternative means of accomplishing that goal and the effects can be meaningfully evaluated."

■══■

Quicknotes

INJUNCTION A court order requiring a person to do, or prohibiting that person from doing, a specific act.

■══■

Thomas v. Peterson

Conservation group (P) v. Forest service (D)

753 F.2d 754 (9th Cir. 1985).

NATURE OF CASE: Appeal from summary judgment in action to enjoin construction of a timber road.

FACT SUMMARY: Thomas (P) protested that the Forest Service (D) did not comply with the National Environmental Policy Act of 1969 (NEPA) in considering the impact of construction of a timber road.

🏛 **RULE OF LAW**
When a road construction project and contemplated timber sales are connected actions, combined treatment in a single environmental impact statement (EIS) that covers the cumulative effects of the road and the sales is required.

FACTS: The Forest Service (D) initiated a road construction project in order to facilitate timber sales. The Forest Service (D) approved construction of the road as well as two timber sales without preparing an EIS because it concluded that the road would not have significant effects on the environment. Thomas (P) brought this action to enjoin construction of the road, alleging a violation of NEPA. NEPA requires an EIS for major federal actions significantly affecting the quality of the human environment. The district court concluded that the Forest Service's (D) procedural violation was insignificant and refused to issue an injunction. Thomas (P) appealed.

ISSUE: Are the road and the timber sales sufficiently related so as to require combined treatment in a single EIS that covers the cumulative effects of the road and the sales?

HOLDING AND DECISION: (Sneed, J.) Yes. The road and the timber sales are sufficiently related so as to require combined treatment in a single EIS that covers the cumulative effects of the road and the sales. The Council on Environmental Quality (CEQ) and this court's precedents both require the Forest Service (D) to prepare an EIS analyzing the combined environmental impacts of the road and the timber sales. Connected actions are to be considered together in a single EIS. The construction of the road and the sale of timber are connected actions because the timber sales cannot proceed without the road, and the road would not be built but for the timber sales. This is evidenced by the road being characterized as a logging road, by statements in the environmental assessment (EA) for the road, the cost-benefit analysis done for the road, and the letter from the Regional Forester to the Forest Supervisor. Cumulative actions are also to be considered together in a single EIS. The road and the timber sales will have cumulatively significant impacts because of the deposits of sediments in the Salmon River and the destruction of the habitat for the endangered Rocky Mountain Gray Wolf.

EAs and/or EISs for the individual timber sales are not sufficient to satisfy NEPA because they will be done after the road has already been approved.

▶ **ANALYSIS**

The CEQ's regulations on cumulative impact were held to apply to private acts on private lands in *Sierra Club v. U.S. Forest Service*, 46 F.3d 835 (8th Cir. 1995).

■══■

Quicknotes

SUMMARY JUDGMENT Judgment rendered by a court in response to a motion by one of the parties, claiming that the lack of a question of material fact in respect to an issue warrants disposition of the issue without consideration by the jury.

■══■

Sierra Club v. Peterson

Environmental group (P) v. Forest service (D)

717 F.2d 1409 (D.C. Cir 1983).

NATURE OF CASE: Appeal from summary judgment upholding agency decision not to prepare an environmental impact statement (EIS).

FACT SUMMARY: The Sierra Club (P) challenged the United States Forest Service's (the Forest Service's) (D) implementation of an oil and gas lease program without first preparing an EIS.

🏛 RULE OF LAW
An agency may not institute a program which prevents it from prohibiting environmentally disruptive action without first completing an environmental impact statement (EIS).

FACTS: The Forest Service (D) created a lease program whereby oil and gas rights of "highly sensitive lands" and "non-highly sensitive lands" were leased. Under the program, the Forest Service (D) could set conditions designed to mitigate damaging effects of the drilling in the nonhighly sensitive lands but relinquished its right to prevent any drilling. The lease program was enacted without first performing an EIS since the agency determined an EIS was unnecessary given that environmental conditions were included in the leases. The Sierra Club (P) filed suit, claiming the Forest Service's (D) conditions were not in compliance with the National Environmental Policy Act of 1969 (NEPA). The district court upheld the lease program. The Sierra Club (P) appealed.

ISSUE: May an agency institute a program which prevents it from prohibiting environmentally disruptive action without first completing an EIS?

HOLDING AND DECISION: (MacKinnon, J.) No. An agency may not institute a program which prevents it from prohibiting environmentally disruptive action without first completing an EIS. An agency has a great deal of discretion in determining when an EIS is required, and its decision will only be overturned when the decision is arbitrary and capricious. However, a court still must examine whether the agency did, in fact, take environmental factors into serious consideration before making such a decision. The fact that the program in this case established procedures to fix any damage done by drilling does not absolve the Forest Service (D) from its obligation to analyze what that impact will be before they give away their authority to prevent it. The purpose of requiring the EIS prior to leasing is to allow the agency to weigh the environmental impact of a decision when it still has ample options at its disposal. Reversed.

▶ ANALYSIS

The court establishes a four-part test to determine whether an agency was justified in finding "no significant impact." The court must ascertain: (1) whether the agency took "a hard look" at the problem; (2) whether the agency identified the environmental issues; (3) whether the agency's position was convincing; and (4) whether the agency established that a truly significant impact was sufficiently reduced by project changes. The court found that the Forest Service (D) had satisfied the first two criteria but not the remaining two.

■■■

Quicknotes

MOTION FOR SUMMARY JUDGMENT Judgment rendered by a court in response to a motion by one of the parties, claiming that the lack of a question of material fact in respect to an issue warrants disposition of the issue without consideration of the jury.

■■■

Hanly v. Kleindienst

Resident (P) v. Government agency (D)

471 F.2d 823 (2d Cir. 1972).

NATURE OF CASE: Action for injunction.

FACT SUMMARY: The United States ordered commencement of a nine-story federal jail in Manhattan across the street from an apartment house where Hanly (P) and others resided.

⚖ RULE OF LAW

The threshold determination, by a federal agency, as to the need for an environmental impact statement in a particular case, should be based upon consideration of (1) the extent to which the action will cause adverse environmental effects in excess of those created by existing uses in the area affected by it, and (2) the absolute quantitative adverse environmental effects of the action itself, including the cumulative harm that results from its contribution to existing adverse conditions or uses.

FACTS: This is the second appeal of a case (originally *Hanly v. Mitchell*) involving interpretation of the National Environmental Policy Act of 1969 (NEPA). Briefly, the case began when the U.S. General Services Administration (the GSA) commenced construction of a nine-story federal jail across the street from the apartment house where Hanly (P) and others resided. Fearing an adverse effect on the neighborhood, Hanly (P) et al. filed an action for an injunction against construction on the ground that the GSA had failed to properly consider and file an environmental impact statement pursuant to the NEPA of 1969. A preliminary injunction was issued and the GSA ordered to make a showing that it had considered all factors concerning the quality of life for city residents. Pursuant to this order, the GSA submitted to the court a 25-page "Assessment of Environmental Impact" discussing such things as extent of citizen-inmate contact, traffic problems, noise problems, and various types of pollution which might result. In the end, the GSA concluded that no environmental impact statement was necessary. Hanly (P) disagreed and renewed his action for an injunction. This appeal followed.

ISSUE: Does full consideration by a federal agency of all factors concerning the environment suffice, by itself, to uphold such agency's decision that an environmental impact statement is not necessary in a particular case?

HOLDING AND DECISION: (Mansfield, J.) No. The threshold determination, by a federal agency, as to the need for an environmental impact statement in a particular case, should be based upon full consideration of "(1) the extent to which the action will cause adverse environmental effects in excess of those created by existing uses in the area affected by it, and (2) the absolute quantitative adverse environmental effects of the action itself, including the cumulative harm that results from its contribution to existing adverse conditions or uses"; but such determination, even if properly made, will not be upheld unless the responsible agency has given prior "notice to the public of the proposed major federal action and an opportunity to submit relevant facts which might bear upon the agency's threshold decision." NEPA requires a federal agency to file an environmental impact statement whenever contemplating major federal actions "significantly affecting the quality of the human environment." Inclusion of the word "significantly" by Congress clearly evidences an intent to give federal agencies the power to make threshold determinations regarding the necessity of an environmental impact statement, in order to weed out "insignificant" federal actions. The court is convinced that the two above-mentioned factors should be the criteria for making such determination. Here, the GSA 25-page statement almost meets them. Unfortunately, it fails to consider the potential for crime on the community. Such is fatal. Furthermore, the GSA has failed to permit any public participation in its deliberations, as no notice, etc., was given.

DISSENT: (Friendly, C.J.) The court today has rewritten NEPA to require a "mini-impact" statement for each threshold determination made by a federal agency under NEPA. The court sets too high a floor on when a statement is necessary, since it is clear that Congress intended that a statement be made any time the environmental impact is even arguably significant. Further, the court then bogs down the whole process by requiring procedures for the threshold determination which should not arise unless a statement is needed. The GSA here should file a statement.

▶ ANALYSIS

This case points up an example of an attempt by a federal court to construe the admittedly vague terms of NEPA. Note that the two criteria adapted by the court are not derived from either any legislative or administrative ruling. Rather, they are adopted by judicial fiat (based on sketchy legislative history). Note also that § 102(2)(B) of NEPA requires all federal agencies to "identify . . . and develop methods and procedures . . . which will insure that presently unquantified environmental . . . values may be given appropriate consideration in decisionmaking." *Kleindienst* stands for the proposition that this section extends minimum due process (notice and opportunity to be heard) to those affected by federal agency decisions. Note, however, that neither *Hanly*

Continued on next page.

decision really addressed the question of when, as a matter of law, a federal action was sufficiently "significant" as to require the filing of an environmental impact statement.

■══■

Quicknotes

INJUNCTION A court order requiring a person to do, or prohibiting that person from doing, a specific act.

■══■

Dept. of Transportation v. Public Citizen

Federal agency (D) v. Citizen (P)

541 U.S. 752 (2004).

NATURE OF CASE: Appeal from judgment that a federal agency's regulations violated the National Environmental Policy Act of 1969 (NEPA) and the Clean Air Act (CAA).

FACT SUMMARY: The Federal Motor Carrier Safety Administration (the FMCSA), a federal agency within the Department of Transportation (the DOT) (D), contended that because it had limited statutory authority regarding motor vehicle carrier registration, the entry of Mexican motor carriers into the United States was not an "effect" of its regulations that permitted cross-border operations of the Mexican vehicles, and, therefore, the FMCSA did not need to consider in an environmental assessment (an EA), pursuant to NEPA and CAA mandates, any environmental impacts that might be caused by the increased presence of Mexican trucks in the United States.

🏛 RULE OF LAW
A federal agency, which lacks discretion to prevent cross-border motor vehicle operations and which issues regulations that permit such crossings subject to the satisfaction of regulatory mandates, does not violate NEPA and CAA by issuing those regulations after concluding that it is not required to evaluate the environmental effects of such cross-border operations.

FACTS: The FMCSA, a federal agency within the DOT (D), is charged with establishing minimum levels of financial responsibility for motor carriers and prescribing federal standards for motor vehicle safety inspections. The FMCSA has only limited discretion regarding motor vehicle carrier registration: It must grant registration to all domestic or foreign motor carriers that are "willing and able to comply with" the applicable safety, fitness, and financial responsibility requirements. The FMCSA has no statutory authority to impose or enforce emissions controls or to establish environmental requirements unrelated to motor carrier safety. In connection with promulgating new application and safety monitoring rules for Mexican motor carriers—the lifting of a Presidential moratorium on cross-border Mexican operations was contingent on the issuance of these regulations—and pursuant to a mandate under NEPA, the FMCSA issued a programmatic EA. Because the FMCSA concluded that the entry of the Mexican trucks was not an "effect" of its regulations, it did not consider any environmental impact that might be caused by the increased presence of Mexican trucks within the United States. Instead, the EA focused on pollution created by roadside inspections, which the FMCSA concluded could be mitigated by the inspection process and reduced entry of vehicles due to more stringent safety requirements. Accordingly, the EA concluded that the issuance of the proposed

regulations would have no significant impact on the environment. Based on this conclusion, the FMCSA issued a finding of no significant impact (a FONSI) and thus declined to prepare an environmental impact statement (an EIS). After the regulations were issued, public citizens (P) sued, contending that the regulations were promulgated in violation of NEPA and CAA. The court of appeals agreed with the public citizens (P), finding that the EA was deficient because it failed to give adequate consideration to the regulations' overall environmental impacts. The Supreme Court granted certiorari.

ISSUE: Does a federal agency, which lacks discretion to prevent cross-border motor vehicle operations and which issues regulations that permit such crossings subject to the satisfaction of regulatory mandates, violate NEPA and CAA by issuing those regulations after concluding that it is not required to evaluate the environmental effects of such cross-border operations?

HOLDING AND DECISION: (Thomas, J.) No. A federal agency, which lacks discretion to prevent cross-border motor vehicle operations and which issues regulations that permit such crossings subject to the satisfaction of regulatory mandates, does not violate NEPA and CAA by issuing those regulations after concluding that it is not required to evaluate the environmental effects of such cross-border operations. Under NEPA, an agency is required to provide an EIS only if it will be undertaking a "major Federal actio[n]," which "significantly affect[s] the quality of the human environment." Here, the relevant question under NEPA is whether that increase in cross-border operations of Mexican motor carriers, and the correlative release of emissions, is an "effect," of the FMCSA's rules; if not, the FMCSA's failure to address these effects in the EA did not violate NEPA, and the FONSI's issuance cannot be arbitrary and capricious. The public citizens' (P) argument that the EA had to take the increased cross-border operations' environmental effects into account because of a statutory expenditure bar that made it impossible for any Mexican truck to operate in the United States until the regulations were issued, and hence the trucks' entry was a "reasonably foreseeable" indirect effect of the issuance of the regulations, is unconvincing; that argument overlooked the FMCSA's inability to countermand the President's lifting of the moratorium or otherwise categorically to exclude Mexican trucks from operating in the United States. Because the FMCSA must comply with all its non-conflicting statutory mandates, the public citizens (P) must rely on "but for" causation, where an agency's action is considered a cause of an environmental effect even when the agency has no authority to prevent the effect. However, "but for" causation is

Continued on next page.

insufficient to make an agency responsible for a particular effect under NEPA and the relevant regulations. NEPA requires a "reasonably close causal relationship" akin to proximate cause in tort law. Also, inherent in NEPA and its implementing regulations is a "rule of reason," which ensures that agencies determine whether and to what extent to prepare an EIS based on the usefulness of any new potential information to the decision-making process. The underlying policies behind NEPA and Congress's intent, as informed by the "rule of reason," make clear that the causal connection between the proposed regulations and the entry of Mexican trucks is insufficient to make the FMCSA responsible under NEPA to consider the environmental effects of entry. Neither of the purposes of NEPA's EIS requirement—to ensure both that an agency has information to make its decision and that the public receives information so it might also play a role in the decision-making process—will be fulfilled by requiring the FMCSA to consider the environmental impact at issue. Since the FMCSA has no ability to prevent such cross-border operations, it lacks the power to act on whatever information might be contained in an EIS and could not act on whatever input the public could provide. This analysis is not changed by the Council of Environmental Quality regulation requiring an agency to evaluate the "cumulative impact" of its action, since that rule does not require the FMCSA to treat the lifting of the moratorium itself or the consequences from that lifting as an effect of its rules' promulgation. Reversed.

▶ *ANALYSIS*

In this unanimous opinion, the Court also held that the CAA was not violated by the FMCSA's failure to determine that emissions from cross-border operations of Mexican motor carriers would be in conformity with existing air quality standards since the FMCSA was powerless to stop the emissions. The Court also ruled that the plaintiffs had forfeited any objection to the EA on the ground that it did not adequately discuss potential alternatives to the proposed action because the plaintiffs never identified in their comments to the rules any alternatives beyond those the EA evaluated.

■═■

Quicknotes

MORATORIUM Suspension of legal remedies or proceedings.

■═■

Center for Biological Diversity v. NHTSA

Public interest organization (P) v. Federal government (D)

538 F.3d 1172 (9th Cir. 2008)

NATURE OF CASE: Appeal to Ninth Circuit for review of rule issued by the National Highway Traffic Safety Administration (the NHTSA).

FACT SUMMARY: The NHTSA promulgated a rule regarding fuel economy for "light trucks" for model years 2008 to 2011.

🏛 RULE OF LAW
The NHTSA's rule regarding light trucks is arbitrary and capricious because of its failure to monetize the value of carbon emissions, failure to close the SUV loophole, and failure to promulgate fuel economy standards for vehicles in the 8,500 to 10,000 weight class.

FACTS: Title V of the Energy Policy and Conservation Act of 1975 (the EPCA) promulgated fuel economy standards for vehicles. The EPCA defines the "average fuel economy standard" as the minimum level of fuel economy for a particular model and model year. This is often referred to as the CAFE standard. The NHTSA promulgated a rule regarding fuel economy for "light trucks" for model years 2008 to 2011. Eleven states, the District of Columbia, and four public interest groups petitioned the Ninth Circuit for a review of the rule, on the grounds that the rule was arbitrary and capricious and not consistent with the EPCA.

ISSUE: Is the NHTSA's rule regarding light trucks arbitrary and capricious because of its failure to monetize the value of carbon emissions, failure to close the SUV loophole, and failure to promulgate fuel economy standards for vehicles in the 8,500 to 10,000 weight class?

HOLDING AND DECISION: (Fletcher, J.) Yes. The NHTSA's rule regarding light trucks is arbitrary and capricious because of its failure to monetize the value of carbon emissions, failure to close the SUV loophole, and failure to promulgate fuel economy standards for vehicles in the 8,500 to 10,000 weight class. The NHTSA's failure to monetize the reduction of carbon emissions in its analysis supporting the rule was arbitrary. The value of reduction of carbon emissions is not zero, as the NHTSA contends. The EPCA also does not prevent the NHTSA from assessing overall environmental impacts of its rule. The NHTSA does have the authority to act on information contained in an environmental impact statement (an EIS), including effects on climate change generally. The accompanying environmental assessment (EA) did not consider the actual environmental impact resulting from emissions from light trucks. The NHTSA must assess the impact of the rule in relation to past or future actions of other entities that contribute to global climate change. The NHTSA cannot simply say a reduction in the rate of carbon emissions for light trucks will have a minimal effect on climate change, without assessing the impact in relation to the government's efforts as a whole to reduce emissions. Therefore, we remand the case to the NHTSA to prepare a revised EA or EIS in accordance with this opinion.

▶ ANALYSIS

This decision is significant because it requires agencies to review the impact of a proposed rule on climate change generally. It is not enough for an agency to state that a rule itself will have a minimal effect on climate change. The agency must assess the environmental impact in conjunction with other federal efforts to combat climate change.

■═■

Quicknotes

EPCA The Energy Policy and Conservation Act of 1975 that promulgated fuel economy standards for vehicles.

■═■

Vermont Yankee Nuclear Power Corp. v. NRDC

Nuclear power company (D) v. Environmental organization (P)

435 U.S. 519 (1978).

NATURE OF CASE: Appeal from finding of a violation of National Environmental Policy Act of 1969 (NEPA).

FACT SUMMARY: The National Resources Defense Council (NRDC) (P) claimed that Vermont Yankee Nuclear Power Corporation's (D) environmental impact statement (EIS) did not meet statutory requirements since it failed to take energy conservation into account.

🏛 RULE OF LAW
An agency's EIS need not take into account every alternative available in order to meet the requirements of NEPA.

FACTS: The Atomic Energy Commission (Commission) (D) licenses nuclear power plants. It granted such a license to Vermont Yankee Nuclear Power Corporation (D) based on an EIS describing the alternatives available to the planned action. The NRDC (P) filed suit, claiming the Commission (D) failed to meet its statutory mandate because the EIS did not discuss the alternative of energy conservation. The court of appeals rejected the EIS, and the Commission (D) appealed.

ISSUE: Must an agency's EIS take into account every alternative available in order to meet the requirements of NEPA?

HOLDING AND DECISION: (Rehnquist, J.) No. An agency's EIS need not take into account every alternative available in order to meet the requirements of NEPA. The requirement of a "detailed statement" does not require a meaningless listing of all alternatives conceivable but rather a careful examination of the relevant alternatives available at the time the EIS was created. The EIS at issue here was created prior to the energy crises of the early 1970s. Prior to those events, energy conservation was a practically unheard-of alternative. The Commission's (D) failure to examine an alternative which was irrelevant at the time the document was prepared is not fatal to the grant of the license. While the courts must ensure that agencies are actually giving precedence to environmental concerns, that duty does not extend to allowing courts to second-guess rationally based decisions. Reversed.

▶ ANALYSIS

The Council on Environmental Quality (CEQ) has set out guidelines for determining the scope of an EIS. An agency should consider at least three alternatives: the effect of no action, reasonable alternatives to the proposed action, and measures that would decrease any damage cause that was not included in the proposal.

■■■■

Sierra Club v. United States Army Corps of Engineers

Environmental agency (P) v. Government agency (D)

701 F.2d 1011 (2d Cir. 1983).

NATURE OF CASE: Appeal from injunction of project pending preparation of final environmental impact statement (EIS) supplement.

FACT SUMMARY: The Sierra Club (P) contended that the United States Army Corps of Engineers (Corps) (D) had not made a serious attempt to discover, or to make a permitting decision based on, reliable fisheries information in connection with the Westway highway project.

> ## 🏛 RULE OF LAW
> A court may rule an EIS unacceptable if the agency has made an inadequate compilation of relevant information, has not analyzed it reasonably, and has ignored pertinent data.

FACTS: Following preparation of draft and final environmental impact statements, the Federal Highway Administration (FHWA) (D) announced its decision to fund Westway, a highway that was to run along the Hudson River past Manhattan. Based on the final environmental impact statement (FEIS), the Corps (D) issued a permit allowing discharge of fill material into the river. Three federal agencies—the Environmental Protection Agency, the National Marine Fisheries Service, and the Fish and Wildlife Service—objected to the EISs and to the permit. They contended that the EISs had relied on outdated fisheries information to reach the conclusion that fill from the Westway project would not adversely impact on fish. They argued that a new study showed rich populations of fish existed in areas that the EISs had characterized as biological wastelands. Nevertheless, the FHWA (D) and the Corps (D) chose not to prepare a supplemental EIS. The Sierra Club (P) challenged the issuance of the permit, and the district court enjoined the Westway project. The Corps (D) appealed.

ISSUE: May a court rule an EIS unacceptable if the agency has made an inadequate compilation of relevant information, has not analyzed it reasonably, and has ignored pertinent data?

HOLDING AND DECISION: (Kearse, J.) Yes. A court may rule an EIS unacceptable if the agency has made an inadequate compilation of relevant information, has not analyzed it reasonably, and has ignored pertinent data. Under the National Environmental Policy Act of 1969 (NEPA), an EIS must set forth sufficient information for the decision-maker to make a reasoned decision by balancing the risks of harm to the environment against the benefits of the proposed action. A decision that relies on false information cannot be accepted as a "reasoned" decision. Here, the FHWA (D) ignored the criticisms of its sister agencies and instead stood by its EISs without performing any new studies or collecting any additional information regarding fisheries impact. Therefore, the FHWA's (D) issuance of the FEIS, and the Corps' (D) reliance on the FEIS, violated NEPA and the Clean Water Act. Accordingly, the district court's requirement that the FHWA (D) or the Corps (D) must prepare a new EIS on fisheries information before Westway may proceed is upheld. Affirmed.

▶ ANALYSIS

Courts may not express an opinion on the substantive merits of permits. If an agency decision is procedurally adequate under NEPA and Corps regulations, it will pass judicial muster. An agency's procedural duty under NEPA, however, does not refer to the duty to hold hearings or observe other procedures. It means the duty to comply with the procedures mandated by NEPA for the preparation of an EIS so that the decision-maker can base his decision on a reasoned analysis. The above case demonstrates how the failure to listen can be fatal to a project; Westway was never built.

■=■

Marsh v. Oregon Natural Resources Council

Government agency (D) v. Environmental organization (P)

490 U.S. 360 (1989).

NATURE OF CASE: Appeal from order requiring preparation of a supplemental environmental impact statement.

FACT SUMMARY: The United States Army Corps of Engineers (Corps) (D) refused to prepare a second supplemental environmental impact statement (EIS) regarding a dam project despite new information regarding the project's adverse environmental impacts.

🏛 RULE OF LAW
An agency must prepare a supplemental EIS if new information shows that the remaining major federal action will affect the quality of the human environment in a significant manner.

FACTS: In 1980, the Corps (D) released a "Final Environmental Impact Statement Supplement No. 1" (FEISS) for a three-dam project on the Rogue River. The Oregon Department of Fish and Wildlife and the U.S. Soil Conservation Service subsequently released two documents concluding that the project would have greater adverse impacts than previously thought. Nonetheless, the Corps (D) refused to prepare a second supplement EIS. The Natural Resources Council (P) contended, and the Ninth Circuit agreed, that the Corps (D) was required to prepare a supplemental EIS. The Corps (D) appealed.

ISSUE: Must an agency prepare a supplemental EIS if new information shows that the remaining major federal action will affect the quality of the human environment in a significant manner?

HOLDING AND DECISION: (Stevens, J.) Yes. An agency must prepare a supplemental EIS if new information shows that the remaining major federal action will affect the quality of the human environment in a significant manner. An agency need not supplement an EIS every time new information comes to light. Otherwise an agency would be continually awaiting updated information. However, depending on the value of the new information, an agency must take a hard look at the effects of its planned action, even after a proposal has received initial approval. In this case, analysis of the new information released by state and federal agencies required a high level of technical expertise and informed discretion. Thus, unless the Corps' (D) decision not to supplement the FEISS was arbitrary or capricious, it should not be set aside. In this case, the Corps (D) made a reasoned decision based on its evaluation of the significance of the new information. Reversed.

▶ ANALYSIS

Note that the National Environmental Policy Act of 1969 (NEPA) itself does not provide a standard of judicial review for courts to apply in NEPA cases, nor does the meager legislative history of the Act provide meaningful guidance from Congress. Therefore, courts are forced to rely on the "arbitrary and capricious" standard provided in the Administrative Procedure Act. This standard, which was promulgated to protect agency decisions from encroachment by the judiciary, essentially gives the benefit of the doubt to the agency.

Quicknotes

ADMINISTRATIVE PROCEDURE ACT (APA) Enacted in 1946 to govern practices and proceedings before federal administrative agencies.

Preservation of Biodiversity

Quick Reference Rules of Law

TVA v. Hill

Government authority (D) v. Scientist (P)

437 U.S. 153 (1978).

NATURE OF CASE: Appeal from permanent injunction restraining violation of the Endangered Species Act (the ESA).

FACT SUMMARY: Hill (P) argued that operation of theTellico Dam by the Tennessee Valley Authority (the TVA) (D) would jeopardize the snail darter, an endangered species.

RULE OF LAW
The Endangered Species Act requires that highest priority be given to the preservation of endangered species, whatever the cost.

FACTS: The TVA (D) began constructing the Tellico Dam on the Little Tennessee River in 1967. When the Tellico Dam was nearly complete and ready for operation, a scientist discovered a previously unknown species of perch, called a snail darter, living in the portion of the river that would be completely inundated by the reservoir created once the dam was operational. In 1975, the snail darter was formerly listed as an endangered species. Hill (P) subsequently filed suit to enjoin operation of the dam on the ground that the dam would violate the ESA by directly causing the extinction of the snail darter. The district court dismissed the complaint, but the court of appeals reversed, ordering that the operation of the dam be enjoined until Congress either exempted Tellico from compliance with the Act or the snail darter was declared nonendangered. The TVA (D) appealed, and the Supreme Court granted review.

ISSUE: Does the ESA require that highest priority be given to the preservation of endangered species, whatever the cost?

HOLDING AND DECISION: (Burger, C.J.) Yes. The ESA requires that highest priority be given to the preservation of endangered species, whatever the cost. Section 7 of the Act plainly commands all federal agencies "to insure that actions authorized, funded, or carried out by them do not jeopardize the continued existence of an endangered species . . . or result in the destruction or modification of [its] habitat." Even though construction on the Tellico Dam began long before Congress passed the 1973 Endangered Species Act, the TVA (D) cannot now operate the dam without eradicating the snail darter, in complete contradiction to the plain language of the ESA. Moreover, the Act does not allow courts to balance the loss of the $100 million invested in the dam against the loss of the snail darter. Indeed, the value of endangered species, and the biodiversity they represent, is incalculable. Therefore, the completion of the dam must be enjoined. Affirmed.

ANALYSIS

The ramifications of this landmark ESA case are still being felt. In response to *Hill*, Congress created a two-level procedure to exempt qualified activities from the Act's "no jeopardy" rule. The process culminates in the cabinet-level Endangered Species Committee, or "God Squad." The God Squad may grant an exemption if it determines that there are no reasonable alternatives to an agency action and that the benefits of the action outweigh the benefits of less harmful alternatives. Although the God Squad refused to exempt the Tellico Dam Project, Congress did so in a subsequent appropriations rider.

Quicknotes

ENDANGERED SPECIES An animal, bird, fish, plant or other species that is in danger of extinction throughout all or a significant portion of its range.

National Association of Home Builders v. Babbitt

Trade association (P) v. Government agency (D)

130 F.3d 1041 (D.C. Cir. 1997).

NATURE OF CASE: Appeal from decision holding that the taking provision of the Endangered Species Act (the ESA) applies to the Delhi Sands Flower-Loving Fly (the Fly) as proper exercise of Congress's Commerce Clause power.

FACT SUMMARY: National Association of Home Builders (Association) (P) contends that the Commerce Clause does not grant the federal Government (D) the authority to regulate wildlife, nor does it authorize federal regulation of nonfederal lands.

> ## 🏛 RULE OF LAW
> The ESA's taking prohibition constitutes a valid exercise of Congress's authority to regulate interstate commerce under the Commerce Clause.

FACTS: This dispute arose when the Fish and Wildlife Service (the FWS) placed the Fly, an insect native to the San Bernardino area of California, on the endangered species list. The listing of the Fly forced San Bernardino County (the County) to alter plans to construct a new hospital on a site that the FWS had determined contained Fly habitat. The FWS and San Bernardino County agreed on a plan that would allow the County to build the hospital and a power plant in the Fly habitat area in return for modification of the construction plans and setting aside of nearby land as Fly habitat. The FWS issued a permit to allow construction of the power plant. However, the County then notified the FWS that it planned to redesign a nearby intersection to improve emergency vehicle access to the hospital. The FWS informed the County that expansion of the intersection would likely lead to a "taking" of the Fly in violation of the ESA. The County ultimately filed suit in district court challenging the application of the ESA's taking provision to the Fly.

ISSUE: Does ESA's taking prohibition constitute a valid exercise of Congress's authority to regulate interstate commerce under the Commerce Clause?

HOLDING AND DECISION: (Wald, J.) Yes. The ESA's taking prohibition constitutes a valid exercise of Congress's authority to regulate interstate commerce under the Commerce Clause. In *United States v. Lopez*, 514 U.S. 549 (1995), the Court explained that Congress could regulate three broad categories of activity: (1) the use of the channels of interstate commerce, (2) the instrumentalities of interstate commerce, or persons or things in interstate commerce, even though the threat may come only from intrastate activities, and (3) those activities that substantially affect interstate commerce. As the second category does not apply here, only the first and third will

be examined. The prohibition against the taking of an endangered species is necessary to enable the government to control the transport of the endangered species in interstate commerce. The taking prohibition falls under Congress's authority to keep the channels of interstate commerce free from immoral and injurious uses. It can also be viewed as a regulation of the third category. This requires an analysis of whether the regulated activity substantially affects interstate commerce. Congress could rationally conclude that the intrastate activity regulated by the ESA substantially affects commerce because the provision prevents the destruction of biodiversity and thereby protects the current and future interstate commerce that relies on it. Furthermore, the provision controls adverse effects of interstate competition. Each time a species becomes extinct, the pool of wild species diminishes. This has a substantial effect on interstate commerce by diminishing a natural resource that could otherwise be used for present and future commercial purposes. The taking of the Fly also substantially affects interstate commerce because it is the product of destructive interstate competition. Interstate competition provides incentives to states to adopt lower standards of endangered species protection in order to attract development vis-à-vis other states.

CONCURRENCE: (Henderson, J.) The "taking" prohibition in § 9(a)(1) of the ESA constitutes a valid exercise of Congress's authority to regulate under the Commerce Clause. However, this validity does not derive from some uncertain medical or economic value that this entirely intrastate species may offer in the future. Rather, given the interconnectedness of species and ecosystems, it is reasonable to conclude that the extinction of one species affects others and their ecosystems and that the protection of a purely intrastate species will therefore substantially affect land and objects that are involved in interstate commerce.

DISSENT: (Sentelle, J.) A creative and imaginative court can certainly speculate on the possibility that any object cited in any locality no matter how intrastate or isolated might some day have a medical, scientific, or economic value which could then propel it into interstate commerce. There is no stopping point. If we uphold this statute under Judge Wald's first rationale, we have not only ignored *Lopez* but made the Commerce Clause into what Judge Kozinski suggested: the "hey-you-can-do-whatever-you-feel-like clause."

Continued on next page.

▶ *ANALYSIS*

Not all endangered insects are protected under the ESA. Congress specifically excluded from the statutory definition of "endangered species" any "species of the Class Insecta determined by the Secretary to constitute a pest whose protection under the provisions of this chapter would present an overwhelming and overriding risk to man."

■━━■

Quicknotes

COMMERCE CLAUSE   Article 1, section 8, clause 3 of the United States Constitution, granting Congress the power to regulate commerce with foreign countries and between the states.

ENDANGERED SPECIES   An animal, bird, fish, plant or other species that is in danger of extinction throughout all or a significant portion of its range.

■━━■

Gibbs v. Babbitt

Landowner (P) v. Government agency (D)

214 F.3d 483 (4th Cir. 2000).

NATURE OF CASE: Appeal of summary judgment.

FACT SUMMARY: Gibbs (P) challenged the federal Government's (D) authority to protect red wolves on private land alleging that it exceeded Congress's power under the interstate Commerce Clause.

> 🏛 **RULE OF LAW**
> The anti-taking regulation as applied to the red wolves occupying private land does not exceed Congress's power under the interstate Commerce Clause.

FACTS: The taking provision of § 9(a)(1) prevents landowners from harassing, harming, pursuing, hunting, shooting, wounding, killing, trapping, capturing, or collecting any endangered species. An experimental population of red wolves, subject to this provision, was introduced into North Carolina. A red wolf may be taken under § 17.84(c) on private property if it is in defense of human life, if the wolf is killing livestock or pets, or if efforts to take the wolf by the Service have been abandoned. Similarly, the red wolf may be harassed so long as such harassment is not lethal or injurious to the wolf. Gibbs (P) challenged the federal Government's (D) authority to protect red wolves on private land. He alleged that the wolves were a menace and North Carolinians were unable to defend their property. The district court ruled in favor of Babbitt (D) on cross-motions for summary judgment, and Gibbs (P) appealed.

ISSUE: Does the anti-taking regulation as applied to the red wolves occupying private land exceed Congress's power under the interstate Commerce Clause?

HOLDING AND DECISION: (Wilkinson, C.J.) No. The anti-taking regulation as applied to the red wolves occupying private land does not exceed Congress's power under the interstate Commerce Clause. The regulation is part of the federal scheme to protect, preserve, and rehabilitate endangered species, thereby conserving valuable wildlife resources important to the welfare of the country. Regulations have been upheld when the regulative activities arise out of or are connected with a commercial transaction which viewed in the aggregate substantially affects interstate commerce. The taking of red wolves in the aggregate implicates a variety of commercial activities and has a sufficient impact on interstate commerce. The taking of red wolves on private land is an economic activity because the protection of commercial and economic assets is a primary reason for taking the wolves. Farmers and ranchers take wolves to protect their property and their investments in the land. Furthermore, without red wolves, there would be no red wolf–related tourism, red wolf scientific research,

and no commercial trade in pelts. The red wolves are part of a $29.2 billion national wildlife-related recreational industry that involves tourism and interstate travel. The regulations of takings on private land are essential to the entire program of re-introduction and restoration of the species because so many wander onto private land. Scientific research generates jobs and deepens knowledge of the world which results in the development of modern medicines. Furthermore, Congress had the renewal of trade in fur pelts in mind when it enacted the ESA. The taking of red wolves is connected to interstate markets for agricultural products and livestock. It is for Congress, not the courts, to balance whether the negative effects on interstate commerce from red wolf predation are outweighed by the benefits to commerce from a restoration of the species. This regulation is also sustainable as an essential part of a larger regulation of economic activity, in which the regulatory scheme could be undercut unless the intrastate activity was regulated. Formal congressional findings that the regulation affects interstate commerce are not necessary in order to sustain a statute or regulation. Informal congressional findings have emphasized the importance of endangered species to interstate commerce. The regulated activity at issue here does not involve an area of traditional state concern, but rather is an area of federal regulation. Affirmed.

DISSENT: (Luttig, J.) The killing of the red wolves on private property would not constitute an economic activity to be of concern to the Commerce Clause. Even if it were an economic activity, it would not have a substantial effect on interstate commerce.

▌ *ANALYSIS*

The U.S. Supreme Court refused to grant review of this decision.

■══■

Quicknotes

COMMERCE CLAUSE Article 1, section 8, clause 3 of the United States Constitution, granting Congress the power to regulate commerce with foreign countries and between the states.

SUMMARY JUDGMENT Judgment rendered by a court in response to a motion by one of the parties, claiming that the lack of a question of material fact in respect to an issue warrants disposition of the issue without consideration by the jury.

■══■

Thomas v. Peterson

Conservation group (P) v. Forest service (D)

753 F.2d 754 (9th Cir. 1985).

NATURE OF CASE: Appeal from summary judgment in action to enjoin construction of a timber road.

FACT SUMMARY: Thomas (P) protested that the Forest Service (D) did not comply with the Endangered Species Act (the ESA) in considering the impact of construction of a timber road on the endangered gray wolf.

🏛 RULE OF LAW
Once an agency is aware that an endangered species may be present in the area of its proposed action, it must make a biological assessment to determine whether the species is likely to be affected.

FACTS: The Forest Service (D) initiated a road construction project in a former roadless area in order to facilitate timber sales. Under the ESA, an agency proposing to take an action must first inquire of the Fish and Wildlife Service (the FWS) whether any endangered species may be present in the area of the proposed action. The Forest Service (D) did not make such an inquiry, however, because it was already aware that wolves were present in the roadless area. Thomas (P) sued to enjoin construction of the road based on allegations that the Forest Service (D) had violated the Act. The district court concluded that the Forest Service's (D) procedural violation was insignificant and refused to issue an injunction. Thomas (P) appealed.

ISSUE: Once an agency is aware that an endangered species may be present in the area of its proposed action, must it make a biological assessment to determine whether the species is likely to be affected?

HOLDING AND DECISION: (Sneed, J.) Yes. Once an agency is aware that an endangered species may be present in the area of its proposed action, it must make a biological assessment to determine whether the species is likely to be affected. In this case, the Forest Service (D) did not prepare such an assessment prior to its decision to build the timber road. Therefore, it cannot be determined whether the proposed project will result in a violation of the Act's substantive provisions. This is not a de minimis violation. Rather, it is comparable to failing to prepare an environmental impact statement under National Environmental Policy Act (NEPA). Thomas (P) has met his burden of establishing that the circumstances triggering a procedural requirement of the Endangered Species Act exist, and the Forest Service (D) has not followed those procedures. Therefore, construction of the road must be enjoined pending compliance. Affirmed in part, reversed in part, and remanded.

▶ *ANALYSIS*

Under the ESA, if the biological assessment discussed above determines that a threatened or endangered species is likely to be affected by the agency action, then the agency must formally consult with the FWS. The FWS must then issue a "biological opinion." If the opinion concludes that the action will jeopardize the species, the action may not go forward unless the FWS can suggest a more benign alternative.

■=■

Quicknotes

CONDITION PRECEDENT The happening of an uncertain occurrence, which is necessary before a particular right or interest may be obtained or an action performed.

ENDANGERED SPECIES ACT Prohibits the destruction of the habitat of endangered species.

■=■

National Ass'n of Home Builders v. Defenders of Wildlife

Trade association (D) v. Advocacy group (P)

551 U.S. 644 (2007).

NATURE OF CASE: Appeal from Ninth Circuit Court's decision in favor of the plaintiffs.

FACT SUMMARY: In 2002, the Environmental Protection Agency (the EPA) approved the State of Arizona's application to administer the National Pollutant Discharge Elimination System (NPDES). Defenders of Wildlife (P) contend that prior to that approval, the EPA did not consult with the Fish and Wildlife Service as mandated by statute.

RULE OF LAW

Because § 7(a)(2) of the Endangered Species Act (the ESA) only applies to discretionary federal involvement, and because the transfer of NPDES's permitting authority is not discretionary, but mandated once a state has met the criteria for transfers under § 402(b) of the Clean Water Act (CWA), the transfer of NPDES authority does not trigger § 7(a)(2)'s consultation requirement.

FACTS: In 2002, the EPA approved the State of Arizona's application to administer the NPDES. Section 402 of the CWA governs such approvals. Specifically, § 402 mandates that once a state has met nine requirements under the statute, the EPA "shall" approve the transfer of authority of the NPDES to the state. [The portion of the decision in the casebook did not list or describe the nine factors.] All parties concede that the state satisfied the Section 402's nine requirements. Defenders of Wildlife (P) filed a petition with the Ninth Circuit Court of Appeals. The advocacy group argued § 7(a)(2) of the ESA mandated that the EPA consult with the Fish and Wildlife Service and obtain an opinion regarding the impact on any endangered species affected by the EPA's action. The Ninth Circuit agreed with the Defenders of Wildlife (P), finding that the EPA must comply with the mandatory provision of § 7(a)(2). The Association appealed.

ISSUE: Because § 7(a)(2) of the Endangered Species Act only applies to discretionary federal involvement, and because the transfer of NPDES permitting authority is not discretionary, but mandated once a state has met the criteria for transfers under § 402(b) of the CWA, does the transfer of NPDES authority trigger § 7(a)(2)'s consultation requirement?

HOLDING AND DECISION: (Alito, J.) No. Because § 7(a)(2) of the Endangered Species Act only applies to discretionary federal involvement, and because the transfer of NPDES permitting authority is not discretionary, but mandated once a state has met the criteria for transfers under § 402(b) of the CWA, the transfer of NPDES authority does not trigger § 7(a)(2)'s consultation requirement. In effect, the Ninth Circuit's decision adds a tenth requirement to § 402's list of nine requirements that states must satisfy prior to EPA approval. However, a regulation from the Fish and Wildlife Service states that "Section 7 and the requirements of this part apply to all actions in which there is *discretionary* federal involvement or control." 50 CFR Section 402.03 (emphasis in text). Therefore, § 7 does not apply when mandatory federal agency action is involved. Here, once the EPA determined that Arizona met the nine requirements, the EPA had no discretion to not grant the permit transferring authority of the NPDES over to the state. Reversed.

DISSENT: (Stevens, J.) Under *TVA v. Hill*, Section 7 of the ESA has no exceptions. Section 7(a)(2) applies to all agency actions, whether discretionary or nondiscretionary. Therefore, it should apply to the EPA's consideration of the state's request to administer the NPDES. There are also two other ways to harmonize the statutory provisions. First, the federal agencies should be allowed to consult with the Fish and Wildlife Service. Second, the states should be required to enter into an agreement with the EPA to list their endangered species.

▶ ANALYSIS

Some commentators have argued this decision weakens the ESA considerably by removing the strong presumption in favor of the Act. In addition, the nature of the scope of agency action under Section 7 has become more paramount. Here, the Court did not examine that issue in detail. Thus, in regards to the applicability of § 7, it will be up to the district courts to determine if an agency action is discretionary or nondiscretionary.

■■▬■

Quicknotes

CLEAN WATER ACT Federal statute regulating water pollution that imposes a maximum penalty of $10,000 per day for placement of fill in navigable water.

ENDANGERED SPECIES ACT Prohibits the destruction of the habitat of endangered species.

ENDANGERED SPECIES ACT, § 7 Requires that all federal agencies ensure that actions do not endanger certain species.

■■▬■

Carson-Truckee Water Conservancy District v. Clark

Water district (P) v. Secretary of the Interior (D)

741 F.2d 257 (9th Cir. 1984).

NATURE OF CASE: Appeal from judgment upholding agency allocation decision in declaratory judgment action.

FACT SUMMARY: The Water Conservancy District (the District) (P) challenged the Interior Secretary's (Secretary) (D) authority to allocate water to conserve endangered fish and argued that he should sell the water instead.

🏛 **RULE OF LAW**
The Endangered Species Act (ESA) mandates that the Secretary of the Interior actively use programs under his control to conserve endangered species.

FACTS: The federal Washoe Project Act permits, but does not require, the Interior Secretary (the Secretary) (D) to sell water to recover dam construction costs. In order to conserve two endangered species of fish, the Secretary (D) refused to sell water from the Stampede Reservoir in California to municipalities in Nevada. The Carson-Truckee Water Conservancy District (P) sought a declaratory judgment that the Secretary's (D) decision violated the Washoe Project Act. The District (P) argued that § 7(a)(2) of the ESA charged the Secretary (D) with a duty to avoid "jeopardizing" the continued existence of a species but not to take affirmative action to conserve them. The district court disagreed, concluding that the ESA gave priority to conserving endangered species until they were no longer threatened, and the District (P) appealed.

ISSUE: Does the ESA mandate that the Secretary of the Interior actively use programs under his control to conserve endangered species?

HOLDING AND DECISION: (Pregerson, J.) Yes. The ESA mandates that the Secretary of the Interior (D) actively use programs under his control to conserve endangered species. This mandate occurs in §§ 2(b)(c) and 3(3). Section 7(a)(2), on the other hand, only applies when a federal agency undertakes a project that threatens an endangered species. It is inapplicable in this case because the Secretary (D) is actively seeking to conserve endangered species and is not "jeopardizing" them. Here, the Secretary (D) decided to give priority to the fish and chose not to sell the project's water until the fish no longer needed the ESA's protection. His decision is well justified. Affirmed in part and vacated in part.

▶ **ANALYSIS**

In reaching its decision, the court also relied on *TVA v. Hill*, 437 U.S. 153 (1978), the famous case in which the endangered snail darter blocked the operation of the Tellico Dam. Although the *TVA* decision was based on the "no jeopardy" proscription of § 7(a)(2), the *TVA* court also addressed the broader mandate applied in *Carson-Truckee*. It emphasized that Congress intended to halt and "reverse" the trend toward species extinction, whatever the cost.

■═■

Quicknotes

ENDANGERED SPECIES ACT Prohibits the destruction of the habitat of endangered species.

■═■

Babbitt v. Sweet Home Chapter of Communities for a Great Oregon

Secretary of the Interior (D) v. Forest industry groups (P)

515 U.S. 687 (1995).

NATURE OF CASE: Grant of certiorari from declaratory judgment action invalidating an Interior Department regulation.

FACT SUMMARY: Sweet Home Chapter of Communities for a Great Oregon (Sweet Home) (P), a group connected to the forest industry in Oregon, brought a declaratory judgment action against Secretary of the Interior Babbitt (the Secretary) (D), challenging the statutory validity of the Secretary's (D) regulation broadly defining "harm" pursuant to the Endangered Species Act (ESA) as habitat alteration.

🏛 RULE OF LAW
Defining "harm" to include significant habitat modification or degradation that actually kills or injures wildlife reasonably construes the intent of Congress when Congress included "harm" as an example of a taking prohibited by the ESA.

FACTS: Section 9 of the ESA makes it unlawful to "take" any endangered or threatened species. Section 3(19) defines "take" as "to harass, harm, pursue, hunt, shoot, wound, kill, trap, capture, or collect, or to attempt to engage in any such conduct." The ESA does not further define these terms. In a regulation implementing the statute, the Interior Department (D) defined "harm" in the definition of "take" to include significant habitat modification or degradation that actually kills or injures wildlife by impairing essential behavioral patterns. In response to the Secretary's (D) regulation defining "harm," Sweet Home (P), a group of Oregonians dependent upon the forest industry, brought a declaratory judgment in district court attempting to invalidate the regulation. They alleged that application of the regulation to the red-cockaded woodpecker and the spotted owl had injured them economically. A District of Columbia Circuit panel initially rejected the challenge, but six months later one judge on the three-judge panel switched his vote and invalidated the regulation, stating that the definition of "harm" must be read with the other terms defining "take," all of which contemplated direct application of force to individual animals. The Interior Secretary (D) petitioned for certiorari.

ISSUE: Does defining "harm" to include significant habitat modification or degradation that actually kills or injures wildlife reasonably construe the intent of Congress when Congress included "harm" as an example of a taking prohibited by the ESA?

HOLDING AND DECISION: (Stevens, J.) Yes. Defining "harm" to include significant habitat modification or degradation that actually kills or injures wildlife reasonably construes the intent of Congress when Congress included "harm" as an example of a taking prohibited by the ESA. The text of the ESA provides three reasons why the Secretary's (D) interpretation is reasonable. First, a dictionary definition of the word "harm" does not include the word "directly," nor does it suggest that only direct or willful action constitutes harm. While the dissent would focus on the word "take," this word has been defined by Congress; it is "harm," which has been left up to the Secretary (D) to define. Second, the broad purpose of the ESA supports the Secretary's (D) decision to extend protection against the precise harms that Congress enacted the statute to avoid. The intent of Congress in enacting the ESA was to halt and reverse the trend toward species extinction at any cost. Third, the fact that in 1982 Congress authorized a permit process for takings incidental to lawful activity strongly suggests that Congress understood § 9 to prohibit indirect as well as deliberate takings. Legislative history also supports the Secretary's (D) interpretation. In enacting § 10, both the House and the Senate reports identified as the model for the permit process a case in California where a development project threatened incidental harm to an endangered species of butterfly by modification of its habitat. Conflicts between habitat and humans are wide in scope and degree and are best left to lower courts to determine on a case-to-case basis, rather than invalidate this regulation. Reversed.

CONCURRENCE: (O'Connor, J.) Two understandings prompt this occurrence. First, the challenged regulation is limited to significant habitat modifications that cause actual, as opposed to hypothetical, death or injury to listed animals. Second, the regulation's application is limited by ordinary principles of proximate causation, including foreseeability. The dissent argues that habitat modification that impairs breeding does not actually injure animals, only population expansion. This argument fails to consider that preventing breeding injures the individual animal by impairing its ability to conduct its most essential physical function—to pass on genetic material.

DISSENT: (Scalia, J.) The legislation at issue here (1) forbade the hunting and killing of endangered animals, and (2) provided federal lands and funds for the acquisition of private lands to preserve the habitat of endangered animals. The regulation issued by the Secretary (D) does not comport with the ESA because it provides for penalties without proximate causation, and it encompasses injury inflicted not only upon individual animals but also upon popula-

Continued on next page.

tions of the protected species. Regarding the last, impairment of breeding does not "injure" living creatures; it prevents them from propagating, thus "injuring" a population of animals. To "take," when applied to wild animals, means to reduce those animals, by capturing or killing, to human control.

▶ ANALYSIS

While Justice Stevens and, to a greater degree, Justice O'Connor do a reasonably good job of dispensing with Justice Scalia's arguments, the fact is that Justice Scalia's argument would have been a winner before the 1982 amendment adding the § 10 permit process. Justice Scalia is dead-on when analyzing the historical meaning of takings and the purpose of § 5, and the majority's arguments to the contrary are weak. However, a discussion of § 10, and particularly the House and Senate report model butterfly case, are conspicuously absent from Justice Scalia's dissent.

■━━■

Quicknotes

CERTIORARI A discretionary writ issued by a superior court to an inferior court in order to review the lower court's decisions; the Supreme Court's writ ordering such review.

DECLARATORY JUDGMENT An adjudication by the courts which grants not relief but is binding over the legal status of the parties involved in the dispute.

■━━■

CHAPTER 10

Environmental Enforcement

Quick Reference Rules of Law

Sierra Club v. Cedar Point Oil Co.

Environmental group (P) v. Oil company (D)

73 F.3d 546 (5th Cir. 1996).

NATURE OF CASE: Appeal from judgment assessing damages in an action against an oil company for polluting a waterway.

FACT SUMMARY: After the Sierra Club (P) brought suit against Cedar Point Oil Co. (Cedar Point) (D) for violation of the Clean Water Act, the district court assessed a penalty of $186,070.

RULE OF LAW
Violators of the Clean Water Act are subject to a civil penalty not to exceed $25,000 per day for each violation.

FACTS: The Sierra Club (P) brought suit against Cedar Point (D) for not disposing of its produced water in a reinjection well. The district court found that Cedar Point (D) had violated the Clean Water Act. In determining the amount of the penalty, the court considered the seriousness of the violation, the economic benefit (if any) resulting from the violation, any history of such violations, any good-faith efforts to comply with the applicable requirements, the economic impact of the penalty on the violator, and such other matters as justice may require. Multiplying $25,000 per day by 809 days of unpermitted discharge, the court arrived at a maximum penalty of $20,225,000. The court found that the economic benefit to Cedar Point (D) came to $186,070, the amount Cedar Point (D) saved by not disposing of its produced water in a reinjection well. Weighing all the other factors, the district court found the maximum penalty inappropriate, assessing a penalty of $186,070. Cedar Point (D) appealed.

ISSUE: Shall violators of the Clean Water Act be subject to a civil penalty not to exceed $25,000 per day for each violation?

HOLDING AND DECISION: [Judge not stated in casebook excerpt.] Yes. Violators of the Clean Water Act are subject to a civil penalty not to exceed $25,000 per day for each violation. The district court did not abuse its discretion in assessing a penalty in an amount that reflected only the economic benefit to Cedar Point (D). In *Tull v. United States*, 481 U.S. 412 (1987), the Supreme Court described the process of weighing the statutory factors in calculating civil penalties under the Clean Water Act as "highly discretionary" with the trial court. It is clear that the district court considered all of the statutory factors before settling on an amount based only on economic benefit. Considering that the court could have imposed a penalty as high as $20 million, the penalty imposed appears to be a fair and just result. Affirmed.

▶ ANALYSIS

Cedar Point (D) had discharged contaminated water into Galveston Bay without a permit. Section 1319(d) of the Clean Water Act prescribes the amount of the penalty to be assessed, along with the factors to be considered by a court in determining the amount of the penalty. In an attempt to bar the filing of the instant suit, Cedar Point (D) had filed suit against the Sierra Club (P) and the Environmental Protection Agency. That lawsuit was dismissed.

■■■■

Quicknotes

DAMAGES Monetary compensation that may be awarded by the court to a party who has sustained injury or loss to his person, property or rights due to another party's unlawful act, omission or negligence.

■■■■

Harmon Industries v. Browner

Plant operator (P) v. Government agency (D)

191 F.3d 894 (8th Cir. 1999).

NATURE OF CASE:
Appeal from decision holding that civil penalties imposed by the Environmental Protection Agency (the EPA) on a plant operator was improper.

FACT SUMMARY:
The EPA (D) contends that the plain language of the Resource Conservation and Recovery Act (the RCRA) allows the EPA (D) to initiate an enforcement action against an environmental violator even in states that have received authorization under the RCRA.

🏛 RULE OF LAW
The EPA's practice of duplicating enforcement actions, in those states where it has authorized the state to act, oversteps the federal agency's authority under the RCRA.

FACTS:
Harmon Industries (Harmon) (P) operates a plant in Missouri that assembles circuit boards for railroad control and safety equipment. Harmon's (P) manager discovered that its maintenance workers routinely discarded volatile solvent residue behind the plant. Following the discovery, Harmon (P) ceased disposal activities and voluntarily contacted the Missouri Department of Natural Resources (the MDNR). The MDNR investigated and concluded that Harmon's (P) past disposal activities were not a threat to human health or the environment. The MDNR and Harmon (P) created a plan whereby Harmon (P) would clean up the disposal area. Harmon (P) implemented the plan. While Harmon (P) was cooperating with the MDNR, the EPA (D) initiated an administrative enforcement action against Harmon (P) seeking over $2 million in penalties. A Missouri state court judge approved a consent decree entered into between the MDNR and Harmon (P), which released Harmon (P) from any claim for monetary penalties. The MDNR based its decision to release Harmon (P) on the fact that the company promptly self-reported its violation and cooperated in all aspects of the litigation. After the filing of the consent decree, Harmon (P) litigated the EPA (D) claim before an administrative law judge (the ALJ). The ALJ agreed with the EPA (D) that civil penalties were appropriate but only for $586,716. The Environmental Appeals Board affirmed the penalty. Harmon (P) filed a complaint challenging the EPA's (D) decision in federal district court. The district court found that the EPA's (D) decision violated the RCRA and contravened principles of res judicata. The EPA (D) appealed.

ISSUE:
Does the EPA's practice of duplicating enforcement actions, in those states where it has authorized the state to act, overstep the federal agency's authority under the RCRA?

HOLDING AND DECISION:
(Hansen, J.) No. The EPA's (D) practice of duplicating enforcement actions, in those states where it has authorized the state to act, oversteps the federal agency's authority under the RCRA. The EPA's (D) process of duplicating enforcement actions is known as overfiling. The plain language of the RCRA dictates that the state program operate "in lieu" of the federal program and with the "same force and effect" as EPA (D) action. The RCRA therefore precludes the EPA (D) from assessing its own penalty against Harmon (P). An examination of the statute as a whole supports the district court's interpretation. The RCRA specifically allows states that have received authorization from the federal government to administer and enforce a program that operates in lieu of the EPA's (D) regulatory program. The RCRA gives authority to the states to create and implement their own hazardous waste program. The notice requirement in the RCRA also operates as a means to allow a state the first chance opportunity to initiate the statutorily permitted enforcement action. If the state fails to act, then the EPA (D) may institute its own action. This indicates that Congress intended to give states that are authorized to act, the lead role in enforcement under RCRA. Affirmed.

▶ ANALYSIS

Steven A. Herman, EPA's Assistant Administrator for Enforcement and Compliance Assurance, argues that it is important for the EPA (D) to have over-filing authority to prevent states from competing for industry through lax enforcement policies. In the case of *Smithfield Foods*, the company failed to install adequate pollution control equipment, resulting in more than 5,000 violations involving pollutants. Virginia took only minor actions against the violations, which had major impacts on the Pagan River, James River, and Chesapeake Bay. Under the EPA's (D) enforcement action, a federal district court fined Smithfield Foods a record $12.6 million penalty.

■═■

Quicknotes

CONSENT DECREE A decree issued by a court of equity ratifying an agreement between the parties to a lawsuit; an agreement by a defendant to cease illegal activity.

RES JUDICATA The rule of law that a final judgment by a court precludes subsequent litigation between the parties regarding the same cause of action.

■═■

United States v. Weitzenhoff

Federal government (P) v. Waste plant managers (D)

35 F.3d 1275 (9th Cir. 1994).

NATURE OF CASE: Appeal from conviction on six counts of conspiracy and substantive violations of the Clean Water Act (CWA).

FACT SUMMARY: After an investigation, Weitzenhoff (D) and Mariani (D), managers of a community waste treatment plant, were indicted on thirty-one counts of conspiracy and substantive violations of the CWA for telling two employees to dispose of sludge by pumping it directly into the ocean.

> ## 🏛 RULE OF LAW
> Criminal sanctions are to be imposed on individuals who knowingly engage in conduct resulting in a permit violation, whether or not the polluter knows of the requirements or the existence of the permit.

FACTS: Weitzenhoff (D) and Mariani (D), managers of a community waste treatment plant, instructed two employees at the plant to dispose of waste-activated sludge (WAS) on a regular basis by pumping it from the storage tanks directly into the ocean. Most of the WAS discharges occurred during the night, and none was reported to the Department of Health or to the Environmental Protection Agency. In response to complaints from lifeguards at a nearby popular beach, Weitzenhoff (D) and Mariani (D) repeatedly denied that there was any problem at the plant. Following an investigation, Weitzenhoff (D) and Mariani (D) were charged in a thirty-one-count indictment with conspiracy and substantive violations of the CWA. The jury found them guilty on six of those counts. Weitzenhoff (D) and Mariani (D) appealed, arguing that the district court erred in its interpretation of the CWA's "knowingly" requirement.

ISSUE: Are criminal sanctions to be imposed on individuals who knowingly engage in conduct resulting in a permit violation, whether or not they know of the requirements or the existence of the permit?

HOLDING AND DECISION: (Fletcher, J.) Yes. Criminal sanctions are to be imposed on individuals who knowingly engage in conduct resulting in a permit violation, whether or not the polluter knows of the requirements or the existence of the permit. The conclusion that "knowingly" does not refer to the legal violation is fortified by decisions interpreting analogous public welfare statutes. The dumping of sewage and other pollutants into our nation's waters is precisely the type of activity that puts the discharger on notice that his acts may pose a public danger. Improper and excessive discharge of sewage causes cholera, hepatitis, and other serious illnesses, and it can have serious repercussions for public health and welfare. The criminal provisions of the CWA are clearly designed to protect the public at large from the potentially dire consequences of water pollution, and as such they fall within the category of public welfare legislation. Thus, the Government (P) did not need to prove that Weitzenhoff (D) and Mariani (D) knew that their acts violated the permit or the CWA.

DISSENT: (Kleinfeld, J.) This is an exceptional case that warrants rehearing en banc. First, it impairs a fundamental purpose of criminal justice, sorting out the innocent from the guilty before imposing punishment. Second, it does so in the context of the CWA, a statute with tremendous sweep. The harm the court's mistaken decision does is not limited to the CWA, because it dilutes the traditional requirement of a criminal state of mind. The decision, instead, makes felons of a large number of innocent people doing socially valuable work. They are innocent, because the one thing which makes their conduct felonious is something they do not know—something that Congress did not include in the statute. What Congress did include in the statute at issue was that it is a felony, subject to three years of imprisonment, to "knowingly violate[] . . . any permit condition or limitation." Here, under a plain language reading of the statute, the plant managers (D) would have to know that they were violating their permits in order for their conduct to be "knowing." Nonetheless, the court instructed the jury that the government did not have to prove the plant managers (D) knew their conduct was unlawful, and refused to instruct the jury that a mistaken belief that the discharge was authorized by the permit would be a defense. Because of the way the jury was instructed, its verdict was consistent with the proposition that the plant managers (D) honestly and reasonably believed that their National Pollutant Discharge Elimination System (NPDES) permit authorized the discharges. Regardless of whether they were innocent or not, in the sense of knowing that they were exceeding their permit limitation, the court's holding will make innocence irrelevant in other permit violation cases where the defendants had no idea that they were exceeding permit limits. The only thing they have to know to be guilty is that they were dumping sewage into the ocean, yet that was a lawful activity expressly authorized by their federal permit. This contradicts the plain language of the statute, which says "knowingly violates" "any permit condition or limitation." The statute does not say "knowingly discharges pollutants." Moreover, since Congress made negligent violation of the statute a misdemeanor, it does not make sense that Congress would make non-negligent, unknowing violation a felony. Additionally, the court's construction of the statute, even assuming the statute is ambiguous, does not comport with the rule of lenity,

Continued on next page.

which requires that the construction permit a defendant more liberty than less. This is especially true where, as here, the court is characterizing the offense as a "public welfare offense" that is not inherently morally wrong, but is unlawful only statutorily, since persons of good conscience may not recognize the wrongfulness of the conduct when they engage in it. Also, there is a presumption that when Congress makes a crime a felony, Congress did not intend to eliminate a mens rea requirement. The case law support the court uses to bolster its conclusion is clearly distinguishable because it applied to misdemeanors, not felonies, and involved inherently dangerous devices and obnoxious waste materials, neither of which elements are present here. The court's decision will have the undesirable effect of threatening sewage plant workers, or anyone who discharges pollutants pursuant to a permit, with prison for unknowingly violating their permit conditions. The court's decision undermines the foundation of criminal law and deprives individuals of justice.

▶ *ANALYSIS*

The dissenters were also dissenting from the court's rejection of a rehearing en banc. In arriving at its decision, the majority applied the rationale of *United States v. International Minerals & Chem. Corp.*, 402 U.S. 558 (1971). In *International Minerals*, the Supreme Court construed a statute that made it a crime to "knowingly violate any regulation" promulgated by the ICC pursuant to 18 U.S.C. § 834(a), authorizing the agency to formulate regulations for the safe transport of corrosive liquids. The Court held that "where dangerous or deleterious devices or products or obnoxious waste materials are involved, the probability of regulation is so great that anyone who is aware that he is in possession of them or dealing with them must be presumed to be aware of the regulation."

■■■

Quicknotes

CONSPIRACY   Concerted action by two or more persons to accomplish some unlawful purpose.

■■■

Norton v. Southern Utah Wilderness Alliance

Federal official (D) v. Environmental group (P)

542 U.S. 55 (2004).

NATURE OF CASE: Appeal from reversal of decision dismissing an action brought under the Administrative Procedure Act (APA) to compel action by a federal agency.

FACT SUMMARY: The United States (D) contended that the APA did not give federal courts the power to require the United States Bureau of Land Management (BLM) to take action regarding off-road vehicle (ORV) use to protect public lands in keeping with BLM's statutory mandates and its own planning documents.

🏛 RULE OF LAW
The APA does not extend to review by federal courts of BLM inaction that is part of its stewardship of public lands under statutory mandates and its own planning documents.

FACTS: The Southern Utah Wilderness Alliance (SUWA) (P), an environmental group, brought suit under the Administrative Procedure Act contending that BLM failed to take action regarding off-road ORV use to protect public lands in keeping with BLM's statutory mandates and its own planning documents. The APA authorizes suit by "[a] person suffering legal wrong because of agency action, or adversely affected or aggrieved by agency action within the meaning of a relevant statute." 5 U.S.C. § 702. Agency action is defined to include a "failure to act." In § 706(1), the APA provides relief for a failure to act by permitting a reviewing court to "compel agency action unlawfully withheld or unreasonably delayed." SUWA's (P) first claim was that by permitting ORV use in certain wilderness study areas (WSAs), BLM violated its mandate to "continue to manage [WSAs] . . . in a manner so as not to impair the suitability of such areas for preservation as wilderness." 43 U.S.C. § 1782(c). SUWA (P) also relied upon a provision of BLM's Interim Management Policy for Lands Under Wilderness Review, which interprets the nonimpairment mandate to require the BLM to manage WSAs so as to prevent them from being "degraded so far, compared with the area's values for other purposes, as to significantly constrain the Congress's prerogative to either designate [it] as wilderness or release it for other uses." SUWA's (P) second claim was that BLM failed to comply with certain provisions in its own land use plans, thus contravening the statutory requirement in 43 U.S.C. § 1732(a) that it manage public lands in accordance with land use plans when they are available. Two such plans were at issue: the San Rafael plan and the Henry Mountains plan. The district court dismissed, the court of appeals reversed, and the Supreme Court granted certiorari.

ISSUE: Does the Administrative Procedure Act extend to review by federal courts of BLM inaction that is part of

its stewardship of public lands under statutory mandates and its own planning documents?

HOLDING AND DECISION: (Scalia, J.) No. The APA does not extend to review by federal courts of BLM inaction that is part of its stewardship of public lands under statutory mandates and its own planning documents. A § 706(1) claim can proceed only where a plaintiff asserts that an agency failed to take a discrete agency action that it is required to take. The discrete-action limitation precludes a broad programmatic attack, such as that rejected in *Lujan v. Nat'l Wildlife Fed'n*, 497 U.S. 871, (1990), and the required-action limitation rules out judicial direction of even discrete agency action that is not demanded by law. Thus, when an agency is compelled by law to act within a certain time period, but the manner of its action is left to the agency's discretion, a court can compel the agency to act, but has no power to specify what the action must be. As to SUWA's (P) first claim, while § 1782(c) is mandatory as to the object to be achieved, it leaves the BLM discretion to decide how to achieve that object. SUWA (P) argues that the nonimpairment mandate will support an APA suit, so that a court could enter a general order compelling compliance with that mandate, but a general deficiency in compliance lacks the requisite specificity for agency action. The principal purpose of this limitation on the APA is to protect agencies from undue judicial interference with their lawful discretion and to avoid judicial entanglement in abstract policy disagreements which courts lack the expertise and information to resolve. If courts were empowered to enter general orders compelling compliance with broad statutory mandates, they would necessarily be empowered to decide whether compliance was achieved. The APA does not contemplate such pervasive federal court oversight. As to SUWA's (P) second claim, a land use plan is a tool to project present and future use. Unlike a specific statutory command requiring an agency to promulgate regulations by a certain date, a land use plan is generally a statement of priorities; it guides and restrains actions, but does not prescribe them. Ordinarily, it is the first step in the land management process. Unless there is a binding commitment by BLM to adhere to a plan, a statement about what BLM plans to do, if it has funds and there are not more pressing priorities, cannot be plucked out of context and made a basis for a § 706(1) suit. The land use plan statements at issue here are not a legally binding commitment enforceable under § 706(1). The San Rafael plan embraces an immense scope of projected activity and lays the groundwork for more specific implementation

Continued on next page.

decisions and, further, more specific plans. The Henry Mountains plan implies that its implementation is subject to budgetary constraints. While an action called for in a plan may be compelled when the plan merely reiterates duties the agency is already obligated to perform, or perhaps when language in the plan itself creates a commitment binding on the agency, allowing general enforcement of plan terms would lead to pervasive interference with BLM's own ordering of priorities. Such interference would occur here if a judicial decree compelled immediate compliance with the plans. Thus, plan statements to the effect that BLM will conduct "use supervision and monitoring" in designated areas—like other "will do" projections of agency action set forth in land use plans—are not a legally binding commitment enforceable under § 706(1). Reversed.

▶ ANALYSIS

The type of action brought in this case was a citizen suit, also known as a citizen enforcement action, brought under the Federal Land Policy Management Act (FLPMA) and the National Environmental Policy Act (NEPA). Many federal environmental statutes authorize such citizen suits in an effort to supplement government enforcement actions. While citizen suits typically challenge an agency's failure to meet a statutory deadline to take some mandated action, as this case demonstrates, they may also be brought to challenge the legality of agency action—or inaction (where the agency has a non-discretionary duty to take an action). These types of suits usually turn on whether the agency's duty to act is discretionary or not.

■══■

Quicknotes

CERTIORARI   A discretionary writ issued by a superior court to an inferior court in order to review the lower court's decisions; the Supreme Court's writ ordering such review.

■══■

Gwaltney of Smithfield, Ltd. v. Chesapeake Bay Foundation

Meatpacking plant (D) v. Environmental foundation (P)

484 U.S. 49 (1987).

NATURE OF CASE: Appeal from summary judgment in citizen suit for declaratory and injunctive relief from Clean Water Act violation.

FACT SUMMARY: Gwaltney of Smithfield, Ltd. (Gwaltney) (D), a meatpacking plant, had repeatedly violated its National Pollution Discharge Elimination System (NPDES) permit, but the violation ceased six weeks before the Chesapeake Bay Foundation (the Foundation) (P) brought a citizen suit.

🏛 RULE OF LAW
Section 505(a) of the Clean Water Act does not authorize citizen suits for violations that occurred in the past.

FACTS: Gwaltney (D), a meatpacking plant, was issued a NPDES permit to discharge certain pollutants. Although it violated the terms of its permit for several years, Gwaltney (D) was never subject to government enforcement. It gradually remedied its violations. Six weeks after the last recorded violation, the Foundation (P) filed a citizen suit, claiming Gwaltney (D) had repeatedly violated its permit and would continue to do so. Section 505(a) of the Clean Water Act permits private citizens, in the absence of federal or state enforcement, to commence civil actions against any person "alleged to be in violation of" the conditions of an NPDES permit. The district court granted partial summary judgment in favor of the Foundation (P), and the court of appeals affirmed. Gwaltney (D) appealed.

ISSUE: Does § 505 (a) of the Clean Water Act authorize citizen suits for violations that occurred in the past?

HOLDING AND DECISION: (Marshall, J.) No. Section 505 (a) of the Clean Water Act does not authorize citizen suits for violations that occurred in the past. The language of the Act, i.e., "to be in violation," is clearly in the present tense. The language and structure of the rest of the citizen suit provisions in § 505 support the interpretation that the Act authorizes prospective relief only. Furthermore, permitting citizen suits for wholly past violations would undermine the ability of such suits to supplement, not supplant, government enforcement. The proper interpretation is to allow citizen suits for permit violations for present violations or where there is a reasonable belief that the violations will continue. If Congress intended to address past violations, it would have drafted the statute in the past tense, i.e., "to have violated." While there was no present violation in this case, there was some evidence that the Foundation (P) had a reasonable belief that the violations would continue, and thus the district court would have jurisdiction. Remanded for consideration of whether the Foundation (P) has alleged, in good faith, ongoing violations by Gwaltney (D). Vacated and remanded.

▶ ANALYSIS

The Foundation (P) argued that the language "to be in violation" was inadvertent. The Court rejected this argument out of hand, yet when Congress later amended the Clean Air Act, it changed the language to the past tense, apparently to incorporate repeated past violations.

■■■

Quicknotes

INJUNCTIVE RELIEF A court order issued as a remedy, requiring a person to do, or prohibiting that person from doing, a specific act.

NPDES National Pollutant Discharge Elimination System, a program of the Office of Wastewater Management (a division of the Environmental Protection Agency), which regulates the discharge of pollutants into the public water system by industrial, municipal, and other facilities.

SUMMARY JUDGMENT Judgment rendered by a court in response to a motion made by one of the parties, claiming that the lack of a question of material fact in respect to an issue warrants disposition of the issue without consideration by the jury.

■■■

Lujan v. Defenders of Wildlife

Secretary of the Interior (D) v. Environmental group (P)

504 U.S. 555 (1992).

NATURE OF CASE: Review of order denying motion for summary judgment in action challenging administrative rule.

FACT SUMMARY: After the Secretary of the Interior (the Secretary) (D) interpreted § 7 of the Endangered Species Act to apply only to domestic actions, two members of Defenders of Wildlife (Defenders) (P) who had studied species abroad claimed they would suffer harm due to the Secretary's (D) rule and thus had standing to seek review of the rule.

🏛 RULE OF LAW
A person may not challenge an administrative regulation unless she can demonstrate actual or imminent injury and redressability.

FACTS: Section 7 of the Endangered Species Act (the Act) requires federal agencies to consult with the Secretary of the Interior (D) to ensure that the projects they fund do not jeopardize endangered species. The Secretary (D) issued a rule interpreting the consultation requirement of § 7 of the Act to the effect that § 7 of the Act would not apply to agency actions taken in foreign countries. Various environmental interests, including Defenders of Wildlife (P), challenged this interpretation. Two members of Defenders (P) presented affidavits that they had studied endangered species abroad and would now be deprived of that opportunity in the future. The Secretary (D) moved for summary judgment, contending that Defenders (P) lacked standing. The court of appeals held standing to be pre-sent, and the Supreme Court granted review.

ISSUE: May a person challenge an administrative action if he cannot demonstrate actual or imminent injury or redressability?

HOLDING AND DECISION: (Scalia, J.) No. A person may not challenge an administrative action unless he can demonstrate actual or imminent injury and redressability. The Case or Controversy requirement of Article III mandates that, for a litigant to have standing to sue, he must have suffered an injury in fact, which is to say, an invasion of a legal interest that is concrete and particularized, actual and not conjectural, be causally connected to the challenged action of the defendant as well as be redressable by the relief sought. Here, the main thrust of Defenders' (P) argument is that § 7 of the Endangered Species Act should be applied to U.S. acts having an effect on wildlife overseas. The "injury" alleged is that the possible destruction to overseas wildlife would have adverse effects should the affiants choose to travel overseas to observe the wildlife. This is insufficient to confer standing. Such an injury, even if it were injury as is meant in the standing context, is not imminent; it is largely conjectural. Also, Defenders (P) have failed to demonstrate redressability. The agencies funding the projects overseas that allegedly violate the Act are not parties here, and an injunction mandating consultation with the Department of the Interior as required by § 7 may not influence them. Also, even if funding from the United States were cut off, foreign governments could find funding elsewhere. Consequently, under normal standing principles, standing is absent. The court of appeals found standing to also exist under a provision of the Act allowing citizen suits against any agency alleged to be in violation of the Act. However, to the extent this provision creates an exception to the standing requirement, it violates Article III and cannot stand. Reversed.

CONCURRENCE: (Kennedy, J.) Since concrete injury has not been shown here, the issue of redressability did not need to be discussed.

CONCURRENCE: (Stevens, J.) Although § 7 does not apply to foreign activities, a person having a professional interest in wildlife may suffer injury in fact by its destruction.

DISSENT: (Blackmun, J.) Sufficient factual issues exist on the issue of injury in fact to survive a summary judgment motion. Also, Congress can confer standing when none would otherwise exist and stay within the confines of Article III.

▶ ANALYSIS

This case has the potential to place severe limitations on Congress's ability to create new causes of action. Pursuant to this ruling, no act of Congress can enable those who have suffered only generalized, as opposed to concrete, harm to sue in federal court. The case neatly illustrates Justice Scalia's general separation of powers jurisprudence and preference for presidential power without interference from Congress or the courts.

■■■

Quicknotes

ARTICLE III, U.S. CONSTITUTION Limits federal judicial power to cases and controversies.

STANDING Whether a party possesses the right to commence suit against another party by having a personal stake in the resolution of the controversy.

SUMMARY JUDGMENT Judgment rendered by a court in response to a motion by one of the parties, claiming that the lack of a question of material fact in respect to an issue warrants disposition of the issue without consideration by the jury.

■■■

Friends of the Earth v. Laidlaw Environmental Services

Citizen group (P) v. Treatment plant operator (D)

528 U.S. 167 (2000).

NATURE OF CASE: Appeal from decision dismissing suit based on lack of standing and mootness.

FACT SUMMARY: Laidlaw Environmental Services (Laidlaw) (D) contends that the case brought by Friends of the Earth (FOE) (P) is moot because Laidlaw (D) fully complied with the terms of its permit.

🏛 **RULE OF LAW**

A case might become moot if subsequent events made it absolutely clear that the allegedly wrongful behavior could not reasonably be expected to recur.

FACTS: Laidlaw (D) violated its National Pollution Discharge Elimination System (NPDES) permit nearly 500 times by discharging greater than permitted quantities of mercury into the North Tyger River. After FOE (P) filed suit, more exceedances occurred, the last reported one taking place long after the complaint was filed but about two years before the judgment was rendered. The district court issued its judgment finding that Laidlaw (D) had gained a total economic benefit of over $1 million as a result of its extended period of noncompliance with the mercury discharge limit in its permit. The court concluded, however, that a lower penalty was adequate. FOE (P) appealed arguing that the penalty was inadequate. Laidlaw (D) cross-appealed, arguing that FOE (P) lacked standing to bring the suit. The court of appeals reversed. FOE (P) appealed.

ISSUE: Is a claim for civil penalties moot if a defendant complies with its permit after commencement of litigation?

HOLDING AND DECISION: (Ginsburg, J.) No. A case might become moot if subsequent events made it absolutely clear that the allegedly wrongful behavior could not reasonably be expected to recur. The heavy burden of persuading the court that the challenged conduct cannot reasonably be expected to recur lies with the party asserting mootness. The court of appeals justified its mootness disposition by referring to *Steel Co.*, 118 S. Ct. 1003 (1998), which held that citizen plaintiffs lack standing to seek civil penalties for wholly past violations. In relying on *Steel Co.*, the court of appeals confused mootness with standing. A defendant claiming that its voluntary compliance moots a case bears the formidable burden of showing that it is absolutely clear the allegedly wrongful behavior could not reasonably be expected to recur. By contrast, in a lawsuit brought to force compliance, it is the plaintiff's burden to establish standing by demonstrating that, if unchecked by the litigation, the defendant's allegedly wrongful behavior will likely occur or continue, and that the threatened injury is certainly impending. There are circumstances in which the prospect that a defendant will engage in or resume harmful conduct may be

too speculative to support standing, but not too speculative to overcome mootness. Standing doctrine functions to ensure that the scarce resource of the federal courts are devoted to those disputes in which the parties have a concrete stake. In contrast, by the time mootness is an issue, the case has been brought and litigated, often (as here) for years. To abandon the case at an advanced stage may prove more wasteful than frugal. Reversed and remanded.

▶ **ANALYSIS**

Laidlaw (D) closed its plant after the Fourth Circuit rendered its decisions, and argued that this fact had rendered the case moot. The Supreme Court noted that either this fact or Laidlaw's (D) achievement of substantial compliance with its permit might moot the case, but only if one or the other of these events made it absolutely clear that Laidlaw's (D) permit violations could not reasonably be expected to recur. Because the effects of these events were disputed facts, the case was remanded for further consideration.

■═■

Quicknotes

MOOTNESS Judgment on the particular issue would not resolve the controversy.

NPDES National Pollutant Discharge Elimination System, a program of the Office of Wastewater Management (a division of the Environmental Protection Agency), which regulates the discharge of pollutants into the public water system by industrial, municipal, and other facilities.

STANDING Whether a party possesses the right to commence suit against another party by having a personal stake in the resolution of the controversy.

■═■

Summers v. Earth Island Institute

United States Forest Service (D) v. Advocacy group (P)

129 S. Ct. 1142 (2009).

NATURE OF CASE: Appeal from Ninth Circuit Court's decision in favor of the plaintiff advocacy group.

FACT SUMMARY: In 2002, the United States Forest Service (the Service) (D) sought to sell timber from a 238-acre portion of the Sequoia National Forest. Earth Island Institute (P) brought suit, seeking a suspension of a Service regulation that exempted such minor transactions from a public notice and comment period.

> 🏛 **RULE OF LAW**
> Removal of a procedural right without some concrete injury to a group or a member of that group does not provide a petitioner with standing to bring suit.

FACTS: After a fire in the Sequoia National Forest in 2002, the Service (D) sought to sell salvage timber from a 238 acre site that had been damaged in the fire. The Service (D) called this the Burnt Ridge Project. In 1992, Congress enacted the Forest Service Decisionmaking and Appeals Reform Act, which required a period of public comment before action taken by the Service (D). In 2008, the Service (D) enacted regulations that would exempt salvage timber sales of 250 acres or less from the public notice requirement. Earth Island Institute (P) brought suit against the Service (D) to force it to suspend the regulations regarding the exemption. It also challenged several other Service (D) regulations not relevant to the Burnt Ridge Project or this appeal. After the district court granted Earth Island Institute's (P) motion for a preliminary injunction, the parties settled the Burnt Ridge portion of the case. After acknowledging that the Burnt Ridge Project was no longer part of the case, the District Court went on to invalidate many of the Service's (D) regulations, including the one providing the exemption for the Burnt Ridge Project. The Government argued that with that portion of the case settled and no other live controversy before the court, Earth Island Institute (P) no longer had standing to challenge the regulations. The Ninth Circuit affirmed the district court's ruling. The Service (D) appeals.

ISSUE: Does removal of a procedural right without some concrete injury to a group or a member of that group provide a petitioner with standing to bring suit?

HOLDING AND DECISION: (Scalia, J.) No. Removal of a procedural right without some concrete injury to a group or a member of that group does not provide a petitioner with standing to bring suit. Article III of the Constitution limits judicial power to addressing cases or controversies. To have standing, a petitioner must allege some actual or imminent injury to persons caused by a violation of law. As an environmental organization, Earth Island Institute (P) can assert standing based on injury to its individual members. However, general harm to the environment itself will not provide stand-

ing. Once the parties settled the Burnt Ridge portion of the case, there were no further controversies in front of the court for adjudication. Affidavits from individual members regarding their intentions to visit Burnt Ridge in the future were too speculative to qualify for Article III standing purposes. In addition, simply because the Service (D) removed the period of public comment for these types of sales does not provide standing. There must be an actual concrete injury that results from the removal of such a procedural right. Reversed.

CONCURRENCE: (Kennedy, J.) Removal of a procedural right alone does not provide standing. The case would be different if Congress had sought to allow redress for concrete injuries giving rise to a case where none had been present before.

DISSENT: (Breyer, J.) Earth Island Institute (P) has standing. Imagine that Congress has enacted a statutory provision to give Earth Island Institute (P) standing based on the following factors. First, Earth Island Institute (P) has members who use the Burnt Ridge Project site and whom will do so again in the future. Second, the group's members have opposed other timber sales in the past and will do so in the future. Such a statute would not be unconstitutional. In addition, this Court has held that parties have standing when their rights may be harmed at some point in the future. For instance, this Court has held that circumstances in which a petitioner, once subject to a chokehold, feared that it would happen again in the future, would provide a basis to bring suit. That same type of future harm is present here.

▶ *ANALYSIS*

The case seemed fairly straightforward. It is very unusual for a trial court to adjudicate an issue that the parties to the suit had settled. The decision may act as a disincentive to settle if one side or the other seeks a ruling that could have national consequences. Also, the decision obviously makes it more difficult for environmental groups to bring suit, because of the actual harm requirement. Justice Breyer's more relaxed standard of a possible threat in the future, what he termed a "realistic threat," would have allowed more of these cases to proceed.

■■■■

Quicknotes

STANDING The right to commence suit against another party because of a personal stake in the resolution of the controversy.

STANDING TO SUE Plaintiff must allege that he has a legally predictable interest at stake in the litigation.

■■■■

Atlantic States Legal Foundation, Inc. v. Eastman Kodak Co.

Environmental group (P) v. Industrial operator (D)

12 F.3d 353 (2d Cir. 1994).

NATURE OF CASE: Appeal from summary judgment in an action involving violations of the Clean Water Act (the CWA).

FACT SUMMARY: Atlantic States Legal Foundation, Inc. (Atlantic States) (P) alleged that Eastman Kodak Co. (Kodak) (D) had violated §§ 301 and 402 of the CWA by discharging large quantities of pollutants not listed in its State Pollutant Discharge Elimination System (SPDES) permit.

🏛 RULE OF LAW
Polluters within the national or state permit scheme may discharge pollutants not specifically listed in their permits so long as they comply with the appropriate reporting requirements and abide by any new limitations imposed on such pollutants.

FACTS: Kodak (D) operated an industrial facility in the state of New York. A state permit system allowed Kodak (D) to discharge its wastewater into a local river and creek. The SPDES permit established specific effluent limitations for approximately 25 pollutants. Atlantic States (P) brought suit, alleging that Kodak (D) had violated §§ 301 and 402 of the CWA by discharging large quantities of pollutants not listed in its SPDES permit. Atlantic States (P) moved for partial summary judgment. The district court denied Atlantic States' (P) motion, but granted Kodak's (D) cross-motion for summary judgment, dismissing the case. Atlantic States (P) appealed.

ISSUE: May polluters within the national or state permit scheme discharge pollutants not specifically listed in their permits so long as they comply with the appropriate reporting requirements and abide by any new limitations imposed on such pollutants?

HOLDING AND DECISION: (Winter, J.) Yes. Polluters within the national or state permit scheme may discharge pollutants not specifically listed in their permits so long as they comply with the appropriate reporting requirements and abide by any new limitations imposed on such pollutants. Environmental Protection Agency (EPA) regulations do not demand information regarding each of the many thousands of chemical substances potentially present in a manufacturer's wastewater because it is impossible to identify and rationally limit every chemical or compound present in a discharge of pollutants. The EPA has consistently contemplated discharge of pollutants not listed under a permit. The EPA is the federal agency entrusted with administration and enforcement of the CWA. As such, its reasonable interpretations of the Act are due deferential treatment in the courts. Affirmed.

▶ ANALYSIS

The EPA commented that there is still some possibility that a national or state permittee may discharge a large amount of a pollutant not limited in its permit, and the EPA will not be able to take enforcement action against the permittee as long as the permittee complies with the notification requirements. This possibility constituted a "regulatory gap." The final regulations control discharges only of the pollutants listed in the national or state permit application, which consist primarily of the listed toxic pollutants and designated hazardous substances.

■■■

Quicknotes

SUMMARY JUDGMENT Judgment rendered by a court in response to a motion made by one of the parties, claiming that the lack of a question of material fact in respect to an issue warrants disposition of the issue without consideration by the jury.

■■■

CHAPTER 11

Protection of the Global Environment

Quick Reference Rules of Law

Beanal v. Freeport-McMoran, Inc.

Indonesian tribal council leader (P) v. Mining company (D)

197 F.3d 161 (5th Cir. 1999).

NATURE OF CASE: Appeal from decision holding that an alien's environmental torts claims cannot be granted relief under international law.

FACT SUMMARY: Beanal (P) contends that the alleged environmental abuses caused by Freeport-McMoran's (Freeport) (D) mining activities are cognizable under international law.

🏛 RULE OF LAW
It is only where nations of the world have demonstrated that the wrong is of mutual concern by means of express international accords, that a wrong generally recognized becomes an international law violation.

FACTS: Freeport (D) operates an open-pit mine in Indonesia. Beanal (P) is a resident of Tamika in Indonesia. He is also the leader of the Amungme Tribal Council of Lambaga Adat Suki Amungme. Beanal (P) filed a complaint against Freeport (D) in federal district court for alleged violations of international law. He alleged that Freeport (D) engaged in environmental abuses, human rights violations, and cultural genocide. Beanal (P) specifically alleged that Freeport (D) mining operations had caused harm and injury to the Amungme's environment and habitat. Freeport (D) moved to dismiss Beanal's (P) claims. The district court dismissed the claims with leave to amend. Beanal (P) appealed.

ISSUE: Must universal acceptance of environmental standards be articulated through express international accords in order to be cognizable under international law?

HOLDING AND DECISION: (Stewart, J.) Yes. It is only where nations of the world have demonstrated that the wrong is of mutual concern by means of express international accords, that a wrong generally recognized becomes an international law violation. The district court conducted a thorough survey of various international law principles, treaties, and declarations and concluded that Beanal (P) failed to articulate environmental torts that were cognizable under international law. The sources of international law cited by Beanal (P) merely refer to a general sense of environmental responsibility and state abstract rights and liberties devoid of articulable or discernible standards and regulations to identify practices that constitute international environmental abuses or torts. Although the United States has articulable standards embodied in federal statutory law to address environmental torts domestically, federal courts should exercise extreme caution when adjudicating environmental claims under international law to insure that environmental policies of the United States do not displace environmental policies of other governments. Therefore, the district court did not err when it concluded that

Beanal (P) failed to show in his pleadings that Freeport's (D) mining activities constitute environmental torts or abuses under international law. Affirmed.

▶ ANALYSIS

Although Beanal (P) cited the Rio Declaration to support his claims of environmental torts and abuses under international law, the express language of the declaration appears to cut against his claims. The Rio Declaration asserts that states have the right to exploit their own resources under their own environmental and developmental policies, but also have the responsibility to ensure that activities within their jurisdiction or control do not cause damage to the environment or other areas beyond the limits of national jurisdiction.

▬▬■

Quicknotes

ALIEN An individual who is a citizen of a foreign country.

RIO DECLARATION The Rio Declaration on Environment and Development was produced in June, 1992 as the result of a United Nations conference on international environmental policy.

▬▬■

Glossary

Common Latin Words and Phrases Encountered in the Law

A FORTIORI: Because one fact exists or has been proven, therefore a second fact that is related to the first fact must also exist.

A PRIORI: From the cause to the effect. A term of logic used to denote that when one generally accepted truth is shown to be a cause, another particular effect must necessarily follow.

AB INITIO: From the beginning; a condition which has existed throughout, as in a marriage which was void ab initio.

ACTUS REUS: The wrongful act; in criminal law, such action sufficient to trigger criminal liability.

AD VALOREM: According to value; an ad valorem tax is imposed upon an item located within the taxing jurisdiction calculated by the value of such item.

AMICUS CURIAE: Friend of the court. Its most common usage takes the form of an amicus curiae brief, filed by a person who is not a party to an action but is nonetheless allowed to offer an argument supporting his legal interests.

ARGUENDO: In arguing. A statement, possibly hypothetical, made for the purpose of argument, is one made arguendo.

BILL QUIA TIMET: A bill to quiet title (establish ownership) to real property.

BONA FIDE: True, honest, or genuine. May refer to a person's legal position based on good faith or lacking notice of fraud (such as a bona fide purchaser for value) or to the authenticity of a particular document (such as a bona fide last will and testament).

CAUSA MORTIS: With approaching death in mind. A gift causa mortis is a gift given by a party who feels certain that death is imminent.

CAVEAT EMPTOR: Let the buyer beware. This maxim is reflected in the rule of law that a buyer purchases at his own risk because it is his responsibility to examine, judge, test, and otherwise inspect what he is buying.

CERTIORARI: A writ of review. Petitions for review of a case by the United States Supreme Court are most often done by means of a writ of certiorari.

CONTRA: On the other hand. Opposite. Contrary to.

CORAM NOBIS: Before us; writs of error directed to the court that originally rendered the judgment.

CORAM VOBIS: Before you; writs of error directed by an appellate court to a lower court to correct a factual error.

CORPUS DELICTI: The body of the crime; the requisite elements of a crime amounting to objective proof that a crime has been committed.

CUM TESTAMENTO ANNEXO, ADMINISTRATOR (ADMINISTRATOR C.T.A.): With will annexed; an administrator c.t.a. settles an estate pursuant to a will in which he is not appointed.

DE BONIS NON, ADMINISTRATOR (ADMINISTRATOR D.B.N.): Of goods not administered; an administrator d.b.n. settles a partially settled estate.

DE FACTO: In fact; in reality; actually. Existing in fact but not officially approved or engendered.

DE JURE: By right; lawful. Describes a condition that is legitimate "as a matter of law," in contrast to the term "de facto," which connotes something existing in fact but not legally sanctioned or authorized. For example, de facto segregation refers to segregation brought about by housing patterns, etc., whereas de jure segregation refers to segregation created by law.

DE MINIMIS: Of minimal importance; insignificant; a trifle; not worth bothering about.

DE NOVO: Anew; a second time; afresh. A trial de novo is a new trial held at the appellate level as if the case originated there and the trial at a lower level had not taken place.

DICTA: Generally used as an abbreviated form of obiter dicta, a term describing those portions of a judicial opinion incidental or not necessary to resolution of the specific question before the court. Such nonessential statements and remarks are not considered to be binding precedent.

DUCES TECUM: Refers to a particular type of writ or subpoena requesting a party or organization to produce certain documents in their possession.

EN BANC: Full bench. Where a court sits with all justices present rather than the usual quorum.

EX PARTE: For one side or one party only. An ex parte proceeding is one undertaken for the benefit of only one party, without notice to, or an appearance by, an adverse party.

EX POST FACTO: After the fact. An ex post facto law is a law that retroactively changes the consequences of a prior act.

EX REL.: Abbreviated form of the term "ex relatione," meaning upon relation or information. When the state brings an action in which it has no interest against an individual at the instigation of one who has a private interest in the matter.

FORUM NON CONVENIENS: Inconvenient forum. Although a court may have jurisdiction over the case, the action should be tried in a more conveniently located court, one to which parties and witnesses may more easily travel, for example.

GUARDIAN AD LITEM: A guardian of an infant as to litigation, appointed to represent the infant and pursue his/her rights.

HABEAS CORPUS: You have the body. The modern writ of habeas corpus is a writ directing that a person (body) being detained (such as a prisoner) be brought before the court so that the legality of his detention can be judicially ascertained.

IN CAMERA: In private, in chambers. When a hearing is held before a judge in his chambers or when all spectators are excluded from the courtroom.

IN FORMA PAUPERIS: In the manner of a pauper. A party who proceeds in forma pauperis because of his poverty is one who is allowed to bring suit without liability for costs.

INFRA: Below, under. A word referring the reader to a later part of a book. (The opposite of supra.)

IN LOCO PARENTIS: In the place of a parent.

IN PARI DELICTO: Equally wrong; a court of equity will not grant requested relief to an applicant who is in pari delicto, or as much at fault in the transactions giving rise to the controversy as is the opponent of the applicant.

IN PARI MATERIA: On like subject matter or upon the same matter. Statutes relating to the same person or things are said to be in pari materia. It is a general rule of statutory construction that such statutes should be construed together, i.e., looked at as if they together constituted one law.

IN PERSONAM: Against the person. Jurisdiction over the person of an individual.

IN RE: In the matter of. Used to designate a proceeding involving an estate or other property.

IN REM: A term that signifies an action against the res, or thing. An action in rem is basically one that is taken directly against property, as distinguished from an action in personam, i.e., against the person.

INTER ALIA: Among other things. Used to show that the whole of a statement, pleading, list, statute, etc., has not been set forth in its entirety.

INTER PARTES: Between the parties. May refer to contracts, conveyances or other transactions having legal significance.

INTER VIVOS: Between the living. An inter vivos gift is a gift made by a living grantor, as distinguished from bequests contained in a will, which pass upon the death of the testator.

IPSO FACTO: By the mere fact itself.

JUS: Law or the entire body of law.

LEX LOCI: The law of the place; the notion that the rights of parties to a legal proceeding are governed by the law of the place where those rights arose.

MALUM IN SE: Evil or wrong in and of itself; inherently wrong. This term describes an act that is wrong by its very nature, as opposed to one which would not be wrong but for the fact that there is a specific legal prohibition against it (malum prohibitum).

MALUM PROHIBITUM: Wrong because prohibited, but not inherently evil. Used to describe something that is wrong because it is expressly forbidden by law but that is not in and of itself evil, e.g., speeding.

MANDAMUS: We command. A writ directing an official to take a certain action.

MENS REA: A guilty mind; a criminal intent. A term used to signify the mental state that accompanies a crime or other prohibited act. Some crimes require only a general mens rea (general intent to do the prohibited act), but others, like assault with intent to murder, require the existence of a specific mens rea.

MODUS OPERANDI: Method of operating; generally refers to the manner or style of a criminal in committing crimes, admissible in appropriate cases as evidence of the identity of a defendant.

NEXUS: A connection to.

NISI PRIUS: A court of first impression. A nisi prius court is one where issues of fact are tried before a judge or jury.

N.O.V. (NON OBSTANTE VEREDICTO): Notwithstanding the verdict. A judgment n.o.v. is a judgment given in favor of one party despite the fact that a verdict was returned in favor of the other party, the justification being that the verdict either had no reasonable support in fact or was contrary to law.

NUNC PRO TUNC: Now for then. This phrase refers to actions that may be taken and will then have full retroactive effect.

PENDENTE LITE: Pending the suit; pending litigation under way.

PER CAPITA: By head; beneficiaries of an estate, if they take in equal shares, take per capita.

PER CURIAM: By the court; signifies an opinion ostensibly written "by the whole court" and with no identified author.

PER SE: By itself, in itself; inherently.

PER STIRPES: By representation. Used primarily in the law of wills to describe the method of distribution where a person, generally because of death, is unable to take that which is left to him by the will of another, and therefore his heirs divide such property between them rather than take under the will individually.

PRIMA FACIE: On its face, at first sight. A prima facie case is one that is sufficient on its face, meaning that the evidence supporting it is adequate to establish the case until contradicted or overcome by other evidence.

PRO TANTO: For so much; as far as it goes. Often used in eminent domain cases when a property owner receives partial payment for his land without prejudice to his right to bring suit for the full amount he claims his land to be worth.

QUANTUM MERUIT: As much as he deserves. Refers to recovery based on the doctrine of unjust enrichment in those cases in which a party has rendered valuable services or furnished materials that were accepted and enjoyed by another under circumstances that would reasonably notify the recipient that the rendering party expected to be paid. In essence, the law implies a contract to pay the reasonable value of the services or materials furnished.

QUASI: Almost like; as if; nearly. This term is essentially used to signify that one subject or thing is almost analogous to another but that material differences between them do exist. For example, a quasi-criminal proceeding is one that is not strictly criminal but shares enough of the same characteristics to require some of the same safeguards (e.g., procedural due process must be followed in a parole hearing).

QUID PRO QUO: Something for something. In contract law, the consideration, something of value, passed between the parties to render the contract binding.

RES GESTAE: Things done; in evidence law, this principle justifies the admission of a statement that would otherwise be hearsay when it is made so closely to the event in question as to be said to be a part of it, or with such spontaneity as not to have the possibility of falsehood.

RES IPSA LOQUITUR: The thing speaks for itself. This doctrine gives rise to a rebuttable presumption of negligence when the instrumentality causing the injury was within the exclusive control of the defendant, and the injury was one that does not normally occur unless a person has been negligent.

RES JUDICATA: A matter adjudged. Doctrine which provides that once a court of competent jurisdiction has rendered a final judgment or decree on the merits, that judgment or decree is conclusive upon the parties to the case and prevents them from engaging in any other litigation on the points and issues determined therein.

RESPONDEAT SUPERIOR: Let the master reply. This doctrine holds the master liable for the wrongful acts of his servant (or the principal for his agent) in those cases in which the servant (or agent) was acting within the scope of his authority at the time of the injury.

STARE DECISIS: To stand by or adhere to that which has been decided. The common law doctrine of stare decisis attempts to give security and certainty to the law by following the policy that once a principle of law as applicable to a certain set of facts has been set forth in a decision, it forms a precedent which will subsequently be followed, even though a different decision might be made were it the first time the question had arisen. Of course, stare decisis is not an inviolable principle and is departed from in instances where there is good cause (e.g., considerations of public policy led the Supreme Court to disregard prior decisions sanctioning segregation).

SUPRA: Above. A word referring a reader to an earlier part of a book.

ULTRA VIRES: Beyond the power. This phrase is most commonly used to refer to actions taken by a corporation that are beyond the power or legal authority of the corporation.

Addendum of French Derivatives

IN PAIS: Not pursuant to legal proceedings.

CHATTEL: Tangible personal property.

CY PRES: Doctrine permitting courts to apply trust funds to purposes not expressed in the trust but necessary to carry out the settlor's intent.

PER AUTRE VIE: For another's life; during another's life. In property law, an estate may be granted that will terminate upon the death of someone other than the grantee.

PROFIT A PRENDRE: A license to remove minerals or other produce from land.

VOIR DIRE: Process of questioning jurors as to their predispositions about the case or parties to a proceeding in order to identify those jurors displaying bias or prejudice.

Casenote Legal Briefs